MUTIN

MW00756199

AMISTAD

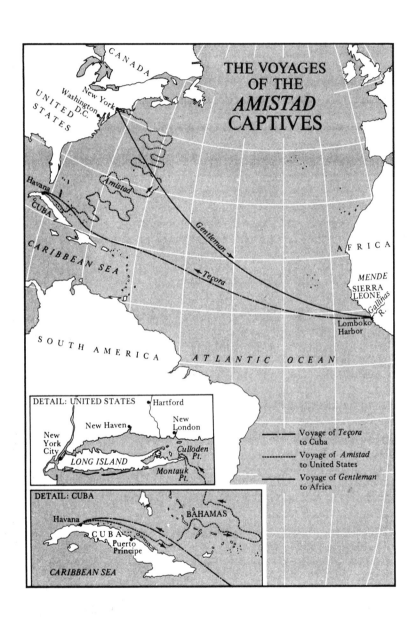

THE VOYAGES
OF THE
AMISTAD
CAPTIVES

CANADA

UNITED STATES

Washington D.C.

New York

Havana

CUBA

Amistad

CARIBBEAN SEA

Gentleman

Tecora

SOUTH AMERICA

ATLANTIC OCEAN

AFRICA

MENDE
SIERRA LEONE
Gallinas R.
Lomboko Harbor

DETAIL: UNITED STATES   • Hartford

New York City

New Haven

New London

LONG ISLAND

Culloden Pt.

Montauk Pt.

—·—·— Voyage of *Tecora* to Cuba

·········· Voyage of *Amistad* to United States

———— Voyage of *Gentleman* to Africa

DETAIL: CUBA

Havana

CUBA

Puerto Principe

BAHAMAS

CARIBBEAN SEA

MUTINY ON THE *AMISTAD*

The Saga of a Slave Revolt and Its Impact on American Abolition, Law, and Diplomacy

HOWARD JONES

OXFORD UNIVERSITY PRESS
New York   Oxford

Oxford University Press

Oxford   New York   Toronto
Delhi   Bombay   Calcutta   Madras   Karachi
Petaling Jaya   Singapore   Hong Kong   Tokyo
Nairobi   Dar es Salaam   Cape Town
Melbourne   Auckland

and associated companies in
Beirut   Berlin   Ibadan   Nicosia

First published in 1987 by Oxford University Press, Inc.,

198 Madison Avenue, New York, New York 10016-4314

First issued as an Oxford University Press paperback, 1988

Oxford is a registered trademark of Oxford University Press

Library of Congress Cataloging-in-Publication Data

Jones, Howard, 1940–
Mutiny on the Amistad.

Bibliography: p.
Includes index.
1. Slavery—United States—Insurrections, etc.
2. Amistad (Schooner) 3. Slavery—United States—
Anti-slavery movements. I. Title.
E447.J66   1986   326′.0973   86-8692
ISBN 0-19-503828-2
ISBN 0-19-503829-0 (ppbk.)

6 8 10 9 7 5

Printed in the United States of America

"CINQUÉ"

The sea calm tonight.

Another night like this we buy
Freedom
        dearly.
We strike
        blood flow
we kill
We win.

We spare two
Take us home
           Africa.
They trick us
We should not trust them
They bring us west
Demand us
        sent to Cuba
Chain and whip
           kill for crime.
America kind
      teach us tell what happen
      give us land grow food
      talk in court
      King with white hair
      talk soft
          convince
      send us tell what happen that
night.
      We make friend
              boy Kali
              they love
    pay for ship

We go home.

The sea calm tonight
Tonight peaceful
        no fighting
        no blood
        just peace.
We go home.

Oscar A. Bouise
Professor Emeritus of History
Xavier University, New Orleans, 1981

Preface

A book is almost always a product of many people's labors, and in this case the generalization holds especially true. Without the assistance of friends and colleagues, any merit that the following work might have would be considerably less.

I was particularly fortunate to have sound advice and encouragement throughout the various stages of this project. Tony A. Freyer shared with me his deep knowledge of American constitutional law and saved me from a number of pitfalls and errors. His continual exhortations were also vital to my completing the manuscript earlier than expected. Maurice G. Baxter carefully read the manuscript and offered many recommendations on style, analysis, and the legal aspects of the *Amistad* and related court cases. Robert E. May also gave the manuscript a close reading and made many helpful suggestions. Forrest and Ellen McDonald provided more assistance than anyone is entitled to receive. Twice they set aside their own work and read my manuscript, making countless recommendations on every aspect of the making of a book. Others who read part of the manuscript or helped in some way included Robert H. Ferrell, Suzanne Freeman, R. Kent Newmyer, David M. Pletcher, Kenneth E. Shewmaker, and Randall B. Woods. Tim Johnson provided invaluable assistance in translating Spanish materials from Madrid and Havana. And, as ever, Guy Swanson repeatedly expressed friendly encouragement and sincere interest in my work.

Archivists in four countries furnished the kind of assistance that helps to make research and writing a pleasure. In the United States, Clifton H. Johnson and his staff at the Amistad Research Center provided expert guidance into the rich collection of *Amistad* materials in New Orleans. Floyd M. Shumway, former executive director of the New Haven Colony Historical Society, was enormously helpful in securing materials relating to the case. David L. Parke, Jr., has continued his predecessor's fine example. Judith Ann Schiff and Patricia Howell provided assistance in finding *Amistad* items housed in the Sterling Memorial Library of Yale University. James K. Owens located legal materials in the circuit and district court records stored in the Federal Archives and Records Center in Waltham, Massachusetts. Others who facilitated my work were John McDonough of the Library of Congress, John D. Cushing of the Massachusetts Historical Society, Tom Canden of the University of Georgia Library, John C. Dann of the William L. Clements Library of the University of Michigan, and the staffs of the National Archives, the New York Public Library, and the University of Alabama Library. In England, the staffs of the British Library, the Public Record Office, and the Royal Historical Manuscripts Commission provided important assistance. My experience in Spain was equally satisfying. José Antonio Martínez Bara and his staff at the Archivo Histórico Nacional in Madrid located the Spanish materials cited in this study. The staffs of both the Archivo General de Indias in Seville and the Archivo General de Simancas assured me there were no *Amistad* materials in their collections. From Cuba, Armando S. Mal-lía B. sent microfilm copies of the few items in the Archivo Nacional in Havana that related to the mutiny. Although these materials did not shape the manuscript, his help is indicative of the spirit of scholarly cooperation that crosses international borders.

Financial assistance from several sources helped in the preparation of this book. The American Council of Learned Societies awarded a grant that, combined with financial help authorized by President Joab L. Thomas and Academic Vice-President Roger E. Sayers of the University of Alabama, allowed me to devote the full academic year of 1984–85 to the *Amistad.* The National Endowment for the Humanities awarded a Summer Stipend in 1984 that relieved me from teaching duties and afforded additional research time. The American Philosophical Society provided assistance that allowed research in Washington, D.C., during the spring of 1985. From the University of Alabama, I received support from the Capstone International Program Center (through the efforts of Edward H. Moseley, its director), the College of Arts and Sciences (through the help of Richard E. Peck, David L. Klemmack, and William D. Barnard), and the Bankhead Fund.

There is no way to express my gratitude to those people with whom I have come into contact at Oxford University Press. Sheldon Meyer believed in the *Amistad* project from its beginning and has continued his enthusiastic support to its completion. Rachel Toor has been a constant source of encouragement, masterfully combining a genuine professionalism with a friendly interest in book and author. Otto Sonntag provided splendid editorial expertise in the last stages of the manuscript's preparation.

Others deserve thanks. Pete Maslowski introduced me to the world of word processors, and Mary Ann, my wife, companion, confidante, and dearest friend, found a way to purchase one for the home. As always, my parents furnished the type of support that can result only from our close relationship. My daughter Shari accompanied me in cars and on planes, trains, and ships in running down materials on the *Amistad* in the United States, England, and Spain. More important, she refused to allow the hours both inside and outside the libraries to become boring. To Mary Ann and our three offspring, Debbie, Howie, and Shari, I dedicate this work with heartfelt appreciation for their patience and understanding.

Whatever good qualities this work may have, I freely share in attribution with all of those mentioned above; the inadequacies I jealously claim as my own.

University, Alabama   Howard Jones
Spring 1986

Contents

Twelve pages of photographs follow page 154.

Introduction

The sun beat down heavily in the late afternoon, sending across his glass a sharp glint of light that made it difficult to see. Lieutenant Richard W. Meade adjusted his sights again, trying to bring form to the moving objects on the beach, over a mile away. From the prow of an American revenue cutter, the USS *Washington,* he had about an hour earlier seen a black schooner with sails torn and tattered, lying low in the water off Culloden Point and less than a mile from Long Island. What was its business in this secluded spot? Meade had scanned the beaches, fighting the glare of the sun as he peered through the glass. At last he saw what appeared to be a dozen men, rushing back and forth across the sand, carrying two trunks from a small boat toward some wagons a few yards up the shore. As Meade finally brought the shoreline into focus, he could see that over half the men were black. Were they smugglers? The evidence seemed clear: wagons for transporting goods; a small boat; two large trunks carried ashore; a ship nearby; hurried activity. But what kind of operation would involve blacks and whites in collusion? Why was there no flag identifying the nationality of the vessel? Somehow, he surmised, the men had commandeered the ship and were now delivering the stolen goods. Clearly they were guilty of piracy, a crime punishable by death under international law.[1]

Meade alerted the commander of the *Washington,* Lieutenant Thomas R. Gedney, who probably welcomed a respite from the tedious duty of surveying the coastal waters. Like Meade, Gedney observed the activity through his glass and immediately suspected those ashore of smuggling. He ordered Midshipman D. D. Porter to take a boat of six armed men and investigate the schooner and the people ashore. Meade volunteered to go with them, and within moments the sailors were under way, rowing as fast as possible under the warm August sun of 1839.

With pistols and muskets ready, the men reached the ship, where Porter quickly led them up the main rigging and, surprisingly, encountered no resistance as he took control amid great excitement and confusion. Meade was shocked by an eerie sight: the sides of the vessel, once colorful with a white streak separating green bottom from black top, now weather-beaten and covered with barnacles; seaweed stringing from the cable and along the water line; topsail yard gone and sails shredded and waving lifelessly in the breeze; the deck strewn with stale remains of food, ripped-open boxes, empty medicine containers, tattered silks, cotton, and other materials. But a worse sight than this was the occupants of the vessel, at first count perhaps fifty of them, all black. One was armed with pistol and cutlass, some had long-bladed knives, many were half-clothed or even naked, and all were clearly desperate from hunger and thirst. Four of the blacks were children—three of them girls, standing around the windlass, and, like the boy, all probably under twelve years of age.

Meade stripped the blacks of their weapons and demanded the ship's papers. Finding that one of the blacks could speak English, but then realizing that this amounted only to a nonsensical string of unconnected words, he ordered all of them below. Meade sent two of his men to search the hold. The ship was a slaver: built for speed, its hatchway wide, five sweeps on each side. Below the large gilt eagle head on its bow, Meade could read *Amistad,* a word he knew meant friendship in Spanish. What calamity had brought this slave ship to New York? More important, where was its captain?

At this point, Meade's men appeared from the hold, accompanied by two haggard white men, severely scarred on their heads and arms from recent injuries. Before Meade could speak, the two men, one in his twenties and the other in his fifties, fell on their knees, crying and exclaiming in Spanish, "Bless the Holy Virgin, you are our preservers." Begging protection from the blacks, the older of the two men became so emotional that he lunged forward and threw his arms around Meade, causing Meade to draw his pistol to the Spaniard's face and threaten to shoot if he failed to let go. Once order returned, someone produced a torn Spanish ensign, which Meade had placed in the main rigging to signal Gedney to send more men because of the possibility of trouble. Meade guessed what had probably happened. Stories had been circulating for weeks of a mysterious black-hulled schooner, manned by black pirates, suspiciously inching its way along the North American coast and stalking defenseless merchant vessels. More than one American sea captain had met resistance upon attempting to investigate the strange intruder and to tow it into harbor. The two white men, perhaps, had at one time been in command of the vessel.

Realizing that the blacks could speak only native African tongues, Meade doubtless wondered if the truth could ever become known. But he could speak Spanish, and one side of the story was better than none. Besides, he found that one of the two Spaniards, José Ruiz, spoke English. Ruiz and his companion, Pedro Montes, claimed to be owners of fifty-three slaves aboard the Spanish vessel. About two months earlier, Ruiz nervously explained, the schooner had departed Havana for the 300-mile coastal voyage to Guanaja, port of entry for Puerto Príncipe in Cuba, where he was to deliver his forty-nine adult male slaves and Montes his four youths. Nothing was illegal about their activities, Ruiz emphasized; he and Montes had purchased the blacks on the public slave market in Havana. Just three days out, during the night of July 1, the slaves, led by Joseph Cinqué, had armed themselves with cane knives and risen in revolt, seizing control of the vessel after killing its captain and owner, Ramón Ferrer, and the cook, Celestino. During the scuffle, Ruiz and Montes put up resistance but were greatly outnumbered and had no chance. Ruiz surrendered, while Montes, who was severely wounded, tried to hide below. Montes was found and returned to the deck. The two crew members disappeared, the two Spaniards declared, presumably murdered and thrown overboard with the other two victims. One black was killed in the melee. By now, in addition to Antonio, the captain's slave and cabin boy, only thirty-nine slaves of the original fifty-three remained alive.

Ruiz explained that he and Montes were alive only because they had navigational skills. Cinqué and his companions had wanted to return to Africa. But, Ruiz explained to Meade, he and Montes tricked Cinqué into believing that the vessel was sailing in the right direction, when in reality the Spaniards were steering it back and forth through the waters, hoping to stay within range of British cruisers patrolling the Caribbean. Though beaten and starved by their black captors, Ruiz proudly proclaimed, he and Montes kept the *Amistad* headed in a general northerly direction toward the United States. The *Amistad* had zigzagged for two months within sight of the American coast, where now, in late August, Lieutenant Meade had just seized the vessel after its remarkable odyssey.

Seemingly satisfied with this story, Meade ordered two sailors to remain with him on the hatches while Porter and the rest of his men went after the others onshore. But five of the blacks who were on the beach at the time saw the approaching boat, jumped into their own craft, and tried to return to the schooner. Before they could paddle halfway across the water, Porter's men were upon them. Panic-stricken, the blacks turned their boat back to shore, whereupon Porter fired a warning shot over their heads and motioned them to the schooner. They made it to the sand, however, followed directly by the sailors with cutlasses drawn. After the white men still onshore nervously explained that their only intention had been to capture the blacks, Porter and his men moved into the brush, where in a few moments they found nine blacks, including the five from the beach, and ordered them to surrender. Facing pistols cocked and aimed, the blacks had no choice. Soon the two small boats were en route to the schooner, one with Porter and his men, the other half-filled with water and beginning to sink, but carrying the black captives, the two trunks Meade had seen from afar, and various other goods.

As the two boats neared the *Amistad,* Ruiz and Montes excitedly declared that one of the captives was Cinqué. An uneasy moment followed as the tall, lightly bronzed, and athletically built young man identified as leader of the revolt climbed aboard with the others and exchanged hard glances with his former prisoners. Meade ordered the blacks to join their companions below. Porter's men threw the contents of the boats on deck: a bottle of gin, sacks of potatoes, the trunks—locked but quickly opened to reveal nothing of value. Meade's men had meanwhile found only a few Spanish doubloons aboard, confirming his belief that Ruiz and Montes had told the truth. The *Amistad* was not a pirate ship but a Spanish slaver, overtaken by black mutineers whom the Spaniards deceived into sailing northward into American waters.

During these lengthy proceedings, Cinqué had become suspicious that the new white captors would ally with the Spaniards and kill him and the rest of his companions. Were not he and his people black and the others white? Who would sympathize with alleged slaves who had taken white lives during a mutiny? Cinqué suddenly leaped up the hatchway past Meade and the others and jumped overboard. Meade ordered a detachment of men after him in a boat. But every time the men approached Cinqué in the water, he dived below, only to surface again a few yards away. After several minutes of this, Cinqué finally became exhausted, and he was captured and returned to the schooner.

Yet the excitement was not over. Meade ordered Cinqué taken by himself to the *Washington;* but once there he showed such a strong desire to return to the *Amistad* that Gedney allowed him to do so. In the hold of the schooner again, his black comrades surrounded him, rejoicing at his safe return. Cinqué began speaking his native language in an animated fashion, apparently intending to stir his fellow blacks into a frenzy and another revolt. This time Meade had Cinqué manacled and returned to the *Washington.* On the next day, Cinqué signified by motions that if his captors would return him to the schooner, he would show them a handkerchief of doubloons he had hidden below. Permitted again to board the *Amistad,* Cinqué went below to receive a welcome even stronger than the one he got the day before. Instead of producing the doubloons, he delivered another impassioned address that alarmed Meade—especially when Cinqué repeatedly turned toward the whites and caused the blacks to yell and jump as if possessed by "some talismanic power."[2] For a third time, Meade had Cinqué returned to the *Washington.* En route to the American vessel, Cinqué stood quietly, his eyes fixed on the *Amistad.* Once aboard the brig again, he resumed staring at the schooner until taken below.

At last in control of the *Amistad* and its occupants, Lieutenant Gedney put his prize into tow, bound for New London, Connecticut, where slavery was legal (unlike New York) and he would file a claim in admiralty court for salvage on his property.

Had it not been for abolitionists in the United States, the excitement over the *Amistad* might have ended quietly in a prize court in Connecticut. But their involvement in the case turned it into a cause célèbre for the abolition movement. New York's Lewis Tappan joined Roger S. Baldwin, Simeon Jocelyn, Joshua Leavitt, and other abolitionists in using the *Amistad* affair as a means of publicizing the evils of the African slave trade and of slavery itself. Doubts arose as to whether the *Amistad*'s blacks were legally slaves. Those versed in international law would point out that in 1817 England and Spain had formally agreed to halt the African slave trade and that the four children on the schooner, who could speak only an African language, were too young to have been brought into Cuba before the treaty went into effect in 1820. If the four youths were not slaves, the legitimacy of the slavehood of the other slaves came into question. The abolitionists, aware of these doubts, would argue in court that all the blacks on the *Amistad* had been kidnapped from Africa and enslaved illegally in Cuba. Personal liberty was at stake in the case, regardless of the color of the persons involved. Should the abolitionists establish the principle that all individuals, white and black, had an inherent right to freedom, it might help erase the color line, inflicting a mortal blow on American slavery by undermining the racial basis of its existence. Indeed, a recent writer insists that before the Dred Scott decision of 1857, no case involving slavery attracted as much nationwide attention as did the *Amistad.*[3]

Abolitionism was part of a broader struggle for equal justice based on natural rights. Looking back over years of abolitionist activity, William Lloyd Garrison, the fiery editor of the Boston *Liberator,* declared in 1852 that the antislavery movement had begun out of concern for blacks but grew into a crusade for the fundamental liberties of all people. Abolitionists saw slavery as unjust not only because it threatened an entire people with bondage but also because it encouraged the development of a class of aristocratic landowners who had conspired to win power by spreading slavery throughout the Southern states. Furthermore, the abolitionist Wendell Phillips warned, the "slaveocracy" would unite with Northern industrial capitalists to form "the Lords of the Lash and the Lords of the Loom."[4] Garrison called for the immediate emancipation of slaves with no compensation to owners.[5] If the state, church, and American Union could not survive the antislavery movement's call for humanity and freedom, he once exclaimed, they deserved to collapse. "If the Republic must be blotted out from the roll of nations, by proclaiming liberty to the captives, then let the Republic sink beneath the waves of oblivion."[6]

Lewis Tappan was a Christian abolitionist who professed a hope to establish a virtuous nation based on the principles of Christian morality. He and others, such as Leavitt and Jocelyn, used evangelical arguments to support their stand against slavery. Tappan realized that the abolitionists were a small minority in the United States and knew that they faced a monumental task in attempting to change a national system that did not permit equal justice to all peoples and relegated some of them to the status of property. Tappan therefore sought to politicize slavery by making it a moral issue and pushing it into the mainstream of American thought. The American courts, however, tried to avert arguments over slavery by searching for a consensus that would quiet the issue and preserve the Jeffersonian-Jacksonian political system of compromise. What seemed clear to Tappan and friends did not seem clear to most other Americans, including those in the North who claimed to oppose slavery. To mobilize an effective movement against the institution, Tappan realized, he and other abolitionists first had to gain the support of moderates. Such a coalition might expose the repugnance of slavery and make an appeal to higher law. The *Amistad* mutiny provided that opportunity.

The *Amistad* affair demonstrates how, at least temporarily, the abolitionists overcame their differences to unite against slavery. Diversity characterized not only the antislavery movement but also the abolitionists. Some trusted solely in "moral suasion," believing that graphic illustrations of the immorality of slavery would turn good people against the institution. Others accepted this approach but added a religious emphasis that made slavery a sin and the slaveholder a sinner; repentance was necessary to end the inhumane, immoral, and unchristian practice. Only a government built on the principles of God, not man, could restore God's sovereignty over man in a proper relationship not subverted by institutions of human bondage. A third group of abolitionists turned to political action, either through the Whig party in particular or by establishing a special party seeking to abolish slavery. Still other abolitionists tried to combine some of the above, or simply moved from one approach to another, hoping that a dramatic incident would awaken the American people to the injustice of slavery.[7] On many occasions the abolitionists bitterly disagreed over their approaches to the problem; in the *Amistad* case they agreed that if they could undercut barriers based on color and racial prejudices, the South would lose its major bases for slavery.

Perhaps the chief reason for the abolitionists' harmony in the *Amistad* case was that there was room for all three approaches. Those emphasizing moral suasion found widespread sympathy for the black captives—even among Americans who had no strong feeling against slavery and who certainly did not advocate racial equality. A paternalistic attitude clearly guided these Americans' thinking once it became clear that the helpless victims on the *Amistad* posed no threat to the white community. After the antiabolitionist violence in the North of the early 1830s, it was difficult to convince Americans that justice for the *Amistad* blacks did not automatically endanger the welfare of everyone around them. Abo-

litionists recognized that they might develop a universal argument
for fair treatment of all people, regardless of color, if they could
demonstrate that black people had human feelings and emotions.
The task would not be easy. Proslavery theorists argued for black
inferiority on the basis of an alleged absence of civilized life in
Africa. Savagery, cannibalism, nongodly worship, the shape of the
head—all were indicative of physical and mental inferiority that
only enslavement could ameliorate.[8] South Carolina's John C. Calhoun declared in the Senate in 1837 that slavery was "a positive
good."[9] To counter racial prejudice, evangelical abolitionists
equated slavery with sin, whereas the more practical members of
the abolitionist movement, those who by the late 1830s were placing more emphasis on political realities, sought to build political
coalitions that would press for a change in the Constitution's sanction of slavery in the states.[10]

The abolitionists' use of the *Amistad* affair paralleled transitions
that occurred in the abolitionist movement as a whole. They first
had to expose the evils of slavery before they could stir substantive
opposition to it. All abolitionists recognized the importance of
revealing the immoral nature of slavery, but not all of them understood that the movement against slavery had to go beyond mere
criticism. To achieve permanent changes in the constitutional
framework of the nation, the abolitionists had to construct bases
of political power. The *Amistad* case illustrates these adjustments
to changing realities. Once the abolitionists had demonstrated the
humanity of the blacks and had publicized the atrocities of the
slave trade and slavery, this stage of the battle was over. For long-
term remedial action, political and legal steps were necessary.

Tappan and other evangelical abolitionists believed that the
Constitution itself was the most serious obstacle to their success in
the *Amistad* affair and other issues involving slavery. The great
document condoned slavery by making it a matter for state constitutions and laws. An amendment for the abolition of slavery was
impossible to obtain because of the need for ratification by three-
fourths of the states. To repeal laws safeguarding slavery, therefore,
one would have to work inside the slave states, which was out of
the question. The only conceivable national powers regarding slavery were those regulating the interstate movement of slaves and
prohibiting it in territories. The day before the *Amistad* case began
before the Supreme Court, that same Court dealt with a case
involving the first of these—*Groves* v. *Slaughter*—and ducked the
issue. The territorial question would arise again and again, but not

until the 1840s, when controversy developed over the Wilmot Proviso, first introduced during the Mexican War. These two approaches to the problem of slavery would ultimately become the abolitionists' most effective weapons; but for Tappan and others during the 1830s, moral suasion was the chief instrument in exposing the injustices contained in the laws of the United States and in combating the evil of slavery.

One wonders what the outcome might have been had more abolitionists searched the Constitution for remedies, rather than criticizing it as a weapon of slaveholders and as being in total violation of the law of nature. Article I, Section 8, Clause 10, empowered Congress to "define and punish ... Offences against the Law of Nations." Since natural law was the foundation of the law of nations, it would have been an interesting situation had the abolitionists taken advantage of the broad definition of international law and raised this point during their struggle against slavery. Believing that there was no legal recourse, they appealed to a higher law—natural law—as had been done (in the abolitionists' view) in 1776. That is what they sought to do in the *Amistad* case.

The following account of the mutiny on the *Amistad* shows that the law of nature went on trial in the United States. The essential issue throughout the affair was a conflict between human rights and property rights—whether natural law as the abolitionists defined it was to take precedence over what they regarded as positive, man-made law. Abolitionists asked whether American law was a guarantor of the nation's ideals. Or did the federal system of government permit a framework for racism that approved the oppression of blacks on the one hand and supported the civil rights of whites on the other? What was the status of free blacks in American society? Did the law of nature permit an attack on slavery, despite the Constitution's tacit approval of it?

More than once, Lewis Tappan alluded to natural law when he spoke of "universal liberty" and called for the "largest liberty for the poor man—for the oppressed." There should be no artificial distinctions in society based on race or color; everyone should have the opportunity to achieve all he was capable of achieving. The only way to reach this goal, Tappan believed, was to establish a government based on the principles of God. Slavery was the most serious of wrongs—indeed, a sin—because it interfered with man's free moral agency and violated God's absolute authority by giving it to man. Tappan sought to go beyond immediate issues in appealing to universal principles of righteousness, thus confronting slave-

holders and their Northern supporters with their own racism and
the inhumanity of the system of slavery it promoted. He and other
evangelicals repeatedly stressed the supremacy of natural rights
over man-made law; they called for a Christian, moral government
admitting to the priority of liberty over property. One of the *Amistad* captives' lawyers, Seth Staples, borrowed from the English philosopher John Locke, in emphasizing the "inherent property of
liberty."[11]

Tappan and other abolitionists derived many lessons from their
attempt to win social justice. In confronting America's racial inequities, they used the courts as a forum in which to condemn social
injustice and to call for equality. Furthermore, they learned what
political and legal paths were open for future battles. Some abolitionists came to realize that despite their appeals to higher law,
they ultimately had to resort to positive law. In that regard, they
would attempt to fight slavery by turning to congressional powers
over interstate commerce and over territories. Americans would
not resolve these moral-legal matters during the 1830s; indeed,
their failure to do so helped bring on the Civil War. And the questions of moral injustice remain today, continuing to divide
Americans.

The *Amistad* mutiny made an indelible mark on history. Besides
being pure drama, the event raised questions about the relevance
of race and slavery to the nineteenth-century definition of liberty.
The affair helped to establish ties between American and British
antislavery groups, while further distinguishing the abolitionists
from other reformers in the United States. It demonstrated not
only black resistance to slavery but also those interracial attempts
to achieve the blacks' freedom. It also led to a level of political
maneuvering by the White House that was both conspiratorial and
illegal. President Martin Van Buren authorized actions that interfered with the judicial process and exceeded the powers of the
executive office—both out of concern about his reelection in
1840. The case strained relations between the United States and
Spain until the outbreak of the American Civil War, often becoming entangled with other issues, including America's growing interest in Cuba. In addition, the diplomatic imbroglio threatened to
involve the British. If the Spanish were guilty of violating treaties
with England against the slave trade, the government in London
would have a pretext for intervening in Cuba and thereby endangering America's interest in the island. Finally, the mutiny became the subject of a trial before the U.S. Supreme Court that pitted former President John Quincy Adams against the federal

government and that may have affected Chief Justice Roger B. Taney's later decision in the famous Dred Scott case. In the *Amistad* verdict of 1841 Associate Justice Joseph Story wrote a decision that helped calm the waters, only to have them become turbulent again when, in the Dred Scott case of 1857, Taney handed down a decree that inadvertently thrust previously avoided issues over slavery into the public arena.

The parallels between the strategy used in the *Amistad* case and that of later civil rights activists are especially striking. Both groups realized that to rid the nation of immoral laws, they first had to expose those injustices before the highest public forum in the land. Their strategy rested on placing the profound differences between positive law and natural law before the American people, hoping they might see the need for changing the Constitution and American laws to comply with the moral principles contained in the Declaration of Independence.

The questions highlighted by the *Amistad* controversy are part of America's national heritage, as provocative to Americans of today as they were to those of the nineteenth century.

1

The Mutiny

I

In early April 1839 the Portuguese slave merchants at Lomboko, on the west coast of Africa, were loading their human cargo onto the *Teçora,* in preparation for the long Middle Passage to Cuba. For weeks this process had been under way, and now, under the blazing equatorial sun, the slave dealers tried to make haste in order to reduce their crew's exposure to African fever, to avoid a seizure by pirates or enemy vessels, and to lessen chances of a slave revolt before the ship could get to sea. Along the tributaries and lagoons of the Gallinas River, most of the factories, crude buildings in which captured blacks were stored until departure, belonged to the house of Martínez in Havana. Indeed, the vessels engaged in the trade—American and Russian as well as Portuguese—flew that house's flag, white with the letter *M* on it. The most notorious slave trader in the area was Pedro Blanco of Havana, who had organized the business in the region during the mid-1820s, and with the help of Europeans and "Settler subagents" he would retire a rich man—after British cruisers had destroyed his factories.[1] Despite British efforts to suppress the trade, in the 1830s, it was still, according to one firsthand observer, the "universal business" of Africa, "by far the most profitable" of all enterprises and sanctioned by the "law of usage."[2]

The factories that were to supply the *Teçora* came alive as the European businessmen closed deals with their black counterparts in Africa. The black captives, largely seized in the continental interior by other Africans, were marched out of the dark, damp, and dingy constructions, their eyes throbbing from the sun. Many had never seen the ocean and were terrified by the roaring surf of the Atlantic, but they were forced into large canoes waiting to carry them to the slave ship. At last, when the *Teçora* was filled, it slowly broke harbor. In the darkened and stifling hold was the slaver's cargo, over five hundred black Africans, mostly women and children, with no one older than the mid-twenties and all of them chained two by two, hands to feet, and packed into layered decks less than four feet high that prevented standing except in a crouch.[3]

Among the blacks was Joseph Cinqué, twenty-five years of age and, like the others around him, horrified by the events that had catapulted him into his present plight. Cinqué's thoughts may well have turned back to the day when four black strangers had seized him while he was at work on a road between villages. He was strong and agile, taller than most of his fellow tribesmen at five feet eight inches, but he had had no chance against superior numbers. Chained by the neck to other blacks, some of whom he recognized, he had been force-marched three days from his Mende homeland in Sierra Leone to the West African coast. The situation was bewildering. He knew that many towns and villages regularly warred on each other for the purpose of selling captives to slave dealers. But he also knew that not all slaves were prisoners of war—that some had been sentenced to slavery for committing crimes punishable by death, whereas others had been captured in the jungle and sold to pay off debts. Cinqué's people were peace loving, and this led him to believe that he himself was the payoff on a debt he owed a business acquaintance. Whatever the truth, Cinqué was now a slave, captured by people he did not know, loaded onto a vessel by strange and hostile white people, and bound for some unimaginable destination. His wife and three children were certainly aware of his disappearance. But, for all they knew, Cinqué had been killed by animals in the African bush.[4]

Cinqué and the others around him would be on the *Teçora* for two months. More than a third would die from sickness and disease caused by inadequate provisions and unsanitary conditions. The slaver carried sufficient rice but not enough water. If the blacks failed to eat all their rice, they were whipped and had vinegar put on their wounds. A common occurrence, according to one of the captives, was to eat so much they vomited. Many of the survivors would never be the same again, either physically or emotionally. None, it seemed certain, would make the return voyage.[5]

At long last, Cinqué could discern by increased activity on deck that the ship was approaching land. *Cuba*—wherever that was—

appeared to mark the end of the journey. He had sensed that the vessel was nearing its destination when, a few days earlier, the captain had ordered his black cargo unchained, brought on deck, bathed, and given clean clothing. Larger quantities of food and water had temporarily lifted the spirits of his fellow captives, although Cinqué and others were immediately fearful of what lay ahead. Hoping to see this new land as the slaver entered the harbor, Cinqué was disappointed when the vessel suddenly came to a halt on the high seas, some distance offshore. The *Teçora* would not make port until dark—for what reason Cinqué could not understand, but the captain's visibly apprehensive crew and officers knew that British cruisers were on anti-slave-trade patrol in the waters surrounding Cuba. The Portuguese slaver was operating in violation of an Anglo-Spanish treaty of 1817, which prohibited the African slave trade and promised death to its violators. Experience dictated an entrance at night.[6]

When darkness fell, only the pale glow of the lights onshore guided the *Teçora* inland. Passing quietly through the still waters, it eased into a secluded inlet along the Cuban shoreline. Once anchored, the vessel gave way to full-scale activity as the captain ordered his men to quickly load the blacks onto small boats and take them ashore. After the entire cargo was on the beach, the crew hustled the captives into the jungle, where after a three-mile march they were jammed into crude dwellings. For almost two weeks, they remained in these warehouses, until one night in June the captain ordered the blacks to form lines and begin another long trek through the thickets. After a while, they came within sight of the city of Havana, where they settled once again, outside the walls, to await morning. At daylight Cinqué and his black companions were put into a barracoon, an oblong enclosure without a roof, which during the day served as a slave market and at night was a prison.[7]

II

Importation of slaves into Cuba was a violation of Spanish law and treaty, although the institution of slavery itself was legal. A paradox had resulted on the island: on the one hand, the slave trade was forbidden; but on the other, if the trader succeeded in getting his merchandise ashore, the blacks, for practical purposes, assumed the status of slaves.[8] The British and Spanish governments had established a mixed commission to enforce prohibitions against the slave traffic, but that body's powers ceased once the cargo reached land. Hence, the Portuguese captain had taken his captives ashore by night and then transported them overland by night, in preparation for the rich profits awaiting him at the slave market.

David Turnbull, an outspoken British abolitionist who was to become consul in Havana in late 1840, only to have the Spanish government secure his withdrawal in less than two years, described the conditions on the island. The Spaniards, he wrote in a journal of his travels in the Caribbean, erected two large barracoons "for the reception and sale of newly imported Africans." Located beneath the windows of the residence of the highest Spanish official on the island, the captain general, one enclosure held up to one thousand slaves, the other fifteen hundred. During Turnbull's time in Havana they were full, serving both as a marketplace and as a prison. The barracoons were situated at the point of "greatest attraction"—at the end of the new paseo, which connected the palace of the captain general with the city. Moreover, a railroad into the interior passed the area, frightening recent arrivals from Africa but allowing passengers to observe the blacks crowded in the barracoons. Indeed, Spaniards often took strangers to the barracoons as a tourist attraction. The slave importer generally treated his captives well, feeding and clothing them, giving them tobacco, providing oil to rub into their skin and make it glisten, encouraging them to exercise in the large courtyard of the buildings. Spirits must remain high; depressed, homesick blacks brought less on the market. The barracoon, Turnbull lamented, was a virtual Spanish monument to Britain's failure to halt the African slave trade.[9]

Turnbull insisted that the barracoons constituted a "well-organized system of kidnapping." Captives of an advanced age were not as adaptable to requirements of the plantation; consequently, slaveowners needed youths for the fields. Their ages appeared to range from twelve to eighteen, and males outnumbered females about three to one because of the greater demand for their labor. Indeed, the planter found it cheaper to increase his labor supply by buying young, recently imported Africans in the barracoons than by depending on procreation. Some estates were filled only with males, forcing their owners to lock them up at night to prevent wanderings. Another reason for slaveowners' wanting to continue the slave trade, Turnbull explained, was the "well-known fact" that children of plantation slaves had less physical strength than those imported from Africa. Black Africans brought more profit on the market.[10]

The situation in Cuba described by Turnbull originated shortly after the Napoleonic Wars ended, in 1815, when Spain's need for African slaves temporarily declined, and its government two years afterward signed a treaty with England outlawing the slave trade. In the spirit of humanity, some argued, the nefarious practice had to end. Others insisted that the advantages to Africans of being exposed to a civilized country like Spain had declined; missionaries could now civilize them in their own lands. The Congress of Vienna in 1815 agreed on the necessity of abolishing the African slave trade. Two years later, the Spanish king announced a treaty with England, which prohibited the purchase of blacks in Africa and declared that as of May 1820, when the pact went into effect, those brought into Spanish dominions became free.[11]

A major flaw in the treaty of 1817 was Article 7, which assured eventual freedom for *emancipados* but in actuality prolonged slavery on the island. According to the system, blacks rescued from captured slavers were to receive certificates of emancipation from the mixed commission before being taken to the government in whose territory the offense had occurred. If British or Spanish cruisers seized a slaver off the Cuban coast, the blacks would go to the government of Cuba, which was to furnish them a place of work for five to seven years as servants or free laborers, with freedom guaranteed at the end of the period. But the system left room for abuse. English officials in Havana realized that the captains general were often *selling* the *emancipados* to planters, who then treated the blacks like slaves. Indeed, firsthand observers argued that the *emancipado* worked harder than the slave. Knowing the *emancipado* was available for only a specific period, many planters worked him into such poor health that he was incapable of taking a place in Cuban society. Furthermore, the *emancipado* system became a thriving business for planters seeking to replace slaves who had died or disappeared. It actually provided another source of slaves on the island.[12]

When the British protested the misuse of the *emancipado* system, the Spanish lamely responded with a hopeful statement that it would eventually work as intended by the treaty. The government in Madrid encouraged the enforcement of the treaty provision by directing Cuban planters to upgrade the treatment of *emancipados* and maintain a register of those freed from slavers. But charges soon spread of falsified information in the register. Planters found it lucrative to sell the *emancipados* as slaves after their service time had expired. British insistence on immediate freedom for those blacks who were released from captured slavers aroused no support from Cuban planters, who argued that an increase in free blacks on the island could set an example conducive to slave uprisings. British proposals to send *emancipados* to Africa likewise met opposition. The process would cost too much, the Cuban government declared, and it would be unchristian to return them to their pagan world. The real reason for wanting to maintain the *emancipado* system was simple: it was enormously profitable to the slaveholders and to Cuban officials who sold the blacks to planters.[13]

During the 1830s a reform movement arose in Cuba that included a call for an end to the slave trade. Primarily influential sugar and coffee planters, the reformers foresaw that the introduction of steam power to the sugar industry in 1819 would soon force a replacement of the African slave with a new kind of laborer: a literate wage earner capable of operating the sugar-processing machines. The addition of more African slaves therefore seemed shortsighted. Moreover, these same Cuban planters suspected the Spanish government of seeking to prolong the slave trade in an effort to promote the increase of blacks on the island and force the planters' continued reliance on leaders in Madrid. Though these Cuban planters by no means composed the majority of the slaveholding groups, they were chiefly from the old class of planters, whose estates had sufficient slaves and who now wanted to end the slave trade and thereby raise the value of slaves in their possession. More important, they feared that the continuation of the slave trade could lead to a larger majority of blacks and eventually cause a general slave insurrection in Cuba similar to the one in Santo Domingo during the 1790s.[14]

Thus several factors obstructed a suppression of the slave trade in Cuba. Spanish officials and merchants had combined with the great majority of Cuban planters who needed a cheap labor force to dampen the reformers' hopes. The government in Madrid profited heavily from Cuban sugar and did not wish to hurt this business by cutting off its source of labor. One reformer highlighted the central problem in the attempt to effect change when he wrote that no one wanted a revolution in Cuba unless its success was certain. In the present situation, he declared, "the *political revolution* is necessarily accompanied by a social revolution and the social revolution is the complete ruin of the Cuban race."[15]

Despite Spain's anti-slave-trade arrangement with England, the illicit business remained widespread. During the 1820s Spain at

times had no more than two ships to patrol two thousand miles of
heavily indented African coast. About fifteen hundred ships
entered Havana every year, making it easy for slavers to hide
among them. Furthermore, there were no laws prohibiting the
shipment of slaves from one Spanish colony to another; this again
allowed one form of business to blend with another. In 1831 the
British foreign minister, Lord Palmerston, demanded that the
Spanish government enforce its laws, but the captain general in
Havana warned that such a move would add to the growing proportion of free blacks on the island and lead to serious social and
political problems. The result was that the government in Madrid
issued public orders to obey treaties yet seemed to connive in the
continuation of the slave trade. Ironically, a major impetus to the
Cuban trade was Britain's decision in 1833 to abolish slavery in its
own West Indies possessions. This move made the Cuban traffic
more important.[16]

A renewal of the Anglo-Spanish agreement in 1835 did not slow
the business, although it led slave merchants to devise new policies
to circumvent the law. The new treaty authorized naval vessels to
act on the basis of prima facie evidence in visiting a suspected
slaver. Slave traders realized that the treaties between England and
Spain applied only to slaves purchased outside Cuba—*not* to those
bought on the island—and they turned even more to importing
human cargo under the cover of night, using deserted coves as
landing sites. Furthermore, they no longer openly fitted vessels in
Cuban ports. Other alterations in the trade became apparent.
Newspapers stopped announcing the arrival and departure times
of ships. Names of slave captains ceased appearing in registers of
the slave exchange in Havana. Slavers replaced Spanish flags with
Portuguese and American colors. The British had little chance of
stopping the trade, because they never had enough ships to patrol
all of Cuba's coastline and because they had no authority on land.
Once the slave merchant made it ashore, his product became legal
and he could ship it anywhere in Spanish territory. The queen of
Spain tried to remedy the situation in November 1838, when she
issued a royal decree urging the captain general on the island to
enforce prohibitions against the traffic and to impose the strictest
penalties allowed by law. This tactic also failed. British abolitionists became frustrated with the situation in Cuba. According to Sir
Thomas F. Buxton in 1840, Spanish officials were guilty of "artifice, violence, intimidation, popular countenance, and official
connivance."[17]

Turnbull was convinced that "political necessity" prevented public officials on the island from enforcing the law. If recently imported slaves had access to the judicial process, they could prove their alleged owners' inability to produce a legal title. Spanish law prohibited ownership of recently imported Africans, he declared; "if the captain-general had not been prevented by secret counter orders from carrying these laws into effect, the trade would long ago have been effectually suppressed." But leaders in Madrid feared that they would lose Cuba if the enforcement of anti-slave-trade laws created a free black class and encouraged slave rebellions on the island. "Conceal it as they may," Turnbull wrote, "the true and simple key to the whole policy of the Spanish government" was that the captain general and others in Cuba had the "official sanction" of the mother country in ignoring the law.[18]

In truth, the Spanish government faced a dilemma. A clampdown on island authorities would satisfy the British, but strong measures would alienate Cuban plantation owners—the richest, most powerful group on the island. Madrid's officials repeatedly assured the British that they were doing their best to halt the slave trade, whereas in reality they turned the other way, allowing regular violations of law and treaty. America's consul in Havana, Nicholas Trist, believed that the slave trade was "a pursuit denounced in every way by the Law, and upheld by an overwhelming Public Opinion."[19]

Another business had developed from Spain's haphazard enforcement of the law: Cuban authorities accepted illegal payments for ignoring importations of slaves from Africa. From the captain general down to customs officers at the ports, bribes in the form of "fees" became a standard practice. Since Spanish law forbade such assessments, officials referred to them as voluntary. According to Turnbull, these officials were "sharers in a common enterprise." In Havana the money was "paid from habit, as a matter of course." So many public officials were involved that slave importers found the payment difficult to evade. Yet the tax did not appear to result either from an act of the Spanish legislature or from royal decree. As evidence for this statement, Turnbull noted that "the parties who pay it have never yet succeeded in obtaining anything in the nature of a receipt or other written acknowledgment for the money."[20]

Once the slaves were sold in the barracoons, the captain general signed the *trespassos,* or passports, which permitted the purchaser to transport his human property to another spot on the island.

Spanish law referred to those slaves who had lived on the island long enough to be Spanish subjects and to speak the Spanish language as *ladinos.* Blacks brought illegally onto the island as slaves were *bozales,* for they had never been domiciled and were unable to speak Spanish. Over the captain general's signature, and for a small fee, slave buyers were able to secure passports that classified their slaves as *ladinos,* regardless of their age or language.[21]

In late 1840 Charles Butler, a longtime resident of Cuba who had studied Spanish law and was a barrister, explained the system to Congressman John Quincy Adams of Massachusetts. Abuses of the law started a few years ago, Butler pointed out, when the captain of a British man-of-war in Havana found a large number of freshly imported slaves leaving in a steamboat. He had to let them go when the captain of the steamer produced a passport from the captain general giving the names of the blacks and the estates they came from, along with their destination. Since that time, Butler explained, slaveowners carried passports from the proper authorities. He had seen these documents countersigned by a naval officer or a justice of the peace, even though there was no doubt that the slaver had unloaded a fresh African cargo. And yet the passport always stated that the slaves had come from some "contiguous estate." The government refused to suppress this business, he lamented to Adams.[22]

The government in Spain was particularly concerned about England. Several officials suspected the British of trying to enhance the value of their Asiatic dominions by disrupting the trade of the West Indies. By the late 1830s the Spanish feared that British efforts to expand the powers of the mixed commission were part of an abolitionist attempt to end the slave trade and divert the blacks' allegiance to the British themselves. A further complication was that England might take advantage of Spain's perennial political problems, exacerbated by revolts and counterrevolts that swept the country for four decades following the mid-1830s. The slavery issue in Cuba thus provided a pretext for British interference in the Caribbean.[23]

This was the confused situation, one that had become a well-oiled system, by the time Cinqué and his fellow Africans arrived in Cuba in 1839.

III

In late June two Spanish dons, José Ruiz (known as Pepe) and Pedro Montes, joined the crowd of slave patrons at the barracoons in

Havana, bartering for slaves to take to plantations in Puerto Príncipe, located about two days' sailing distance on the northwest coast of the island. Ruiz was only twenty-four years old and Montes fifty-eight, but both men were seasoned and wealthy businessmen who knew their trade. Ruiz, accompanied by the Portuguese captain of the *Teçora,* carefully narrowed his choices and called for the blacks to stand in a row so that he might examine their bodies and teeth. Satisfied, he paid $450 apiece for forty-nine adult males, including Cinqué. At the same time, in another part of the yard, Montes bought four young children, three of them female. On June 22 Montes secured a passport from the captain general that authorized him to transport his "black Ladinos" to Puerto Príncipe by sea; four days later Ruiz did the same. Cinqué and his companions had been in the barracoons for ten days.[24]

Two nights later, on June 28, Ruiz and Montes accompanied the newly purchased Africans on foot through Havana, headed for a vessel they had chartered—the *Amistad,* a small and sleek black schooner with two masts, built and fitted in Baltimore for the coastal slave trade. At eight o'clock that evening, with only the glow of the harbor lamps lighting the dock, Ruiz and Montes ordered the fifty-three blacks to come aboard. Though the *Amistad* had for three years operated legally in the coastal slave traffic, the two Spaniards knew that the vessel was subject to British search procedures anywhere in the Caribbean. Hence they had taken the precaution of loading at night. Despite their passports, duly signed by the captain general, they did not want to take a chance. Their captives were not *ladinos:* none knew Spanish; all spoke only African tongues; and the four children were too young to have been slaves in Cuba before the anti-slave-trade law went into effect in 1820. Nonetheless, the passports contained descriptions of each black, along with false Spanish names assigned to them by their purchasers. Under the command of Ramón Ferrer, the vessel's captain and owner, the *Amistad* departed at midnight for Puerto Príncipe, carrying Ruiz and Montes, their fifty-three blacks unchained but in the hold, two sailors as crew members, the captain's sixteen-year-old cabin boy and slave, Antonio, a mulatto cook named Celestino, $250 in cash, and cargo and provisions worth about $40,000.[25]

Captain Ferrer and his two Spanish companions prepared for a routine trip. The weather was hot and humid. Once clear of the harbor Ferrer followed his usual practice of dragging his mattress up the stairs and onto the deck. A few moments later, one of the sailors heard some of the blacks noisily coming up the hold to the forecastle. After a reprimand, he ordered them back below. The

following day the winds shifted, lengthening the voyage and leading to a decision to forgo any trips ashore for more provisions.
Thus each black was allotted only one banana, two potatoes, and
a small cup of water per day. Tempers shortened in the tropical
heat. Ruiz and Montes had allowed a few of the blacks at a time
to gain relief on deck. When one of the captives, Burnah,
attempted to take more water than allotted, Ruiz had him flogged
by a crew member.[26]

Cinqué became increasingly restless in his concern over the
Spaniards' intentions. On one occasion while on deck, he used sign
language to ask the cook what would happen to them. In cruel jest,
Celestino grinned and pointed to barrels of beef across the room
and then to an empty one behind him. Upon arrival in Puerto
Príncipe, he indicated with his fingers, the Spaniards planned to
slit all the slaves' throats, chop their bodies into pieces, salt them
down, and eat them as dried meat. Cinqué stumbled out of the
kitchen, stunned by Celestino's crude revelation and yet furious
with himself and with the cook's arrogant manner. Cinqué should
have known better than to talk to him; Celestino had once struck
him for no apparent reason. Finding a nail, Cinqué hid it under his
arm, determined at the first opportunity to pick the lock on the
iron collar around his neck and make a strike for freedom.[27]

On the third night at sea, July 1, Cinqué worked closely with a
fellow captive named Grabeau in making preparations for an
insurrection. After freeing themselves and then the others from the
irons, they found boxes below that contained weapons: sugar cane
knives with handles consisting of square pieces of steel an inch
thick, and attached to blades two feet long that gradually widened
to three inches at the end. Stealing up the hatchway, they prepared
to storm the captain where he slept on deck.[28]

Captain Ferrer had retired at a little past 11:00 P.M., just as the
moon was rising. A storm soon hit, blackening the night and forcing the crew to lower the sails for hours until it passed over.
Around 4:00 A.M., with the sky still rainy and darkened by heavy
clouds, Ruiz and Montes were suddenly awakened by loud noises
and the scuffle of many feet on the deck, followed by screams of
"Murder!" Jumping from their bunks, they rushed outside to join
the two sailors who were running toward the sound of trouble. At
first they were barely able to discern the figures moving only a few
feet before them, but the four men finally distinguished Cinqué
and other blacks near the captain, armed with cane knives and
closing in on him and his slave Antonio. "Throw some bread at

them!'' the captain yelled in desperation while wielding his dagger. But Cinqué ignored the basket at his feet and with his heavy steel blade struck the captain to the floor, leaving the others to strangle him to death. Through the misty darkness, Ruiz and Montes could see that the captain had perhaps killed one of his assailants and wounded two others; to the right they saw a ring of blacks surrounding the boat where Celestino regularly slept and angrily thudding hatchet blows onto his crumpled and already lifeless body.[29]

Ruiz and Montes frantically tried to regain control. Montes drew his knife and joined one of the sailors swinging a stick to drive some of the blacks behind the foresail, while Ruiz stood before the galley, ordering others back into the hold. The second sailor yelled at Montes to throw him the cook's knife. "Kill them all!" the sailor screamed as he groped for the weapon now at his feet. Montes slashed a few of the blacks, trying to frighten them and break the mutiny. But the sight of their own blood drove the blacks into a frenzy. As they advanced toward him, Montes swung at the blacks with knife in one hand and pump handle in the other, forcing them to retreat behind the foresail, but not before they had wounded him with sticks and cane knives. Seeing one of the blacks reaching for an oar under the foresail, Montes grabbed the flat end and pulled desperately against the man now tugging the handle. But two other blacks also grabbed the oar while others whacked Montes repeatedly on the legs and body with another oar, causing one of the sailors to exhort him to let go before they killed him. Montes dropped his knife in the struggle, and as he bent down to find it he took a hard blow on the head with a cane knife, which drove a deep gash above his ear and knocked him senseless to the deck. Barely able to rise, he staggered below to the hold, his bloody frame falling headlong to the floor. He had to hide. Crawling through the darkness, he squeezed behind a food barrel and pulled an old sail over him.[30]

Cinqué, along with Grabeau and Burnah, had taken command of the *Amistad.* The captain and cook were dead. Ruiz had surrendered after sustaining several mild wounds. Antonio had begged for mercy and remained alive, tied to the anchor. The two sailors had disappeared, probably drowned after jumping overboard and trying to swim the long distance to shore.[31] The only one unaccounted for was Montes; but he could wait the short time until daybreak. In minutes the mutiny had succeeded.

As dawn lighted the skyline, Montes dazedly heard what sounded like two people running down the steps leading below, crashing into objects, angrily searching in the pale light for him. Montes attempted to lie still, but he was breathing heavily and shaking uncontrollably. Suddenly his cover was thrown off, and Cinqué was revealed standing over him with raised cane knife, ready to bury it in Montes's body. Montes screamed and begged for his life while trying to escape the rain of blows. But before Cinqué could inflict a mortal wound, Burnah grabbed his arms and after a heated exchange persuaded him not to take the Spaniard's life.[32]

Only dimly conscious, Montes was dragged on deck, where he realized that his life had been spared for one purpose: to sail the vessel to Africa. He saw Ruiz, also bleeding and now sitting on the deck with hands tied. Cinqué and his companion tied one of Ruiz's arms to one of Montes's, threatening to kill them if they tried to escape. After some time they loosened the two men's bonds, took off their blood-covered clothes, and used the key to their trunks to find clean ones. Cinqué, the acknowledged leader of the mutineers, had communicated his aim by signs. Though lacking navigational skills, he recalled that the slave ship he and others had been on during the passage from Africa to Cuba had sailed away from the rising sun. To return home, Cinqué ordered Montes, who had once been a sea captain, to sail the *Amistad* into the sun. But the two Spaniards, talking in Spanish, which none of the blacks could understand, devised a plan whereby Montes would during the day steer the vessel in the proper direction but at night turn northward. Surely, they thought, a British cruiser on anti-slave-trade patrol would rescue them.[33]

Now at the helm, Montes gazed around him at the remains of the mutiny: Cinqué issuing orders to drag the bodies of the captain and cook to the side and throw them overboard; other blacks washing down the deck, stained red with blood; the ghostly silence that always seems to accompany death now prevailing over the eerie sounds of mast creaking and sails rustling in the breeze; the two sailors not in sight; only himself, Ruiz, and Antonio alive. As the *Amistad* cut through the warm, azure waters, Montes wondered how long he might fool Cinqué into believing that the vessel was sailing toward Africa.[34]

IV

The next two months were tumultuous for the *Amistad* voyage. For days Montes kept the vessel near the Bahamas before beginning an erratic north and northeast course toward the United States. To further obstruct the voyage, Montes kept the sails flapping in the wind, causing the vessel to make little headway during the day. As the moon rose during the first night following the insurrection, a violent storm blew from land, forcing Montes to have all sails lowered except the foretopsail. By this time the blacks were terrified at the thought of dying at sea. But when the squall passed and daybreak came, Cinqué began to suspect that the vessel was heading back toward Havana. Calling a hurried council in the cabin below, he and others apparently decided to kill the two Spaniards. As Cinqué approached Montes with a dagger, the Spaniard immediately fell to his knees, pleading for mercy. Cinqué again spared his life but kept one of the blacks with him at the masthead for the remainder of the voyage.[35]

Conditions steadily worsened aboard ship. At one anchor in the Caribbean, a small fishing boat approached, its owner thinking that the schooner needed a pilot to steer it ashore. But when the boat got within hailing distance, the blacks raised their cane knives and frightened their visitors away. For the next seven days, Montes sailed back and forth through those waters, vainly hoping that the fishermen would report the incident and prompt an investigation. Though the *Amistad* passed merchantmen and other vessels, Montes was unable to signal distress. Meanwhile, supplies were about gone, rough winds had nearly destroyed the sails, and some of the blacks, delirious from thirst, had consumed the liquid contents of bottles found below, only to sicken and die from the medicines stored in some of the containers. Gloom and despair cast a heavy pall over the *Amistad* as the total of blacks who had died reached ten.[36]

Several sea captains had sighted the *Amistad*, but they hastily retreated upon seeing a large number of blacks, armed with long knives, dressed in alien costumes, and obviously desperate. In one instance, the captain of an American merchant vessel had come sufficiently close to exchange a few words with Burnah, who knew enough English to make the blacks' needs known. The captain gave them a keg of water and some apples, but when he prepared to take the *Amistad* in tow, Cinqué became suspicious and seemed ready to board the vessel, causing its captain to cut the line and flee from what appeared to be pirates.[37] By late August the *Amistad* had caused considerable stir along the North American coast as the vessel approached waters off the state of New York.[38] Indeed, commanding officers at the Brooklyn Navy Yard had ordered two vessels to search for the mysterious ship.[39]

Finally, as the situation aboard ship worsened, Cinqué had no choice but to order the *Amistad* close to shore; he would go with Grabeau, Burnah, and others to find food and water.[40] Cinqué anchored the badly weather-beaten schooner off Long Island, joined eight of his comrades in a small boat, and headed ashore for provisions. On that day, August 25, they wandered from one isolated dwelling to another, frightening most residents but managing to purchase two dogs, a bottle of gin, and some sweet potatoes with the Spanish gold doubloons they had found on the *Amistad*.[41]

By late afternoon five white men who had seen the schooner offshore arrived in wagons and approached Cinqué and his companions on the beach. Henry Green and his friends, all seamen from the immediate area, confirmed by sign language that the blacks had come from the schooner lying nearly a mile out. Were there Spaniards in this land? the blacks wanted to know. After Green shook his head no, they asked if there were slaves. Again told no, the blacks immediately jumped up and down with delight—so much that they scared Green and the others into running to their wagons for weapons. But Cinqué quickly assured them that he meant no harm, and as proof he gave them two guns, a knife, a hat, and a handkerchief. Green wondered what the blacks wanted. Burnah indicated that they would pay the whites in gold doubloons for taking them to Sierra Leone. Surprised by the offer, Green suspected that the vessel contained something of value and tried to lure all the blacks ashore so that he could seize it as a prize. Might he and his friends board the schooner? Cinqué, however, had become suspicious of their motives and tried to put them off until the following day. In the meantime he would show them two trunks from the vessel. Cinqué had planned to get the *Amistad* under way the next morning, a decision reinforced by the actions of these white men.[42]

But early the following day Green spotted an American naval vessel on the horizon and feared that it would seize the schooner and deny him the salvage he thought was his. When the blacks prepared to leave, he warned that two men-of-war nearby would capture them and make them slaves.[43] At this point Lieutenant Meade on board the USS *Washington* saw the activity ashore and at Lieutenant Gedney's orders seized the schooner, the cargo, and the blacks.[44] Perhaps because New York had abolished slavery, Gedney took his prize to New London, Connecticut, where slavery was legal. There he would seek salvage on the *Amistad* and its cargo, including the blacks as property.

Popular excitement about the *Amistad* spread shortly after its arrival in New London the following day. The accuracy of the newspaper reports was doubtful at best. Some of the press spoke of the black pirates, who had murdered the captain and crew and, but for Gedney's bravery, would have continued preying on American merchant vessels and coastal dwellers.[45] Other newspapers, however, argued that since the slave trade was illegal under American law, the blacks had possessed a natural right to win freedom.[46] Cinqué, some of them noted, struck an impressive figure: the "son of an African chief" who dealt in slaves, an erroneous story, and possessed "sagacity and courage" not often associated with his race.[47] The United States marshal in New Haven, Norris Willcox, took Gedney's report and immediately notified the federal district judge of Connecticut, Andrew T. Judson. Willcox and Judson left that day for the *Washington.*[48]

Judson at once conducted an inquiry on board the American brig in New London harbor. After hearing the testimony of Ruiz, Montes, and Antonio, the slave belonging to the slain captain and owner of the *Amistad,* Judson temporarily halted the proceedings as Cinqué was brought into the cabin. Manacled and with a cord around his neck holding a snuffbox, Cinqué wore a red flannel shirt and duck pantaloons, and seemed calm and in control. At first smiling and making hand motions showing that he expected to be hanged, he then turned and stared intensely at Montes and Ruiz. At that point Judson resumed the inquiry by examining the vessel's papers and finding that they upheld the Spaniards' story: the *Amistad* was a Spanish slaver, legally authorized to transport fifty-three *ladinos* as slaves belonging to Ruiz and Montes from Havana to Puerto Príncipe. The slaves had mutinied and were apparently guilty of piracy and murder. Ruiz and Montes asked the judge to sanction the delivery of the *Amistad,* its cargo, and the slaves to the Spanish consul in Boston; all items were their property, the two Spaniards argued. Judson, however, decided to hold the thirty-nine black adult males for the next meeting of the grand jury of the United States Circuit Court, scheduled in Hartford, Connecticut, for September 1839. At that time, he explained, the court would make a ruling on the property claims and decide whether the blacks should stand trial for mutiny and murder. Antonio and the four black children were not involved in the mutiny and would appear as witnesses. Since no one posted bond for the youths, Judson directed the marshal to transport all the blacks to the New Haven jail.[49]

In carrying out his orders, Willcox noted with curiosity that none of the blacks answered to the Spanish names on the warrant, even though the clerk had carefully copied those names from the passports issued in Havana.[50]

More legal action followed. Gedney filed a libel suit in behalf of himself and others on board the *Washington* for salvage of the *Amistad,* its cargo, and the black passengers. On the basis of the "meritorious service" of Gedney and his men, the suit alleged, the court should award compensation for saving the Spaniards' property from certain total loss.[51]

These immediate legal issues were important in themselves, but before the circuit court could convene, American abolitionists became interested in the case as a way to publicize the evils of the slave trade and perhaps of slavery itself, and they would soon raise questions involving human and property rights and the relationship of morality to law. The series of events about to unfold in Connecticut constituted a severe test of America's ideals. The abolitionists would ask how one could reconcile the enslavement of human beings in a nation founded on natural rights and fundamental principles of personal liberty. Their intention was to challenge Americans to mesh positive with natural law in protecting individual freedom.

2
Abolitionists and "This Matter of Color"

Cinqué and his companions could not have known, but the timing of their arrival in the United States was fortunate: the nation was experiencing a widespread reform movement that, on the surface at least, exalted the common man and emphasized equality of opportunity. Although Andrew Jackson was no longer in the White House, his presidency had left an imprint on the nation that carried into the administration of his successor, Martin Van Buren. Questions have arisen over democratic myth and reality in the Jacksonian period, but numerous Americans claimed that they were serious about ending undemocratic practices and redeeming the grand promises contained in the Declaration of Independence.

The greatest evil of the age, according to the small but vocal group of antislavery activists called abolitionists, was the enslavement of human beings. Slavery, they argued, was symbolic of all that was wrong in the United States and living proof of the hypocrisy of a people who could proclaim the unalienable rights of mankind while practicing slavery and racial discrimination. The abolitionists decided that the time had come to rid the nation of slavery. As Cinqué and the other captives of the *Amistad* were victims of the situation in Cuba, so might they become beneficiaries of a reformist mood that was not confined to the United States but permeated England as well.

I

Less than a week after the *Amistad*'s arrival in New London, American abolitionists decided to use the mutiny in their campaign against slavery. Antislavery sentiment was part of the reform age of the 1830s, but it had not yet raised its head above other causes. Abolitionists were few in number and differed among themselves over methods and over the issue of the black's position in society but were united in believing that all men had a right to freedom.[1] Abolitionists were more radical than the larger number of Americans who merely opposed slavery. Whereas many Northerners were moderately antislavery and were satisfied to confine the institution to its current borders and force it into slow decline, the abolitionists demanded immediate emancipation without compensation to the owners.[2] Perhaps many of the "immediatists" privately conceded that implementation of such a plan was not feasible and that what they wanted was an immediate commitment to emancipation through agitation, but their basic belief was that slavery violated the most sacred principles of a Christian civilization by inflicting the worst kind of injustice on human beings.[3] The seeking of advantages at the expense of the weak and unfortunate had destroyed the nation's ideals and caused some people to question whether America itself could survive.[4] The *Amistad* case might bring these great issues into focus.

Abolitionists recognized that the *Amistad* affair had the potential for causing an emotional debate over slavery in the United States. A young Connecticut lawyer, E. W. Chester, summarized the issue in a letter to the *Emancipator,* the official organ of the American Antislavery Society. In the *Amistad* case, he insisted, "*color* cannot alter the rights or liabilities of the accused." Africans had to stand before the courts in the same way Europeans or Americans would stand. These people could be regarded "only as persons, as moral agents, owing allegiance to this law of nature when on the high seas, and liable to be dealt with for its violation by any jurisdiction within which they may afterwards be found."[5] If the abolitionists demonstrated that color was not a legitimate obstacle to a person's natural right to freedom, they would lay the basis for a major assault on slavery that might vindicate their larger aims.

Many abolitionists were convinced that the end to slavery depended upon a prior end to racism in the United States.[6] Abolition would succeed, the evangelist Theodore Dwight Weld declared, only in proportion to a decline in racial prejudice.[7] A black abolitionist, the Reverend Hosea Easton, had warned in 1837 that after slavery died the abolitionists would have to fight the spirit of prejudice that made color "a mark of degradation."[8] Gradual emancipation would not work. Racial feelings were too deeply embedded in Americans to be rooted out with time and patience. Nor was sending black people to Africa the answer, abolitionists believed, for they dismissed the American Colonization Society as a tool of racist Americans who wanted to safeguard slavery by ridding the nation of free blacks. The only remedy was an appeal to morality based on Christian principles and to individual liberties grounded in natural law.[9]

Many of the abolitionists had been trained for the ministry, and to those guided by religious evangelism the antislavery cause assumed both spiritual and temporal meanings.[10] The evangelicals' main goal was to convert everyone to Christianity and return the United States to God's grace.[11] To preserve the Christian basis of America, they had to expose the most flagrant evidence of this sickness—the hatred and violence stemming from slavery. Abolitionists asked searching questions. How could liberty and equality coexist with slavery and racial prejudice? Was it necessary to stand society on its head to awaken a national consciousness that would drive out slavery and racism? How could one establish a Christian world unencumbered by the enslavement of human beings?[12] These questions had personal and immediate implications as well as those of a visionary and international nature. As the abolitionist Wendell Phillips declared in 1851, "My friends, if we never free a slave, we have at least freed ourselves in the effort to emancipate our brother man."[13]

The abolitionists' growing belief in immediatism by the 1830s stemmed from evangelical Christianity, and for that reason their movement against slavery rested on emotions that had potential social, political, and economic consequences. The "Christian abolitionists," as some writers have called them, believed that they had to convert people from within, by appealing to their sense of morality.[14] In trying to destroy social evils, they argued that sin was a rebellion against God and therefore required repentance. Only through the soul's regeneration could a Christian launch an inner drive for perfection that would manifest itself in attempts to reform society.[15] Abolition became a religious act grounded in the revivalist feeling of the times. For nearly two thousand years Christians had considered sin a form of slavery; now they were arguing that slavery itself was a sin.[16] One could not abolish slavery gradually, any more than one could abolish sin gradually. To compensate slaveowners for losses would be to compromise with evil. As the evangelicals argued, conversion itself was compensation, for it meant a bestowing of God's favor.[17] Nonabolitionists warned that any attempt to end slavery with a sudden sweep would cause nationwide upheaval.[18]

Abolitionists during the 1830s aimed primarily at converting Northerners to their cause. The main objective of the movement, according to the *National Anti-Slavery Standard* of New York, was to "reform the white man, so that the colored man may be safe by his side." Conversion of Southern slaveholders seemed hopeless, leading most abolitionists to believe that to succeed they had to widen their narrow base of followers to include antislavery moderates in the North who regarded slavery as injurious to economic expansion and to democratic ideals.[19] But these moderates lacked fervor, and abolitionists bitterly attacked those who refused to make a total commitment to the cause.[20]

Opposition to slavery, whether intense or mild, was not necessarily devoid of racism. Many Northerners who were antislavery in feeling nonetheless feared that immediate abolition would lead to racial troubles. Antislavery groups disagreed over the methods and time required to reach the goal, and over the types of social adjustment necessary during the postslavery period. Anti-abolitionists were concerned that abolition would force a choice between racial war and racial amalgamation.[21] The South, they feared, could not survive the social and economic upheaval caused by abolition. Furthermore, such a revolution would have serious ramifications in their own section of the country. Another wave of violence stemming from the slavery issue—similar to that which had occurred in the early 1830s—could permanently divide the country.[22]

Probably because of widespread racial feelings, no antislavery group, including the abolitionists, had formulated a plan for social, political, and economic adjustment after slavery came to an end.[23] Most Americans seemed to agree that sentiment against slavery did not automatically lead to a push for equality between the races. Abolitionists themselves differed over how far the reform movement should go beyond ending slavery. Whereas some proclaimed it poor strategy to argue about details when great principles were at stake, others were not willing to advocate a racially integrated society. More than a few had not given thought to the matter.[24]

Abolitionists believed that the essential weakness in the antislavery cause was that Northerners had stubbornly failed to take a stand against the greatest wrong of the day.[25] The reason for this reluctance, they thought, was that few Northerners had confronted slavery on its own terms. Instead of accepting the slaveholders' arguments about the ameliorative qualities of the institution, Northerners should examine the central depravity fostered by slavery: the degradation of both master and slave resulting from one man's ownership and exploitation of another man as property.[26] Abolitionists believed that a dramatic event was required to awaken their countrymen to the sordid nature of slavery. The mutiny on the *Amistad* provided that signal opportunity.

II

Shortly after Judge Judson's hearing on the USS *Washington,* Dwight P. Janes, an abolitionist from New London, informed friends in the cause that none of the black captives on board the *Amistad* was legally a slave belonging to José Ruiz or Pedro Montes. Janes had been on board the *Washington* during the inquiry, and Ruiz had made this admission to him in the cabin. Furthermore, Janes had secured confirmation of this information from Marshal Willcox. A slaver had violated Spanish laws against the African slave trade by transporting the blacks from Africa to Cuba, where Ruiz and Montes, with full knowledge of the situation, had purchased them at the public slave market.[27] The blacks' status was of no concern to Ruiz. He had bought them legally.

Janes wrote to two allies in the abolitionist cause, the Reverend Joshua Leavitt of New York, a Yale graduate, lawyer, and editor of the *Emancipator,* and Roger S. Baldwin, a lawyer from New Haven who had already become known as a defender of justice for the less fortunate. After recounting the details of the mutiny to both men, Janes argued that the *Amistad*'s blacks could be neither slaves nor Spanish subjects. They had not been in Havana long enough to be domiciled. They could not speak Spanish. Their languages were clearly African. Spanish law labeled the African slave trade an act of piracy, punishable by death. For these reasons, the captives on the *Amistad* had a legal right to liberty at any cost. Janes asked Leavitt to investigate the vessel's papers in New York, with the intention of establishing that the Spaniards had no legal title to the blacks as slaves. He also suggested that Leavitt attempt to find someone in New York who could speak the Africans' languages and go to New Haven to determine their side of the story. Finally, he urged Leavitt to persuade Baldwin to take the case. "Perhaps I over-rate the importance of this affair," Janes wrote, but "all the abolitionists here feel as I do."[28]

Janes explained the abolitionists' strategy. He first asked that Baldwin act on behalf of the *Amistad*'s blacks in filing a claim for the vessel and the cargo as their legal property. The objective was to charge the two Spaniards with piracy and then to gather evidence by locating native Africans who could speak the languages of the blacks of the *Amistad*. The case had aroused great interest in New London. Most Americans, he believed, did not think the blacks guilty of murder and opposed returning them to Spanish officials to stand trial. The best solution was to set them free or return them to Africa. Janes added that the latter option appeared to be the responsibility of the American Colonization Society, which would be, he sarcastically remarked, "the *only* legitimate work which has yet been offered them." If Baldwin could establish that the blacks were not legally slaves, the inherent right of self-defense would justify their seizure of the *Amistad*.[29]

Janes insisted that the abolitionists sought only "humanity and justice" for the blacks. Baldwin should refer to them as "citizens of Africa," for the burden of proof would then rest on the prize master and the two Spaniards to show that slavers had taken the blacks to Havana before the slave trade became an act of piracy. Failure to provide such proof might establish that the schooner was engaged in an illegal activity that had begun in Africa, and that the blacks had a right to liberty. Besides Ruiz's admission, there was the statement to Janes by the young cabin boy, Antonio, that the blacks on the *Amistad* had arrived in Cuba only recently. The passports secured by the Spaniards in Havana proved the local government's involvement in a "bad business." The papers could not legalize the voyage to Puerto Príncipe unless the Spaniards first established that the blacks' entrance into Havana was legal.[30]

Janes advised prompt action out of concern that the Spanish government might secure a quiet arrangement with the Van Buren administration in Washington that provided for the return of vessel, cargo, and blacks to Spanish authorities. Although the Spanish consul in Boston had said he did not believe that his government would demand their return, Janes feared that the consul's policy was to play down the issue while negotiating a settlement with Secretary of State John Forsyth. Janes was aware of Forsyth's strong proslavery feelings (the secretary was a slaveholder from Georgia), and he knew that the Van Buren administration would not want the *Amistad* matter to erupt on the political scene—especially with a presidential election coming soon. Janes recommended that Baldwin pursue whatever legal means were necessary to require the United States marshal in New Haven to hold the vessel, its cargo, and the blacks until a full investigation could take place. Indeed, Ruiz and Montes themselves had enough money to settle the salvage matter with Lieutenant Gedney; this would eliminate the only obstacle to a delivery of the prize to Spanish officials. Could not Baldwin start a legal action against Gedney based on "unlawful detention" of the blacks?[31]

Baldwin was no novice in the field of constitutional liberties. He was born in New Haven in 1793, into a family tracing its lineage from Puritan emigrants and having a long history of participation in public affairs. His mother was the daughter of Roger Sherman, one of the signers of the Declaration of Independence, a later delegate to the Constitutional Convention in Philadelphia, and, ironically, a key figure in the protecting of slavery in the Constitution. At the age of eighteen, Baldwin graduated with honors from Yale College, and after studying law he was admitted to the bar in 1814. Soon afterward he won a fugitive slave's freedom by securing a writ of habeas corpus by establishing him as a person and successfully arguing the case before the superior court. Before becoming governor and later United States senator from Connecticut during the 1840s, Baldwin was interested in the cause of abolition. With Simeon Jocelyn, a Congregational minister in New Haven, he had in 1831 confronted an angry mob resisting their attempts to build a black training school near Yale College.[32]

Now Jocelyn asked Amos Townsend, Jr., a prominent banker in New Haven, to persuade Baldwin to take the case. Jocelyn was the minister of New Haven's first church for blacks, a founder of the city's antislavery society, and a conductor of runaways in the underground railroad. Recognizing that the case would require more than one counsel, he secured help from Seth Staples, who later founded Yale Law School and now, because of the importance of the issue, agreed to accept an indemnity only for his time. In the meantime Townsend accompanied another abolitionist from Connecticut, John F. Norton, to talk with Baldwin about handling the case. After a two-hour discussion in Baldwin's office, he agreed to do so. Baldwin was reluctant to discuss terms because he was not sure he would charge anything for defending the "injured fellow beings." At this time he advised Townsend that a writ of habeas corpus would not be necessary, because even the president of the United States lacked authority to turn the blacks over to Spanish authorities without allowing them their day in court.[33]

By early September abolitionists in Connecticut had established contact with friends in New York City, who made an important move in securing the aid of Lewis and Arthur Tappan. The two brothers, descendants of Benjamin Franklin, were successful merchants who had experienced firsthand the resistance to the abolitionism that pervaded much of the North. Lewis had left Boston to join Arthur in New York in 1826, and the following year Arthur established the *Journal of Commerce* to exert moral influence against slavery. Arthur had earlier been instrumental in founding the American Antislavery Society. Public reaction to the Tappans' antislavery activities had been swift. In 1834 a mob disrupted a meeting of the society in New York and went on to break into Lewis's house, throwing furniture into the street and burning it. The mob then threatened to do the same to the store of Arthur Tappan and Company, but iron shutters protected the windows, and thirty clerks armed with muskets frightened off the mob. The following year an unnamed person offered $100,000 for the bodies of the Tappans, payable upon delivery into any slave state. They heard stories of gangs waiting for them; they were burned in effigy and attacked in the press; insurance companies declined to insure family property; and they received mail containing threatening letters, pieces of rope suggesting the gallows, and, at one point, a slave's ear. These and other events had subjected the Tappan brothers to trial by fire. When friends of Arthur's urged him to resign as president of the American Antislavery Society, he declared, *"I will be hung first."* Lewis meanwhile armed himself with his only weapon—a copy of the New Testament in his breast pocket.[34]

And yet, Arthur Tappan showed an ambivalence toward color that was probably characteristic of many Americans. He was not racially prejudiced but was undecided about free blacks' place in American society. After an incident of 1834, in which church members were incensed over his appearance with a fair-skinned black minister, he refused to associate publicly with blacks except for business purposes. Years afterward he made a distinction between emancipation and mixture of the races. Although Christians had to disregard color, he wrote to a friend, he saw the need for "great prudence" in seeking changes in the public's attitude on race. Tappan insisted that his own feelings did not preclude public association with a "well educated and refined colored person, male or female," but he added, "I felt that their best good would be promoted by refraining from doing so till the public mind and conscience were more enlightened on the subject."[35] Whether this was a rationalization is impossible to say; but Tappan's longtime public support for the cause suggests that he was confronting the same dilemma that faced many. Serious social, political, and economic consequences awaited people who morally condemned slavery and the racism that was its underpinning.

Lewis Tappan's feelings toward slavery were indicative of the strong evangelical strain running through the abolition movement. He was a puritan who constantly faced the problem of wanting to change the world while having to live in it. An admitted Christian abolitionist, he would not compromise with either slavery or racial prejudice. Firmly believing slavery a moral wrong, he condemned both those who participated in the act and those who permitted the practice by ignoring it. Unlike his brother, he openly opposed racial discrimination. Even in marriage, he insisted, religious unity was more important than race. Amalgamation did not concern him. By the "present system of bleaching," he wrote a friend, both blacks and whites would in a thousand years be "copper colored, the original color of this climate."[36] And he was an uncompromising moralist: all sins, in his view, involved rebellion against God, and slavery was evidence of a whole range of sins. Slavery, he wrote his brother Benjamin, a senator from Ohio, was "the worm at the root of the tree of Liberty. Unless killed the tree will die."[37]

Tappan did not want balance. His stereotypes, which idealized blacks and condemned the South, were necessary tools for uprooting the deeply entrenched institutions that were morally irreparable. The black became a noble savage, victimized by morally corrupt Southerners and by morally calloused Northerners. Tappan saw slavery solely in moral terms, and for that reason he could not compromise with social, political, or economic realities. Such concessions would be tantamount to making amends with evil.[38]

III

In early September, New York abolitionists appointed Lewis Tappan, Joshua Leavitt, and Simeon Jocelyn as the "*Amistad* Committee," which was assigned the task of raising money for the blacks' legal counsel and for their needs while in the New Haven jail.[39] This was not the first time the three men had served the cause together. In 1831 they were on a committee in New York that tried—but failed—to establish a national antislavery society.[40] Leavitt differed with Tappan over the place of political action in the abolitionist movement but for the time being joined forces

with him and other evangelicals.[41] Indeed, the *Amistad* affair perhaps suggested that the sentiment against slavery was widening
because later events united many opponents of the institution who
were not always abolitionists and who often disagreed with one
another. The committee ran advertisements in the newspapers,
asking "Friends of Liberty" to make donations. According to the
committee, the president of the United States would choose to surrender the blacks to Spanish authorities in an effort to take "the
victims out of sight with the least observation." Since black Africans had killed a white Spaniard, no one would see the need for
further inquiries. The committee declared that the Africans' right
to freedom derived from the law of nature, international laws
against the slave trade, and "the voice of humanity and liberty."
Almost immediately, contributions began to arrive.[42]

Meanwhile, the blacks' legal team continued to grow. The abolitionists had attempted to secure the services of Rufus Choate of
Boston, but the prominent attorney declined. Though citing previous commitments, Choate was a Whig who believed that abolitionists were radicals whose agitations could disrupt the Union.
The abolitionists did succeed in persuading one other attorney to
join Baldwin and Staples in defending the *Amistad* captives: Theodore Sedgwick, an antislavery Democrat whose office was located
in the same building in New York City as Staples's and who,
according to Lewis Tappan, was "an active & talented young lawyer." Baldwin was assigned the responsibilities of preparing the
case and giving the opening argument in court.[43]

Townsend was worried that the *Amistad* matter was coming
under too much visible control of the abolitionists. He feared that
the widespread favorable impression of the blacks could disappear
because of the animosity for Tappan and other abolitionists. The
wisest course, Townsend thought, was to call a meeting of "gentlemen" to appoint a committee to handle the case. They should
keep their work distinct from Tappan's fund so that the effort
on behalf of the blacks would not "smell too strong of Abolition." If managed correctly, the case could change the public's
attitude toward slavery and the slave trade. But if abolitionists
appeared to claim the "virtue of exclusive sympathy," many
Americans would turn away in disgust. The New York *Daily
Express,* Townsend pointed out, had already denounced Tappan's
advertisement as an effort by abolitionists to cause trouble. It
would be wise to enlist the help of those who were not "professed

abolitionists" and who could exert a favorable influence on the case.[44]

Before Townsend could carry out his recommendation, Tappan assumed a leading public role in the case by locating three native Africans in New York and immediately taking them to New Haven to talk with the *Amistad* captives. One of them, John Ferry, was a native of the Kissi tribe in the continental interior who had been kidnapped at the age of about twelve and liberated in Colombia by Símón Bolívar. Ferry could speak Mandingo but was more fluent in Gallinao, which some of the prisoners could speak. After Tappan delivered an impromptu sermon to the blacks (which they could not comprehend), Ferry engaged in limited conversation with a few of the blacks. He concluded that the four children were Africans by birth, one of them being Congolese, the other three Mandingoes. Though most of the story remained untold because of difficulties in communication, Ferry claimed that at least the youths had been kidnapped in Africa and illegally sold into Cuban slavery.[45] This was enough to confirm the abolitionists' position.

Realizing that the blacks' greatest asset was public sympathy, the *Amistad* Committee did everything possible to keep attention focused on their plight. Leavitt and Tappan visited the blacks in New Haven on at least three occasions, returning to write long public letters for the newspapers that further aroused the feeling of readers. The press printed every detail, no matter how seemingly obscure and unimportant. The blacks were not "man-eaters," Tappan declared in trying to dispel stories in some of the newspapers. One of the blacks, Konoma, was a Congolese with teeth that protruded markedly. However, he was not a cannibal. Rather, as the abolitionists later reported, Konoma was a likable young man who had disfigured his teeth to attract women. Tappan insisted that the blacks were human beings, possessing the same wants and needs as whites. These details were of enormous interest to people in Connecticut and elsewhere, many of whom had never seen black people and visited the jail to view the captives firsthand.[46]

According to the accounts by Leavitt and Tappan, all the prisoners except Cinqué lived quite comfortably in four apartments—the men in three different rooms and the four children in a room by themselves—under the care of United States Marshal Norris Willcox and the jailer, Colonel Stanton Pendleton. Cinqué was in a room with others charged with various crimes, "savage looking fellows, black and white." Problems existed in all the dwellings. Fresh air and exercise were lacking, and a physician had found evi-

dence of disease and malnutrition. Tappan reported that though
the blacks were generally in good health, one had died a few days
earlier and two or three were seriously ill. The Mandingoes among
them, Tappan declared, were "robust" and at times "full of hilar-
ity," but all were generally "quiet, kind and orderly." Leavitt
agreed that most of the blacks appeared to be of "quiet minds" and
"mild and cheerful temper" with "no contentions" among them.[47]
The marshal had secured decent food and clothing for the prisoners, despite some of the newspapers' charges that they had nothing
to wear on their arrival in New Haven. Leavitt explained that the
basis for these accusations probably lay in the blacks' decision to
remove most of their clothing because of the heat of the hold on
board the *Amistad.* Tappan noted that the men were dressed in
dark striped cotton trousers and striped cotton shirts, whereas the
girls were in calico frocks and had shawls that they made into
turbans.[48]

Most public interest was focused on Cinqué, who had become a
romanticized figure. He greatly resembled the prints already on
sale around the streets, Leavitt declared. Cinqué was "like another
Othello," Tappan wrote, of "fine proportions," who carried himself with a "noble air" and a "good degree of gracefulness and
native dignity." Asked whether he believed in God, Cinqué had,
according to Tappan, expressed "some idea" of a "good Spirit"
and of an "evil Spirit." If men lied, Cinqué asserted through Ferry,
the evil spirit would "take them somewhere, they knew not
where." He declared, "God is good," and insisted, "Me tell no
lies—me tell the truth." Asked where God was, Cinqué pointed
upward. Tappan hired divinity students from Yale College to work
with Ferry in giving the blacks religious instruction. Tappan soon
realized that the captives from the *Amistad* regarded Cinqué as
their chief. When receiving permission to visit Cinqué, they called
him "massa" and gave him money received from visitors. But Cinqué turned over the money to his brother, one of the prisoners,
before reentering his cell—probably because he worried that one
of his fellow inmates would take it from him, Tappan thought.[49]

Even the shape of Cinqué's head drew the attention of those
pseudoscientists of the nineteenth century who claimed that they
could determine his character from it. A phrenologist, L. N. Fowler, examined Cinqué and reported his conclusions in a journal
article that revealed strong racial overtones even though the thrust
of the argument was favorable to his subject. The base of Cinqué's
brain, Fowler declared, was smaller than the other parts, meaning

that "lower animal propensities" did not dominate his character. In temperament Cinqué liked mental and physical exercises and was nervous and restless. He was blessed with a "strong constitution" and "great powers of endurance" and had a "love of liberty, independence, determination, ambition, regard for his country, and for what he thinks is sacred and right." Shrewd, tactful, a good manager, and a man of moral courage, pride, and self-esteem, Cinqué possessed strong leadership qualities and could handle power and command respect. He did not seem to be "*naturally* cruel, malicious, or even selfish," but his disposition changed if his liberty and rights were in jeopardy. He refused to be subject to others, and although at times "tyrannical and dictatorial," he could show "humanity, kindness, and sympathy for the happiness of others." His "cerebral organization," Fowler remarked, seemed "superior to the majority of negroes" in the United States. Indeed, Cinqué's intellect was "generally well-balanced, and better developed than most persons belonging to his race."[50]

After some discussion the jailer allowed a professor of linguistics at Yale College, Josiah W. Gibbs, to accompany Tappan, Baldwin, and Ferry in talking with Cinqué. Gibbs had visited the blacks a few days earlier, and after learning some of the numbers in their languages, he searched the waterfronts of New York and New Haven, hoping to find a native African who might recognize the languages. He finally came across two Africans employed on the British warship *Buzzard,* then in New York: James Covey, a former slave from Sierra Leone, and Charles Pratt, a native of Mende who had been seized by a Spanish slaver about seven years earlier. Gibbs took them to New Haven on September 9.[51]

Cinqué was at first reluctant to talk with his visitors, but he finally consented. He confirmed what the other blacks had told Ferry—that most of them were from Mandingo. Gaining confidence as he spoke, Cinqué declared with great feeling that he was born in Africa about sixty miles inland, the son of one of the "principal men" of his country, but not of a king or a chief. During his business dealings, he had bought some goods but was unable to pay the entire amount. Seized by his own tribesmen as payment for the debt, he had been sold to King Sharks, who reigned in the Gallinas area about fifteen miles from the Atlantic. After a while Spaniards, he thought, bought him and took him to Havana, forcing him to leave behind his parents, wife, and three children. Asked whether he had ever helped enslave his countrymen, he staunchly replied, "I would never take advantage of any one, but would always defend myself." He asserted that during the voyage of the *Amistad* the captain was "very cruel and beat them severely." After the revolt, the Spaniards, he bitterly remarked, "made fools of us and did not go to Sierra Leone." Cinqué did not realize that the vessel was in America until Captain Green told him. Although Cinqué was willing to give up everything, Green refused to take the blacks to Sierra Leone. When asked whether the *Amistad* had carried gold, Cinqué claimed that the two trunks taken ashore and shown to Green had rattled and clanked with doubloons. But after Lieutenant Gedney had seized the vessel and cargo, Tappan wrote, the gold was never found. At one point, Cinqué drew his hand across his throat, asking whether his captives planned to kill him. Reassured that he was among friends and would soon go home, he showed noticeable relief.[52]

Cinqué had not told all the truth, probably because he did not trust white people. Most of the blacks, Cinqué included, were from Mende, not Mandingo, and Cinqué later admitted in court that the *Amistad* carried only a few doubloons, not as many as he wanted Tappan and the others to believe. Perhaps he feared additional assaults from slave traders on his people still in Mende. On the gold question, he perhaps hoped to divide the whites or thought that by alleging knowledge of the wealth, he would assure his fellow captives' lives. The reasons Cinqué may have had for these fabrications remain a matter for conjecture. Almost two years later, however, the *Amistad* blacks admitted to having agreed among themselves not to reveal their homeland, because they trusted no one.[53]

The *Amistad* Committee wanted the court to release the prisoners unless officials brought formal charges, and it urged Baldwin to seek a writ of habeas corpus before the Van Buren administration intervened and delivered them to the Spanish government as property under the terms of Pinckney's Treaty of 1795. Tappan recommended that Baldwin take "every precautionary measure," including, the committee noted, seeking the writ "in case of necessity." As Tappan pointed out, the Spanish minister in Washington had referred to Pinckney's Treaty in demanding the blacks' return to Cuba, and the White House would undoubtedly comply. He recommended that Baldwin talk with Governor William W. Ellsworth about the steps the Connecticut state government might take in case the federal government tried to "interfere unlawfully." Some "trusty man" should watch the marshal and give immediate warning if anyone tried to remove the blacks from jail. Henry B.

Stanton, a well-known lawyer and abolitionist from Boston, agreed with Tappan that the American government would return the Africans to the Spanish upon demand. Ellis Gray Loring, another abolitionist from Boston, who was an avid follower of William Lloyd Garrison and who served as the Tappans' attorney, also urged Baldwin to use a writ of habeas corpus to prevent such an event. As Jocelyn scribbled on the outside of a letter from Leavitt to Baldwin, a writ of habeas corpus seemed advisable because "it may save the Africans and us [the abolitionists] great respect." "Who will trust the present administration in regard to law," he asked, "when none but the lives of foreign blacks are concerned?"[54]

One careful observer of the proceedings was John Quincy Adams, member of the House of Representatives from Massachusetts and former president. Though not an abolitionist, he hated slavery for what it had done to the American fabric of freedom. The blacks, he wrote to William Jay—an evangelical abolitionist, a legal and constitutional expert, and the son of John Jay—had "vindicated their own right of liberty" by "executing the justice of Heaven" upon a "pirate murderer, their tyrant and oppressor." Adams refused to believe that if the Spanish government demanded the blacks, the United States would comply. Such a move would turn them over to "slavetrading justice and mercy." No executive officer of the United States would be "daring enough" to return them to the "mockery of a tribunal of slave-smugglers."[55]

To discourage any effort to surrender the blacks to Spain, the abolitionists appealed to the president to allow the courts to handle the matter. In a letter to Van Buren, Staples and Sedgwick urged him to refrain from an exercise of "executive discretion" and permit the judiciary to determine the facts in the case. The treaty of 1795 did not authorize the submission of conflicting property rights to "mere official discretion"; that decision belonged to the tribunals always relied upon to guarantee civil rights. Nothing in the treaty authorized their delivery to Spain. Moreover, international law did not require the president to give in to demands. The Spanish had no legal title to the blacks as slaves. The government in Madrid had forbidden the African slave trade by agreeing to a treaty with England in 1817 and by issuing a royal decree under the queen's name in November 1838. Ruiz and Montes could not have acquired legal ownership over blacks illegally imported into Cuba. The inherent right of self-defense had allowed the captives to free themselves from "illegal restraint." Staples and Sedgwick asked that the president refuse to have the matter decided "in the recesses of the cabinet," where these "unfriended men" could present no evidence in their behalf.[56]

The abolitionists intended to push the *Amistad* issue into the public arena. To do this, they had to wrest it from the president's private negotiations with Spain and to take the case into the courts, where, they hoped, it would become a national concern.

3
The Politics of Justice

Had not a presidential election and racial feelings entered the controversy, the *Amistad* matter might have come to a close during the autumn of 1839. If newspapers were any indication, many Americans seemed to concede the blacks' right to freedom. But this feeling met rigid opposition from the Van Buren administration in Washington, scattered spokesmen in the American press, especially in the South, and the Spanish government in Madrid. Political and racial considerations soon combined to force a White House policy regarding the *Amistad* that ignored fundamental liberties and called for an end to the matter by returning the vessel and its cargo to the Spanish government. If the president had doubts about the issue, his Southern constituency probably removed them. The blacks were Spanish subjects, according to the Charleston *Mercury*. The moment a slave was sold in Cuba, the American government was obligated to recognize him as Spanish property. America's laws against the slave trade could not apply to Spanish subjects. Otherwise, the United States would have approved the "monstrous English doctrine" that municipal law was part of the law of nations. The Richmond *Enquirer* declared that the administration's only duty was to return the blacks to Cuba once the Spanish provided proof of ownership. The United States had no right to inquire into Spanish law.[1] The "Southern" argument made sense to the White House: no debates over slavery would develop; the president's chances for reelection would increase; Southerners would not feel threatened by federal interference; the surrender to Spain would uphold a treaty and maintain good relations. The answer seemed simple to the White House— and it might have been, had not the abolitionists intervened.

I

At first glance the abolitionists appeared to have a chance for success when some Northern newspapers repeatedly declared that the blacks had been kidnapped in Africa and should go free on the basis of the universal right of self-defense. Had the *Amistad* fallen in with either a British or a Spanish cruiser, according to the New York *American,* the blacks would have been *"injured freemen,"* and the whites who took them would have been hanged as pirates. Had the mutineers on the *Amistad* been Englishmen and their masters dark-skinned Algerines, "what would have been their reception in a country born of Revolution, and where life, *liberty,* and the pursuit of happiness, are declared to be the equal and inalienable rights of all men?" The leader of such a revolt would not have been held for piracy and murder but have been received as a hero for choosing freedom over slavery.[2]

But even amid the widespread clamor for the blacks' freedom, racial prejudice created a climate in which slurs were cast at them. While admitting that the *Amistad* captives had a moral and Christian right to freedom and that Cinqué was as much a man as was William Tell, the New York *Sunday Morning News* declared that blacks in the United States were "happier and better in a state of subjection." The New York *Evening Star* remarked that even though the African slave trade was abhorrent, the Africans were receiving more sympathy than white men would have gotten in a similar position. Blacks and whites should have "equal justice." The New York *Daily Express* declared that the questions in the case were "purely legal" and should not go before the "excitability of a Jury trial." Besides, the *"property"* was poor in quality, for the blacks were "hardly above the apes and monkeys of their own Africa, and the language they jabber [was] incomprehensible here."[3] Indeed, the *Evening Star* moaned, "certain persons" always defended the blacks, even when they rebelled and killed white men. Blacks seemed to "to be privileged to commit such outrages."[4]

Some American commentators sensed a reverse kind of racism fostered by abolitionists that discriminated against whites. The *Evening Star* declared that the mutiny on the *Amistad* was a "Godsend to the ultra abolitionists," for it raised their "failing energies." Debtors were starving in the "Egyptian Catacombs" (the city's prison), but they were *"white men"* and attracted little attention. Lewis Tappan had appealed to Americans to ignore laws and treaties in an effort to "shield the accused because they [were] blacks and [had] been sold to slavery in a foreign land." His love of notoriety, according to another paper, was "insatiable." Tappan was a "quack in religion and in every other matter" he touched, a man with a "morbid vanity, at the expense of order and the welfare of society." Whereas abolitionists would not help "accused white men," they would do everything for these Africans in the claim that law and justice could not save them. A letter to the editors of the New York *Commercial Advertiser* expressed resentment for the "officious interference" of "certain prominent abolitionists" who could prejudice the public against the blacks. The true supporters of the blacks, the writer believed, wished that the "self-styled" *Amistad* Committee would realize that it did not represent the "public liberality." The abolitionists' attempt to make "abolition capital" out of the case would "dry up the public bounty" that favored the blacks.[5]

The abolitionists' involvement in the case drew out strong racial sentiments. The New York *Morning Herald* noted that Cinqué was "as miserably ignorant and brutalized a creature as the rest of them." All of the blacks' reputed speeches and statements were the "pure invention" of the abolitionists. A correspondent from New Haven wrote to the paper that Tappan lied in asserting that the blacks were intelligent and in remarking that Cinqué had the dignity and grace of Othello: "I never saw a human being who was not an idiot, that approximated to the average of these negroes in point of hopeless stupidity and beastly degradation." Cinqué was a "blubber-lipped, sullen looking negro, not half as intelligent or striking in appearance as every third black you meet on the docks of New York." Abolitionists would do anything to promote their "unholy schemes." The "God of nature" never meant the black race to live with whites "in any other relation than that of master and slave." Africans knew only how to eat and steal. One of the *Amistad* blacks was a "pretended cannibal," but he really was a "helpless imbecile" or "absolute idiot" who, like the rest of them, wore a "baboon-like expression." Ruiz was correct in claiming that had the captain killed one of those "great cowards" at the outset of the mutiny, they would have returned to the hold without further resistance.[6]

If justice were to prevail in the *Amistad* case, it would have a difficult time because, among other reasons, the abolitionists were in the forefront of a struggle that involved both political and racial issues. The Van Buren administration refused to take any stand that might alienate its constituency, and that meant avoiding all matters relating to slavery. Racial attitudes in both the North and the South demonstrated that even those Americans willing to grant freedom to the *Amistad* blacks did so with great hesitancy. Few spokesmen would do anything to further an abolitionist cause that to them breathed fanaticism and sectional division—not to mention certain defeat at the polls. To the abolitionist, the American Republic of the 1830s appeared to belong to the slaveholders and their sympathizers.

Political and racial matters had magnified the importance of a case that the abolitionists found it convenient to exploit; but then the *Amistad* mutiny gained an international dimension that further highlighted events in New Haven. On September 6 the Spanish minister in Washington, Angel Calderón de la Barca, presented Secretary of State John Forsyth a series of demands calling for the surrender of the blacks to his government in Madrid. Calderón praised the commander of the USS *Washington* for saving the *Amistad* and insisted that the American government should now return the captives to allow them to stand trial in Cuba for mutiny and murder. The failure to punish the "crime in question" would cause more "revolt and evasion" among blacks in Cuba, many of whom worked American property and were often transported from one part of the island to another.[7]

On the surface, Calderón had a convincing argument—or so it seemed to an administration in Washington that wanted to comply. Under Pinckney's Treaty of 1795, he demanded immediate delivery of the vessel and its cargo to their owners, with no expenses deducted as salvage. Article 8 of that treaty provided that if one of the signatory nation's ships entered the other's port "through stress of weather, *pursuit of pirates or enemies, or any other urgent necessity*" (emphases here and afterward were added by Calderón), that ship should receive good treatment, help, protection, and provisions *"at reasonable rates."* Most important, it *"shall no ways be hindered from returning out of the said ports."* Article 9 of the same treaty declared, "All ships and *merchandise, . . . which shall be rescued out of the hands of any pirates* or robbers on the high seas," shall be taken to the port's officials *"to be taken care of, and restored entire"* to owners. And Article 10 stated that any ship "wrecked, foundered, or otherwise damaged" on the coasts or in territorial waters of the other should receive *"the same assistance which would be due to the inhabitants of the country where the damage happens, and shall pay the same charges and dues only as the said inhabitants would be subject to pay in a like case."* Furthermore, Calderón insisted, American courts had no jurisdiction over Spanish subjects or over crimes committed on Spanish vessels in Spanish waters. He based his government's claim on the law of nations, on Pinckney's Treaty, which was later upheld by the Adams-Onís Treaty of 1819, and on good feelings between the nations.[8]

A Spanish newspaper in New York, *Noticioso de Ambos Mundos,* summarized the Madrid government's position regarding the *Amistad.* Private feelings about slavery and the slave trade could not interfere with law and justice. All nations had the right to govern themselves when their actions did not violate treaties with other nations. The treaties of 1795 and 1819 contained the governing principles in this case. Ruiz and Montes had brought the schooner into the United States by "stratagem and on purpose" to save their lives and property from mutineers and murderers on the high seas. They sought asylum and protection. The United States welcomed them as a "social duty" among friendly nations that rescued them from "savages." Pinckney's Treaty allowed the completion of the *Amistad*'s voyage without exacting any salvage other than what Americans would normally have received had it been an American vessel. The United States had no right to interfere with Spanish officials enforcing Spanish laws, nor could it question whether the blacks were slaves. The latter point could not come up for discussion except with the general governments, and the administration in Washington could not assume powers inconsistent with treaties or the law of nations. The United States could not legally inquire into the matter of whether the blacks were legally slaves; it had no treaty with Spain for suppressing the slave trade, and the practice was not contrary to the law of nations.[9]

The Spanish paper appealed to the administration's tendencies to take the Southern position on matters relating to slavery. Could the United States approve the "principle that robbery and murder are not crimes when committed by slaves for the purpose of regaining their freedom?" The United States condoned slavery in many states and in its capital city; it had recently forbidden abolitionist petitions from appearing in Congress. The Spanish paper supported its position by quoting the famous jurist Chancellor James Kent of New York, who declared, "[E]very State is bound to deny an asylum to criminals, and upon application and due examination of the case to surrender the fugitive to the foreign State where the crime was committed. The guilty party cannot be tried and punished by any other jurisdiction than the one, whose laws have been violated; and therefore the duty of surrendering him applies as well to the case of the State surrendering as to the case of subjects of the State demanding the fugitive."[10]

The paper offered assurances to those Americans who feared that returning the captives to Cuba meant automatic execution. If Spanish tribunals on the island determined that the blacks had been illegally imported, they would take these circumstances into consideration in "extenuation of their crime and punishment." Since the blacks were accused criminals, the paper emphasized, the United States's sole responsibility was to deliver them to Spanish authorities.[11]

The Spanish government's demand for surrender of the *Amistad* and its cargo was attributable both to national honor and to apprehension that the British would use an alleged violation of the Anglo-Spanish treaties against the slave trade as a pretext for intervening in Cuba. The Spanish knew that no nation could draw respect from others if it could not enforce its own laws. Torn by civil war at home, the government in Madrid could not appear weak in international affairs and encourage more opposition to its authority. It had to take a strong stand, if only to save face.

But Spain could not emerge from this situation unscathed. One can conjecture that if the United States had returned the blacks to Spain, the ensuing trial in Cuba (assuming one had taken place) would have led to a ruling against the blacks. Various interests on the island would have resisted acquittal for fear of setting a precedent for freeing mutinous slaves who had killed their masters. More important, the threat of execution would have provided the British with exactly the pretext for intervention that the Spanish most dreaded. And yet, if the *Amistad* case had gone to trial in the United States, any outcome would have been conducive to British intervention. If the court had either freed the blacks or returned them to Africa, such a verdict would have rested on the finding that Spain *had* violated the anti-slave-trade treaties; but had it affirmed Spain's demands and returned the captives to Cuba, British involvement on the island would have become more likely because the blacks' lives would have been at stake.

In retrospect, British intervention in Cuba was highly improbable during this period; but neither the Spanish nor the Americans could have been sure. England had problems at home and abroad, including more and more difficulties with the United States over the Canadian boundary and related matters. The American diplomatic position on Cuba and general European meddling in the Western Hemisphere was also clear by the 1820s. Nevertheless, the Van Buren administration was aware of British commercial interests in the Caribbean, and the government in Madrid feared that British abolitionists would stir the island's blacks into rebellion and force Spain to relinquish all claims to Cuba. Indeed, Spanish leaders believed that the British were intent upon controlling the Caribbean as part of a drive toward world power. Whether the perceptions of the Americans and the Spanish were correct is not crucial; they *believed* that the British were capable of some form of intervention in Cuba. That belief was a major determinant in each nation's policy toward the island.[12]

The reaction of the White House to Spanish demands was what the abolitionists expected: it sought to avoid a confrontation with Spain that could in some way relate to slavery. President Van Buren was a moderate on slavery issues but not on political aims. The greatest challenge facing his administration that autumn was the approaching presidential election of 1840. His Democratic party rested on a coalition of Northerners and Southerners, who would remain in alliance as long as the slavery issue lay dormant. Van Buren's predecessor, Andrew Jackson, had encountered that danger during the mid-1830s, when his friend Sam Houston sought Texas's admission to the Union as a state. Forces on both sides of the slavery issue warned of a bitter fight that would undermine the Democratic party. Jackson took the political course of refusing Houston's request and evading a confrontation over slavery. When the Texas question arose again during Van Buren's tenure in office, he had followed Jackson's example and once more averted the issue. Surely the same approach would work with the *Amistad.*

Some observers drew analogies between the *Amistad* case and earlier maritime incidents involving American coastal slavers forced into British ports. In 1830 the *Comet* was carrying slaves from Virginia to Louisiana, when it ran into a storm and had to beach in the Bahamas. Four years later the *Encomium* left Charleston, only to suffer the same fate. The following year a storm drove the *Enterprise* into Bermuda. Over American protests, British officials in the islands freed all the slaves. The secretary of state during the controversy over the *Comet* was Van Buren himself. When the United States sought indemnification in 1836 for all three vessels, Andrew Stevenson, the minister in England and a Virginia slaveholder, encountered great reluctance in London. The British foreign secretary, Lord Palmerston, finally agreed to meet American claims for the *Comet* and the *Encomium,* but not for the *Enterprise,* because it had entered Bermuda after August 1, 1834, the day British emancipation in the West Indies went into effect. Stevenson immediately rejected Palmerston's reasoning, declaring that American law authorized the coastal slave trade and was backed by international law, which superseded British law in the West Indies. In the Senate later on, John C. Calhoun likewise denounced Palmerston's distinction, arguing in resolutions on March 4, 1840, that under international law a ship engaged in legal commerce— the interstate slave trade—was under the exclusive jurisdiction of its government, even while on the high seas and even if forced into a foreign port. The British owed an indemnity for the *Enterprise,* Calhoun insisted. Now, since the Spanish government authorized the coastal slave trade in Cuba, the United States by its own reasoning appeared to have no choice but to comply with Spain's demands for the *Amistad* and its cargo.[13]

But a careful examination of these three cases and that of the *Amistad* shows that no valid comparison existed: whereas no questions arose about the legitimacy of the American coastal vessels' business, the voyage of the *Amistad* caused enough suspicion to justify an inquiry into its papers. Furthermore, in the earlier maritime controversies the major American demand was for indemnity and not for a return of slaves, especially after parliamentary emancipation. Stevenson had presented the argument, which the British rejected, that a ship was an extension of a nation's territory and thus safe from encroachment because of its flag. He also declared that, on the basis of hospitality, ships of friendly nations forced into foreign ports were to receive help in completing their voyages. But this policy did not apply in instances involving fraud. Whites in control of coastal slavers surely aroused no questions about ownership; but blacks in command of a weather-beaten schooner that carried white prisoners, flew no flag, and was thousands of miles from the Cuban coast certainly raised suspicions. Legal support for an inquiry into the status of the *Amistad* could have come from the commentaries of Justice Joseph Story of the United States Supreme Court. According to his writings of the early 1830s, public officials *could* go beyond prima facie evidence when there was reason to suspect that a ship's papers were fraudulent.[14]

To the Van Buren administration, however, the central consideration in the *Amistad* case was not the law but political concerns that prohibited the discussion of issues conducive to sectional division.[15] The White House did not find it politically expedient to examine the obvious legal infractions in the *Amistad* case and make the expected judgment. Even a superficial inquiry by the Van Buren administration would have created a legal case for believing that both the cargo and the voyage were illegal. But the easy solution was to disregard the evidence and make a political decision—which was what the White House intended to do.

II

It is surprising only at first that the Van Buren administration made no inquiries in Cuba about information relating to the *Amistad* and to the slave-trade question in general. Was the *Amistad* a known slaver? Was illicit slave importation a thriving business? Were Spanish officials on the island in collusion with participants in the traffic? What were the reputations of Ruiz and Montes? Were the barracoons primarily outlets for selling recently imported Africans? An examination of dispatches to Washington from the American consul in Havana, Nicholas Trist, shows no effort on anyone's part to ascertain facts that might have facilitated justice.[16]

Several factors may explain the administration's lapse in securing information on the *Amistad*. Trist was preoccupied with other matters. A still unresolved controversy in America's diplomatic history concerns the allegations that he accepted money for failing to police the issuance of clearance papers to slave traders in Cuba who sought to use the American flag in guarding against a British search. Trist hotly denied the charges, and the president believed him.[17] Conceivably this issue overshadowed all others—including that of the *Amistad*. The Van Buren administration may also have initially thought the *Amistad* issue so inconsequential that neither the White House nor Trist sensed the importance of forwarding relevant information to Washington. Another explanation may be the sheer ineptness of the White House. Yet this is unlikely. Forsyth was a responsible federal official. In addition, the White House, having already made a decision, might not have *wanted* to know any more about the case. Furthermore, it is possible that Van Buren perceived that slavery as an issue could wreck not only the Democratic party but the Union itself, and that he therefore wanted it kept out of politics.

The administration's lukewarm attitude toward the African-slave-trade question also helps to explain its stance on the *Amistad* issue. In early 1837, shortly after Van Buren became president, the

British invited the United States to join them and the French in a treaty establishing an international force to suppress the traffic along the African coast. Forsyth refused the offer of mutual search for several reasons: the United States feared a loss of maritime rights, preferred to enforce its laws in American waters only, and wanted to act alone in halting its citizens' participation in the trade. Moreover, the proposed arrangement would harm American commerce. Whereas British and French nationals would have courts close by, Americans would have to return to the United States for trial. Finally, a mutual search treaty carried dangerous implications for American slavery. Later, in October 1839, Henry S. Fox, the British minister in Washington, sent a note to Forsyth complaining of America's failure to halt the slave trade. The United States, Fox urged, had to permit the right of mutual search in stopping the practice. Forsyth denied that America was responsible for the failure of the anti-slave-trade arrangement, and blamed the signatory nations for their duplicitous practices. Forsyth repeatedly directed Stevenson in London to protest British naval officers' searching American vessels suspected of engaging in the slave trade. Palmerston provided no satisfaction.[18]

Forsyth's proslavery and states' rights views doubtless affected his stand in the *Amistad* controversy. A former Georgia congressman and governor, he had been minister to Spain from 1819 to 1823. He owned slaves, but his modest wealth allowed him no more than a few household servants; in 1840 he owned three. As a Southerner, he believed that the federal government should not interfere with slavery, because it was a state matter. During the 1820s he opposed an attempt by a New York congressman to secure a resolution declaring that a free black from New York had a right to live free in any state of the Union. The Southern delegation countered with the resolution, which Forsyth supported, that Southerners had "the right to exclude free People of Color, to eject them, and to limit their privileges," when Southerners allowed free blacks to reside among them. On the African slave trade, Forsyth in the 1820s denounced the business as piracy, advocating prosecution under the law of nations and urging the United States to act independently in suppressing the practice. Only treaties with foreign nations, he insisted, could lead to the search of American vessels.[19]

All the above factors probably influenced the Van Buren administration's attitude toward the *Amistad* case; but the overriding consideration appears to have been its desire to dismiss the matter before it could affect the Democrats' chances for reelection in 1840. Van Buren had no strong feelings about slavery—except that he did not want it to interfere with his remaining in the White House. In a long letter published in the press, the president asserted that the relation of master and slave belonged "exclusively" to each state and that the government in Washington had no right to violate the "Spirit of the compromise which lies at the basis of the Federal compact." The abolitionists, he declared, sought only "to disturb the amicable relations existing between the Slave holding & non-Slave holding States of this Union." They had caused "unmixed mischief," and as a "public man" his duty was "undisguised opposition" to their tactics. The Spanish minister thought that Van Buren's primary concern was political. Calderón believed that in order to bring pressure on the president to free the captives and thus undermine his Southern support, the abolitionists had proclaimed Cinqué and the others "heroes comparable to the Romans."[20]

Forsyth took the lead in formulating the administration's strategy on the *Amistad.* Time would take care of the matter, he believed. On September 5 the United States district attorney in Connecticut, William S. Holabird, asked Forsyth for instructions in the case but appears to have guessed what they would be. "I *suppose,*" Holabird wrote, "it will be my duty to bring them to trial, unless they are in some other way disposed of." Yet less than a week later he explained that after careful examination of the law, he did not believe that American courts had jurisdiction, since the offense had taken place on a vessel "belonging exclusively to citizens of a foreign State, on the high seas, and . . . against subjects of a foreign State." Sensing legal difficulties, he asked whether the United States was party to any treaties that would allow a surrender of the blacks before the circuit court convened. On September 11 Forsyth directed Holabird to make sure that no judicial proceedings permitted the *Amistad,* cargo, and "slaves" to go "beyond the control of the Federal Executive."[21]

With the president out of Washington for a few days, Forsyth discussed the matter with Attorney General Felix Grundy, Postmaster General Amos Kendall, and Secretary of the Treasury Levi Woodbury, who all agreed that the United States should comply with Spain's demands on the basis of Pinckney's Treaty of 1795. Woodbury assured the president by letter that the *Amistad* case was "undergoing full examination" by them all; in a suggestion not followed by the White House, the secretary of the treasury wrote,

"[P]erhaps nothing is lost in point of public feeling by letting the judiciary take all the responsibility in respect to it, which they [*sic*] may choose to exercise." After Van Buren returned to the White House, he approved his cabinet members' recommendation to accept Spain's position in the controversy, and he instructed Grundy, a Tennessee slaveholder, to write an opinion in its support.[22] This business out of the way, the president turned to more important matters—domestic financial difficulties, longstanding Canadian boundary problems with England, and the reelection campaign.

By the middle of October the attorney general had prepared a legal opinion that supported the administration's stand. Grundy insisted that Pinckney's Treaty obligated the president to deliver the vessel, cargo, and blacks to persons designated by the Spanish minister in Washington. The United States, he added, had to give "due faith and credit" to official acts of other nations' "public functionaries." Property titles held by Ruiz and Montes were conclusive and not subject to question in another country's judiciary. The *Amistad* had papers "regularly authenticated" by "proper officers" in Havana. In a statement that contradicted Story, Grundy declared that there was no legal principle justifying American investigation into the validity of those papers. Furthermore, he noted, judicial actions were not the only official acts above scrutiny by another nation. All acts of other nations were binding, whether executive, legislative, judicial, or special. Otherwise, the principle of comity would cease to exist, leaving international law to collapse in disharmony. American intervention in the case would constitute an effort to make decisions on a treaty between England and Spain; only parties to a treaty could judge matters affecting that treaty. Special tribunals existed to deal with violations of treaties.[23]

The *Amistad* affair was not a case of piracy, Grundy declared; otherwise, both the law of nations and municipal law would condone American jurisdiction over the matter. According to one American legal scholar, piracy was "the offense of depredating on the seas, without being authorized by any sovereign State, or with commissions from different sovereigns at war with each other." Pirates were "the common enemies of all mankind" and for that reason were subject to capture and trial by any nation. Chancellor Kent called pirates the "enemies of the human race" and agreed that they deserved "universal hostility." The federal courts, Grundy pointed out, held in *U.S.* v. *Smith* that pirates were "freebooters upon the sea, not under the acknowledged authority, or deriving protection from, the flag or commission of any Government; and, therefore, . . . subject to trial within the United States." But in the *Amistad* case, the ship was Spanish, belonged to Spaniards, was protected by Spanish papers and flag, and was moving from one Spanish port to another. In *U.S.* v. *Palmer,* Grundy noted, the Supreme Court held that piracy, as defined by the congressional act of 1790, did not include robbery on the high seas and on a vessel belonging to subjects of a foreign country. American courts had no jurisdiction in the *Amistad* matter because the uprising was not piracy.[24]

Grundy cited the Supreme Court's *Antelope* decision of 1825 in support of his argument. According to Chief Justice John Marshall, the law of nations sanctioned the slave trade. Grundy admitted that many Americans considered the slave trade inhumane, but he pointed out that both international law and "almost all civilized nations" had declared the practice legal. Though an individual country could declare the business illegal, such decrees were operative only within its territories and only against its subjects. American courts could not judge actions by another country's citizens. The *Amistad* had not been engaged in the African slave trade at the time of the revolt, and just as Americans had the legal right to participate in the interstate slave trade, the Spanish vessel had been legally transporting slave property from one Spanish port to another.[25]

Grundy insisted that since the blacks were Spanish property and the United States could not take action against them as criminals, the only remedy was for the White House to follow Pinckney's Treaty and order the United States marshal in Connecticut to surrender the vessel and the cargo to the Spanish minister. The president had no legal power to return them to Africa, Grundy explained, for congressional acts on the slave trade applied only when violations occurred inside the United States. The Spanish claimants had not entered United States territory with the intention of either selling or enslaving the blacks. It was clear that "no violation" of American laws had been committed and that "no such violation was in contemplation." Furthermore, Grundy noted, the blacks had denied being slaves, and they would not have a chance to prove their innocence if the president surrendered them to Ruiz and Montes. The only safe course was to deliver the blacks to the Spanish minister, who would see that they stood trial before Spanish tribunals. The president's responsibility was to execute the treaty by ordering the marshal to deliver property to persons designated by the Spanish minister. Van Buren's cabinet approved Grundy's opinion.[26]

The flaws in Grundy's analysis were clear to those knowledgeable in international law. Grundy had made an invalid comparison between the *Amistad*'s voyage and that of American vessels engaged in the interstate slave trade in that there were no suspicions that the blacks on board the American ships had come from the illegal African slave trade. Moreover, America's demands in these cases had been for indemnification, not for the return of slaves. The attorney general's effort to show that the *Amistad* mutiny was not a case of piracy led him into a contradiction when he referred to Article 9 of Pinckney's Treaty in arguing that the United States had to return to Spain all merchandise rescued from robbers and *pirates*. Similarly, in refusing to recognize the blacks as pirates and robbers, he again showed inconsistency in argument by inadvertently implying that they were free men, *not* slaves, and entitled to seek liberty. As pirates and robbers, the captives would have had to be slaves, now legally held for an illegal revolt.[27] In addition, Grundy's attempt to define when the African-slave-trade process actually ended was unconvincing. His argument implied that no prosecution could take place unless authorities caught the perpetrator in the act of violating the law. Portuguese slavers had transported the blacks to Havana, where Spaniards bought them and took them to Puerto Príncipe. In effect, he was arguing that the blacks legally became slaves once they entered a Spanish possession even though their entry was illegal. But at what point did the illegal trade terminate and the legal domestic traffic begin? It is arguable that the African slave trade was still under way during the blacks' passage to Puerto Príncipe, leaving them every right to strike for freedom.[28]

The reason for the attorney general's stance was easy to understand: it was politically inexpedient to allow the *Amistad* case to go to trial in the United States. Had he admitted that the uprising was piracy, international law would have taken precedent over Pinckney's Treaty and permitted the American courts to have jurisdiction. Abolitionists would have entered the fray, which would have provoked a heated Southern defense of slavery and split the Democratic party. The alternative course for Grundy would have been to argue that the blacks on the *Amistad* had sought only freedom, eliminating the possibility of piracy and relieving the American judiciary of jurisdiction. And yet this stand would have placed the White House on the side of the abolitionists and created the political problem of a sectionally divisive public debate.

An article in the *Emancipator,* signed "Veto" (actually Theodore Sedgwick, one of the blacks' attorneys), emphasized that the outcome of the *Amistad* case depended upon implementing the "law of the case with a calm and dispassionate eye." Ruiz and Montes could not claim the blacks as property, because the law was not on their side. As Chief Justice Marshall pointed out in the *Antelope* decision, the legality of the seizure of a ship engaged in the slave trade depended upon the law of the country under which that vessel sailed. If the slave trade was legal, compensation was in order; if not, the vessel was subject to settlement by a prize court. Spanish law prohibited the slave trade. The sale of the blacks in Havana did not change their status from "stolen property." No matter how many times the items changed hands, no divestiture of property could have occurred. On the matter of criminal jurisdiction, Veto declared that if the blacks were not property, they could not be guilty of any crime in seeking freedom. The blacks were "free persons illegally restrained of their liberty," and it was "not murder for a free man to kill his kidnapper." The mutiny was neither robbery nor piracy. By the law of nations, Veto claimed, piracy was robbery at sea. But to constitute robbery, there had to be the *"animus"* or the intention. The blacks of the *Amistad* had one objective: to win their freedom and return home, not to plunder the ship's goods.[29]

A writer to the New York *Evening Post* who signed himself "A" argued that the *Amistad* case belonged in the American courts. To bring it before the judiciary, he thought a writ of habeas corpus advisable. Treaties were part of the law of the land, and when their execution involved private rights, one had to look to the judiciary for protection or redress. The Constitution declared that judicial power extended "to all cases, in law and equity, arising under the constitution, the laws of the United States, and treaties made, or which shall be made, under their authority." The executive could not act independently of the judiciary.[30]

The *Emancipator* emphasized that the law had to prevail in the *Amistad* case, although the antislavery paper was pleased that the "old American feeling, in favor of liberty and equal justice to all men, irrespective of clime, caste or color, [was] reviving among us." The paper's greatest objective was that justice might go to the *Amistad* blacks, just as it would go to "any other class of men who forcibly liberate themselves from unlawful captivity," and that this might in turn help to overthrow the slave trade and bring about the introduction of civilization to Africa. The blacks' future was in the hands of the American courts, and this meant that law had to prevail over feelings pertaining to slavery.[31]

Though the abolitionists were convinced that the remedy in the *Amistad* case was to take it before the courts and the American people, they had not counted on politics' interfering with justice. Van Buren's zeal for reelection threatened to override all considerations, including whether it was just to return the blacks to Cuba for what would probably be a mock trial. Forsyth's directive to Holabird of September 11 had provided the first glimmer of an attitude that seemed prevalent in the White House—that the executive possessed a prerogative that might allow interference in the judicial process.

4

"The Inherent Property of Liberty"

The first round of the abolitionists' struggle in the *Amistad* case took place in the United States Circuit Court meeting in Connecticut. The blacks' attorneys hoped to convince the presiding judges, Associate Justice Smith Thompson from the United States Supreme Court and Andrew T. Judson from the district court, that the circuit court lacked jurisdiction in a case where natural law was the guiding principle and that there was nothing to warrant a grand-jury indictment for either murder or piracy. They first tried to secure a separate writ of habeas corpus for the three girls; this would force the prosecution to bring formal charges against them, or see the court excuse them from appearing as witnesses in the case. Their release would result in a courtroom confrontation between the black captives, who had attracted considerable public favor, and the two Spaniards, who had not. Furthermore, the writ would serve as a license to bring into debate the entire question of human rights and property rights pertaining to slavery. If the abolitionists could show that there was no legal basis for holding the youths, they would expand the argument to include the other blacks. If they could establish that the captives were human beings and not property, no one could have property or salvage claims on them and the blacks could go free. Most important, the abolitionists could exert pressure on the Van Buren administration to change its stand on the issue.

The abolitionists' strategy in the *Amistad* affair was to exhaust every legal remedy for securing the blacks' liberty, and their first step was to make a highly tenuous appeal for a writ of habeas corpus to show cause for not releasing the blacks. Such a court order would shield them from unlawful imprisonment unless the Spaniards' counsel filed formal charges. If he did so, the blacks' attorneys could argue that the blacks had been charged as *persons,* not as property, and this would win a major principle in Connecticut that might spread nationwide. To do this, they intended to establish that both Lieutenant Gedney and the United States marshal had acted illegally in detaining the blacks. If they could prove that the blacks were not slaves and therefore not property, both American officials would have violated the blacks' fundamental rights. Dismissal of the case on a writ of habeas corpus would constitute an admission to the abolitionists' most important objective—that natural rights superseded municipal law and guaranteed blacks the liberty inherent to mankind.[1]

The appeal for a writ was the beginning step in the judicial strategy designed to publicize the substantive issue of human and property rights in the circuit court. One abolitionist insisted that the central question was "whether an African [was] a *man,* and of course entitled to all the rights of humanity." Even if the blacks' attorneys failed to win the writ, it was worth the effort, for at the least they could explore the inhumanity of slavery in a judicial and public forum. As Joshua Leavitt later told the General Antislavery Convention in London, the purpose of the writ was "to test their right to personality."[2]

The abolitionists were on shaky legal grounds. Federal judges could inquire into the legality of a person's detention by the executive branch of the American government, but state and local detentions lay outside the jurisdiction of federal courts.[3] Since the passage of the Judiciary Act of 1789, the "Great Writ" supposedly protected individuals against unjust imprisonment by the federal government, but few federal offenses actually called for a defense based on a writ of habeas corpus, for there was little federal criminal law. In the states the writ was important, but few poor people could seek remedy against state actions; besides, state judges were hesitant to issue the writ against state, county, or local officials. The result was that, although the Constitution guaranteed habeas corpus, the importance of the writ before the Civil War was clouded or problematic.[4]

If the court in Hartford issued the writ, the blacks' attorneys intended to argue that their clients were persons who shared constitutional rights with other Americans. If the abolitionists succeeded, the decision would alienate the South by suggesting that American slaves were also persons who could seek a writ of habeas corpus in claiming freedom. The best chance for undermining the

Spaniards' argument lay with the three girls: they spoke only an African language, they attracted great popular sympathy, and their youth made it clear that they were recent imports from Africa. This proceeding in Hartford would form the basis for all succeeding legal arguments in the case.[5]

I

Whether the attraction was mere curiosity, concern over universal principles, or the rumors sweeping the countryside that a mass public hanging was about to take place, the large number of visitors in Hartford converted the usually placid town into a virtual carnival as the time approached for the hearing. Public hotels were filled, the streets jammed, and the courtroom crowded to capacity long before the session was scheduled to convene on the afternoon of September 19. Among the distinguished visitors were the wives of the judges, along with elderly and respected citizens of the community and of towns as far distant as Boston and New York. Ruiz and Montes attracted great interest by arriving in nearby New Haven Bay on a steamboat, accompanied by Lieutenant Richard W. Meade of the USS *Washington*.[6]

The number of visitors in the New Haven jail had increased dramatically over the last few days, now totaling perhaps four thousand (each paying twelve and one-half cents admission). The long streams of strange white faces had frightened the blacks, who nervously passed their hands over their throats in asking whether they were about to die. When repeatedly told no, they were puzzled: "If they don't mean to kill us, why are so many people here to see us?" At one point the four children, in another part of the building, began crying loudly with fear. Lewis Tappan, who happened to be present, learned that Ruiz had recently been in the room. When the youths saw the Spaniard, one of them ran to the matron and all burst into tears. Cinqué had dourly responded to Ruiz's visit by drawing his hand across his throat.[7]

Abolitionists were pleased with the atmosphere in Hartford. They could hardly have hoped for a stronger indictment of slavery than the spectacle of a United States marshal bringing in the three black girls, weeping with terror and desperately clutching the jailer's hands as he tried to calm them with pieces of fruit. Nor could they have asked for greater melodrama than to hear the defense plead for a separate writ of habeas corpus for the girls to release them from jail, only to hear the prosecution stand in opposition and call for bail of $100 on each of them to assure their appearance as witnesses to the mutiny. A "whole posse" of lawyers, according to the Washington *National Intelligencer,* was ready to do battle over the most sacred principles of the Republic. Never, according to another paper, had there been a "greater legal and moral entanglement than this question." Carry on the cause of the *Amistad,* the abolitionist Gerrit Smith joyously exclaimed in the *Emancipator* on the day court proceedings began. "God has ordered them [the abolitionists] to hasten the overthrow of slavery." In the same paper, a lady from Hartford expressed the hope that the trial would "open the eyes of the good people of this State upon our most horrible system of slavery, and the dreadful cruelty of the slave trade." Timed for the opening day of the trial, William Cullen Bryant's poetic lines commemorating what he called the African Chief appeared in the *Emancipator* as an attempt to immortalize Cinqué:

> Chained in a foreign land he stood,
>   A man of giant frame,
> Amid the gathering multitude
>   That shrunk to hear his name—
> All stern of look and strong of limb,
>   His dark eye on the ground—
> And silently they gazed on him
>   As on a *lion* bound.
>
> Vainly, but well, that chief had fought—
>   He was a captive now;
> Yet pride, that fortune humbles not,
>   Was written on his brow.
> The scars his dark broad bosom wore
>   Showed warrior true and brave;
> A prince among his tribe before,
>   *He could not be a slave.*[8]

The Spaniards' counsel emphasized the primacy of property rights in his argument against a writ of habeas corpus. Attorney William Hungerford opposed releasing the blacks on the ground that his clients, Ruiz and Montes, claimed the captives as their property. He invoked the law of nations, American law, and treaties between the United States and Spain. Moreover, Hungerford said, the matter had to come to trial because Lieutenant Gedney also had a libel pending before the district court. The court could not set the law aside because of an appeal to abstract rights allegedly guaranteed by some amorphous higher law.[9]

Judge Thompson, however, allowed arguments on the petition for a writ of habeas corpus, permitting an inquiry into the cause of commitment and furnishing the abolitionists with their first victory by his declaration that all issues in contest could come before the court.[10]

Further entanglements became apparent when other principals spoke. The United States district attorney, William S. Holabird, explained that the Spanish minister in Washington had officially requested the return of the *Amistad* and its cargo as property under Pinckney's Treaty of 1795. To win executive control over the blacks, as Forsyth had instructed, Holabird declared that if the court should find the captives to be slaves, he hoped that it would allow the United States government to comply with the Spanish claim. If the court decreed that the blacks were not slaves but "negroes and persons of Color" taken illegally from Africa, he hoped that it would authorize the White House to transport them to Africa. Henry Green and his four companions, who had first come across Cinqué and the others on the New York beach, had likewise filed a libel in district court for salvage of the *Amistad* and its cargo. According to their attorney, Governor William W. Ellsworth of Connecticut, they had suspected that the blacks had "feloniously obtained" control of the vessel and had therefore forced Cinqué and his accomplices to "surrender up themselves." Had Green and the others not been on the beach at "great risk of life," the argument went, Gedney would have been unable to seize the ship and cargo.[11]

As the proceedings continued to become more complex, Judge Thompson realized that this was no ordinary hearing and that he confronted momentous issues. That same morning, Judge Judson, who had opened the district court proceedings for accepting the filing of libels in the case, strongly implied that salvage claims against the blacks were invalid when he explained at the hearing that only property was liable for salvage and that the state of Connecticut would not regard the blacks as property. He saw no way the district court could order a sale of blacks in Connecticut.[12] Hungerford's partner in the case, Ralph Ingersoll of New Haven, argued against a writ of habeas corpus and tried to shift the thrust of their case from the status of the girls to the criminal charges against the adult males of the *Amistad*. The blacks were slaves, he insisted, and a federal warrant against them for murder and piracy had necessitated the setting of bond to hold the three girls as witnesses. Furthermore, Montes had filed a separate libel in district court for the youths as slaves, claiming he had bought them in Cuba, where slavery was permitted. According to treaties between the United States and Spain, Ingersoll argued, the girls should be returned to his client at no loss. Judge Thompson allowed the blacks' attorneys time to prepare an answer. Court was adjourned until the following morning.[13]

II

Theodore Sedgwick opened the next day's proceedings with a long and passionate argument. Described as an "iron-faced man" from Philadelphia, Sedgwick clearly wrote most of the argument for the blacks. Who could have guessed, the New York *Advertiser & Express* wondered, that the Mandingo words Sedgwick had learned while engaged in the African slave trade would now prove helpful in defending victims of that practice? None of the blacks were legally slaves, Sedgwick declared; they were "natives of Africa," born in the district of Senegambia and seized contrary to international law, the law of nature, and Spanish laws, treaties, and ordinances. After outlining the events leading to the mutiny, he presented the affidavits of John Ferry and Augustus Hanson, both native Africans who after talking with the girls were convinced that they were native Mandingoes. The blacks were not slaves but kidnapped Africans; Ruiz and Montes had no case.[14]

Ingersoll countered with another argument against a writ of habeas corpus. The circuit court, he declared, should not deal with this case while it was pending before the district court. The Spaniards' counsel had libeled the blacks as Spanish property, and the United States had brought a libel suit because of the Spanish minister's demand for their restoration under Pinckney's Treaty. The district attorney's libel also asserted that if these blacks had been illegally imported into the United States for sale as slaves, the congressional act of 1819 authorized the president to send them back to Africa. On these grounds, Ingersoll asked, could the circuit court issue a writ of habeas corpus and "take the whole case out of the hands of the district court?"[15]

At this point Roger S. Baldwin rose to deliver the major argument on behalf of a writ. Its purpose, he declared, was to establish that the authorities illegally held the blacks as property and that the court could not violate their constitutional rights as persons by retaining them in custody while settling other questions. Furthermore, Baldwin asserted, Gedney had no right to seek jurisdiction in Connecticut, for the seizures had taken place in New York: "If a party can, for the mere purpose of changing the jurisdiction, go to another state, he is equally at liberty to go where he thinks it may be most for his interest to have his libel tried." And now Gedney claimed a "meritorious service"—not to "these poor Africans, by saving their lives, but, by reducing to the condition of slavery, men who, when he found them, were free."[16]

Baldwin held that Gedney had had no right to treat the blacks as property before the courts had decided their status. "Every presumption is," he said, "that all beings, who have the form of our nature, are free." The marshal, through a "most liberal construction" of the warrant, took the blacks into custody. His federal warrant authorized seizure of the vessel and the cargo; but he wrongfully supposed the blacks to be slaves and took them under the name of cargo. Did anyone have the blacks in his possession when Gedney arrived? Or were they free, "themselves in the command and possession of property?" Gedney admitted that he had found them in control of the vessel. The blacks were free when seized, Baldwin insisted, and American law prohibited their enslavement. The district court lacked jurisdiction because the blacks were not property but human beings.[17]

Color was the difference, Baldwin lamented: "It is only when men come here with a black skin, that we look upon them in a condition in which they may by any means be made slaves. But, when we find them here from the coast of Africa, the same rule must apply to the black as to the white man." Under the laws of slavery in Connecticut, Baldwin declared, one will *not* find that "every colored man is presumed to be a slave, until the contrary is shown." The *Amistad*'s blacks came to the United States for asylum, he said, adding, "I say there is no power on earth that has a right again to reduce them to slavery."[18]

Baldwin rejected the opposing counsel's argument that the three girls were slaves. They were between the ages of seven and nine, he declared, native Africans incapable of speaking any language other than their own. "Does not this honorable Court see that they cannot be slaves?—They were not born slaves,—they were born in Africa." Baldwin insisted that Montes must have known that the girls were not slaves. He knew they did not speak either Spanish or Portuguese; he knew from their ages that they had probably been brought to Cuba in violation of Spanish law. Baldwin dramatically asserted that Montes bought them from a pirate and was as guilty as the slavers in Africa.[19]

Baldwin cited the *Antelope* case of 1825 in claiming that American courts could decide property titles only in cases of captured fugitive slaves. Two central facts had emerged in that case: the property in question had been taken illegally, and the African slave trade was legal under Spanish and Portuguese law. The court simply restored the blacks to their condition of slavery. But there was a critical difference between the *Antelope* and the *Amistad* cases: by 1839 Spanish, Portuguese, and American law had declared the trade illegal. "What, then," Baldwin asked, "is the pretense for the interference of the Spanish Government?" The blacks are natives of Africa, he insisted, not fugitives from justice. "Are they to be judged by Spanish laws, or by our own laws, or the laws of nature?" The Spanish claimants "deserve the penalty of death for piracy, which would be awarded to any citizen of the United States, who should be found engaged in the same manner."[20]

Baldwin argued that the president could not comply with the Spanish minister's demand; to do so would make Americans into "slave catchers" for a foreign government. "What law," he asked, "has imposed upon the executive of the United States the obligation to hunt up the runaway slaves of Spanish subjects, and restore them?" Baldwin was astounded by the district attorney's claim that the circuit court ought to hold the blacks until it could determine whether the president should return them to Africa: "This is a strange process—imprison them, in order to ascertain that they are free!" The only two laws remotely relevant to this situation were not applicable, because they pertained to slaves brought into the United States on American vessels. If the *Amistad* blacks were slaves, the district court had no authority to order their seizure. If they were not slaves, the executive had no power to send them to Africa. The blacks were not slaves and not property. And yet the prosecution wanted the American government to act as "auxiliary to persons engaged in this foul traffic."[21]

Ingersoll disputed Baldwin's argument. Pinckney's Treaty required the restoration of all ships and merchandise taken by pirates. The United States government at the present time, he insisted, recognized slaves as property. When American vessels wreck in Cuba, Ingersoll pointed out, they seek restoration; when an American ship ends up in British possessions with slaves aboard, the government in Washington calls for their restoration. The Treaty of Ghent in 1814 provided a commission to deal with claims resulting from slaves carried off during the war. The *Antelope* decision upheld the restoration of a captured foreign slaver.

According to international law, the African slave trade was legal to those nations authorizing it. "A foreign vessel, captured in time of peace, engaged in the slave trade, will be restored, even if the nation to which the vessel belonged, had prohibited it."[22]

Ingersoll insisted that a writ of habeas corpus had no bearing on the *Amistad* case. Baldwin had no evidence that the blacks had come from Africa. The only question before this court was whether they were property under Spanish law. To settle this issue, Ingersoll claimed, it might prove necessary to inquire into Spanish laws in Cuba. And yet Baldwin had demanded a writ of habeas corpus that would prevent such investigation by immediately setting them free. It was "utterly unfounded and entirely gratuitous" to argue questions about the slave trade and whether Ruiz and Montes knew that the blacks had come from Africa. The court's only responsibility was to decide whether the treaty of 1795 required restoration of the blacks to their owners, or whether the American law of 1819 called for their return to Africa.[23]

The third attorney for the blacks, Seth Staples, countered with the argument that a writ of habeas corpus was in order because the real issue in the *Amistad* case was individual liberty, not rights of property. The children had asked only that the court protect their personal rights through the "process which renders all our guarantees of civil liberty available—the great palladium of civil liberty." The writ of habeas corpus, Staples asserted, was not concerned with the "lower and more vulgar objects of property." It reached "the higher elements of society—the life, liberty, and safety of the citizen." Arguments over property could not interfere with "this great conservative writ." To his opponents in the courtroom, he dramatically declared, "Go on with your litigation, as to the *Amistad* and her cargo, to your heart's content; but take not these children and deprive them of the habeas corpus, under pretext of a question whether they are brutes or human beings."[24]

At the beginning of the afternoon session, Judge Thompson prepared to give his decision on the jurisdictional question as the grand jury filed into the courtroom. The court, he instructed the grand jury, did not have jurisdiction. Gedney had captured the ship and its cargo in New York, which meant that a trial for murder and piracy could not take place in Connecticut. While the blacks' counsel tried to sort out the ramifications of this apparent victory, Thompson continued. If an offense had occurred, he declared, it had done so "on board a Spanish vessel, with a Spanish crew and commander, and Spanish papers, as a mere coasting vessel, on the Island of Cuba." American courts had jurisdiction only over offenses against American statutes or against the law of nations. Furthermore, there was not enough evidence for a grand jury indictment.[25] A ripple of excitement spread through the court-room as the recognition set in that the captives would not stand trial for murder or piracy.

When order returned, Thompson expressed concern about what would happen to the blacks if released: "The great difficulty is they are now in the custody of the law, and what is to be done with them?" Staples surmised that if the blacks had committed no offense against American law, "nothing [could] be done with them." The claim in this court was that they were property. But if released, the judge pressed further, were there Connecticut laws to provide for them? Staples replied that the state would provide for them as "foreign paupers." The state's citizens, he was sure, would hesitate to give them up to "pretended friends, who might possibly stop short of Africa." When Hungerford objected that the court was not to go into the "merits of the case," Thompson reminded him that when a party brought up a writ of habeas corpus, the court had to examine these matters to determine the true situation. If the blacks were in the custody of the court, it was "necessary to inquire into the process which [held] them."[26]

Probably sensing that the judge was leaning toward the defense argument, the United States district attorney repeated the govern-ment's position that there had been a violation of American laws prohibiting the importation of slaves into the country. The vessel that entered the United States was under the control of Africans, Holabird insisted, adding, "As to the national character of that ves-sel, I contend nothing is yet known." It was common practice for a slaver to sail under another's flag. The vessel might even prove to be American. If an inquiry found it to be American, a violation of American law would have occurred and the court would have jurisdiction. While an investigation was under way, he insisted, the blacks had to remain in jail.[27]

Hungerford believed it unnecessary to inquire into the morality of slavery; the only question before the court was whether his clients had the right to buy property in slaves. Slavery was legal in Cuba. Although an Anglo-Spanish treaty prohibited the slave trade, the United States had a treaty obligation with Spain to return "every species of property" to claimants. If both signatories to the treaty recognized slavery as legal, it followed that if a slave escaped from one territory to the other, the latter was bound to return him. And since slavery was legal in the United States, that party had a right under comity to seek the return of his slave. If the Spaniards were entitled to these slaves, either by principle, comity, or treaty, the United States was bound to deliver them.[28]

Staples argued that the law of 1819 did not permit America's armed vessels "to cruise for slavers." They had to be "instructed, commissioned, authorized." American cruisers could not seize a suspected slaver without specific authorization from the president. No evidence showed that Lieutenant Gedney had such authority. His responsibility was to survey the American coast. Yet Gedney and his men seized the vessel and its cargo as property and demanded salvage. Staples asked, "Can the district attorney avail himself of their act, and say they took it under this law, when they say they did not?" Furthermore, under the law the commander of the vessel seizing a slaver was to take everyone aboard to the district marshal. But the marshal took possession of the blacks under the interpretation he gave to the term *cargo* contained in the warrant. To establish his case, Staples insisted, the district attorney had to show that Gedney was commanding an "armed public vessel, commissioned to do this service."[29]

Staples expressed surprise that Ruiz, who could speak English, had not appeared as a witness. But, of course, neither he nor Montes, Staples remarked, would swear under oath that he did not know that the blacks had just come into Cuba. The dialect of the blacks was the most conclusive evidence that they were native Africans recently imported into Havana; it was spoken nowhere but along the African coast. "And yet I am told that Ruiz will come here and swear that he did not know that they came from Africa," Staples challenged him. "Let him come here and encounter the perils of perjury, if he dare."[30]

Staples concluded with the argument that the burden of proof lay with the people claiming these blacks as slaves. In the circuit court case of *La Jeune Eugénie* of 1822, Justice Joseph Story had declared that a foreign claimant of a vessel seized for engaging in the slave trade had to present evidence of ownership. A court, Staples asserted, could not allow the withdrawal of property from its jurisdiction without proof from the owner. The presumption was that "every man [was] born free." An admiralty court could not be "converted into a court for seizing runaway slaves, and restoring them to foreign claimants." According to one observer, Staples spoke with "impassioned strain" in declaring that the only question of property involved in the *Amistad* case was "the inherent property of liberty"—that "blessing which was next to life itself."[31]

III

The next day, September 21, Judge Thompson warned that the court was not ready to render a verdict but was unwilling to approve a writ of habeas corpus that would release the prisoners. He noted that the attempt to dismiss the case had placed the court in an embarrassing position. The only question before the court was procedural; it could not deal with the "merits of the whole case." Yet consideration of the writ allowed an examination of all issues touching upon the request. If the district court could properly detain the blacks, Thompson asserted, the circuit court could not interfere. The judge digressed for a moment in declaring that personal feelings could not affect the outcome: "However abhorrent it may be to keep these persons in prison, or to view them in the light of property, and however desirous the court might be that they should all be set at liberty, they must not permit their private feelings to govern them in deciding upon the case before them." Justice had to prevail, Thompson insisted, "however painful it might be." Despite the argument by the blacks' attorneys that there was no right of property in human beings, Thompson held that legally there was. Foreign powers had permitted slavery; the United States had signed treaties with them; and the United States Supreme Court had recognized the institution. In the case of the *Antelope,* the Supreme Court was equally divided over the question of property in human beings; but it decreed that the owner bore the burden of proving his property. Thompson declared that "the prisoners could not be taken out of the jurisdiction of the district court on the writ of habeas corpus."[32]

Elated at the judge's findings on the writ, Ingersoll sought to bring the arguments to a close by proposing that counsel for each side prepare a brief so that the court might make a decision. He would confer with his opponents to see whether they might reach agreement by the opening of the afternoon session. If not, they would continue arguments at that time. Thompson adjourned the proceedings until 2:00 P.M.[33]

Judge Thompson opened the Saturday afternoon session by asking counsel on both sides whether they had reached an agreement to furnish briefs. If so, he could take them home and write an opinion. But Ingersoll expressed regret that they had not. Baldwin remarked, "[I]n a case of jurisdiction, where the personal rights of a party are concerned, those who maintain the jurisdiction should come prepared to argue the case." Hoping to keep the issues before the public, he insisted that the matter demanded prompt investigation and declared it inconvenient to prolong the argumentation. Staples agreed. He also had other obligations, but he wanted the issue settled immediately because "forty human beings" were unjustly incarcerated. Thompson replied that he had hoped for more time to examine the case but that if the blacks' attorneys insisted, the arguments would proceed.[34]

Baldwin opened his final argument with the assertion that the only question before the court was whether it had jurisdiction over the persons applying for relief under the writ of habeas corpus. Thompson agreed. In the *Antelope* case, Baldwin explained, the persons found on the Spanish slaver were slaves captured from slave vessels. Authorities seized the slavers because there was reason to believe that they intended to violate American laws on the slave trade. The slavers had prima facie jurisdiction over the slaves, and the capture was legal. The slaver was a Spanish vessel sailing for Havana, carrying regular papers, and holding the slaves as property. The principle was this: in returning the property, the Supreme Court was "restoring things to the condition they were in when the first unlawful act took place." But the *Amistad* case was different because the prisoners were not in the condition of slaves at the time of capture: "They were *prima facie* free when first found, and they must be treated as persons." They had rights given by God. Gedney had begun the case against vessel and property, not against persons. The blacks were not included in the warrant. Indeed, Baldwin asserted, the president himself did not have the power to make decisions relating to personal liberties in the states. If Ruiz and Montes wished to prosecute their claim, they had to do so in the common-law courts of Connecticut, where there was trial by jury. In the meantime, the blacks should go free.[35]

As the antagonists repeatedly hammered out their arguments, there was little indication that anything important would come out of the trial. But the tempo of proceedings was about to change—as a result of actions not by either counsel but by the Van Buren administration itself.

Apparently the White House noted that the growing public sympathy for the *Amistad* blacks could cause political damage, for Holabird made a statement that stunned everyone in attendance. He first explained that he wanted only to see the implementation of the "benevolent intentions" of the law of 1819 relating to blacks illegally introduced into the United States from Africa. "I stand here," he surprisingly exclaimed, "to contend that these blacks are free men—that they have been brought within the jurisdiction of the United States, . . . and if found to be, as I suppose, native Africans, they may be sent to their native land."[36] Clearly the Van Buren administration had discerned its district attorney's inability to prove them slaves and subject to return to Spain under Pinckney's Treaty. It now hoped to show them to be victims of the African slave trade—but still under the president's care. Since popular interest was building to the point that the case threatened to get out of hand, the safest course appeared to be to rid the nation of the blacks by admitting that they were free and subject to return to Africa. Though the strategy had changed, the objective had not: the White House sought to prevent political repercussions.

Staples was incredulous that Holabird now argued that the blacks were free men. In a statement revealing his deep distrust of the Van Buren administration, Staples remarked that the district attorney's stance reminded him of the saying "[S]ave me from my friends, and I will take care of my enemies." Why had the White House suddenly agreed with the abolitionists that the blacks were free? Why had Holabird made a concession undermining the Spaniards' property claims and providing the captives with some hope in the district court? All Staples could mutter was "What now?" He concluded at 7:00 P.M., ending five hours of argument by counsel on both sides.[37]

Indeed, what now? Judge Thompson might have asked himself this question on Monday morning, September 23, as he prepared to give his decision before a jammed courtroom. He denied the motion for a writ of habeas corpus, refusing to release the captives and leaving their disposition to the district court. Yet he noted his desire to have the district attorney accompany one of the defense attorneys to Montauk Point to determine the exact point of seizure by Lieutenant Gedney. Thompson was worried that the complexity of the proceedings had made his single task difficult for the public to understand. Since the community's feelings were deeply involved in the issues, he feared misunderstandings about the real questions before the court. Though the case had taken on the appearance of a fight over slavery, the court would not make a decision on the "abstract right of holding human beings in bondage." "My feelings," the judge asserted, "are personally as abhorrent to the system of slavery as those of any man here, but I must, on my oath, pronounce what the laws are on the subject." Thompson insisted that the question of liberty did not play a role in his decision. The court here could not determine whether the Spaniards had a right to the blacks as property, or whether the matter fell within the slave-trade provisions of the act of 1819. Interested parties could bring suits before the district court, where its decision would be subject to appeal to the circuit and then to the Supreme Court. Before adjourning, Thompson admonished the large number of "note-takers" in the room to relate a "true representation" of the decision.[38]

Immediately afterward, Judge Judson convened the district court in the same room. He directed the district attorney and counsel for the blacks to go to Montauk Point to determine where Gedney had seized the *Amistad.* In the meantime the court would adjourn until the third Tuesday in November, when it would meet again in Hartford. Though the presumption was that the court would allow the blacks' release on bail, it had to be on "appraisement," he explained, and their counsel would not permit an act tacitly admitting their status as property. The *Amistad* captives remained in the New Haven jail, although with a favored incarceration that permitted visitors, religious instruction from Yale faculty members, and exercises on the green.[39]

The reaction to Thompson's decision was mixed and immediate. The reporter for the antislavery society proclaimed that the blacks' attorneys had succeeded in portraying the "hideous bearing" of slavery in a way "calculated to open the eyes of the people in the free states to the extent of their entanglements in the guilt and dangers of slavery." The Charleston *Mercury* criticized the judge for being "as great an abolitionist as the TAPPANS" in his reluctance to admit that American law protected slavery. But the New York *Commercial Advertiser* warned Southerners to stay out of the case and allow the *Amistad* affair to die on its own. Nonetheless, nearly all Southern papers, according to the New York *American,* continued to find "color incompatible with freedom." Distinctions based on color, however, were not confined to the South. The *Morning Herald* of New York rejoiced in the abolitionists' suffering over the decision on a writ of habeas corpus. They now had to "send home their darkies and disperse—love's labor being entirely lost." The *Emancipator* ignored the maze of legal arguments and assailed Thompson for affirming the central reality in the case: that property rights affirmed by positive law had preference over personal liberty drawn from the law of nature. He had dishonored the sacred writ of habeas corpus in evading responsibility for a decision touching the most sensitive issues of the age.[40]

Judge Thompson may not have considered all of the following, but the issuance of a writ of habeas corpus would have had broad legal and political implications that few in the United States could have accepted. It would have set the blacks free, resolving the question of whether they were slaves without permitting a hearing on the libels before the district court. It would have been a tacit admission that the *Amistad* blacks were human beings having rights to liberty by any means, including mutiny. It would have denied the court's jurisdiction in cases similar to the *Amistad* case, implying that no judicial process was available to halt a further influx of mutineers. And it would have invited slaves from other countries to rebel and then seek asylum in the United States. In addition to causing obvious problems, the latter would have been embarrassing on the diplomatic level. At the same time when the American government was protesting British decisions freeing American slaves in the Caribbean, a Supreme Court justice would have been offering freedom in the United States to rebellious blacks. Furthermore, a verdict for freedom would have made the Spanish guilty of violating their anti-slave-trade treaties, providing the British with a pretext for intervening in Cuba and endangering American interests in the island. Granting a writ would also have condoned insurrection among blacks, who, whether or not legally slaves, could argue that the higher law of morality governed human relationships and that, regardless of positive law, the act of enslavement was wrong. Finally, such a decision would have enhanced the argument that human bondage was morally wrong even if it accorded with the laws of a country.

The most important observation about Thompson's decision is that, despite his aversion to slavery, he knew that American law recognized the institution as legal. He also realized that his verdict provided proslavery groups with their strongest defense, and yet, as several abolitionists believed, the only way to destroy slavery was to create a public animosity so strong that it forced a change in the law. Sedgwick had earlier warned that working within the legal system was the only way to defeat slavery. On hearing Thompson's decision, he expressed agreement and remarked to Tappan, "It is too late or rather let us hope too early to contend in the courts of the U.S. that there can be no property in Human Beings—in Africans at least."[41] Tappan still believed that moral suasion could convince Americans that slavery could not exist in a Christian nation. Perhaps success could come from a combined legal-moral approach that stressed the inhumanity of slavery.

To the abolitionists the circuit court ruling was probably no surprise—their objective was to keep the *Amistad* case before the American public, and in that they were successful. Interest in the captives had risen considerably, for even the most racially prejudiced American could feel paternalistic concern over the blacks as long as they were helpless and posed no threat to the white community. Once Northerners were satisfied that expressions of sympathy for the *Amistad* blacks did not automatically mean support for the abolitionists, the affair became a cause that many Americans could adopt, whether for or against slavery. For these Americans, concern for the captives was an act of charity, not a suggestion either to move against slavery or to struggle for racial equality.

The abolitionists had not left Hartford empty-handed. They had made a notable advance on one critical level: many more Americans had become acquainted with the *Amistad* affair. The abolitionists had publicized the enormous gulf between positive and natural law in regard to slavery, their clients had escaped trial on capital charges, and the Van Buren administration had admitted that the captives were not slaves. The outcome encouraged the abolitionists to push for a court settlement on the question of whether the blacks were slaves and, therefore, property.

Thompson had correctly recognized that this was no ordinary trial and that he had indeed faced momentous issues.

5

"A National Matter"

The legal process begun by the abolitionists in Hartford now entered its second phase: the battle in the district court over whether the *Amistad* blacks were slaves and therefore the property of Ruiz and Montes. If it could be established that the blacks were not property, both Lieutenant Gedney and the United States marshal in Connecticut would have acted illegally and the Spaniards would have no legitimate claims. To undermine the property argument, the abolitionists would have to establish that the captives, by Spanish laws and treaties, were not slaves. They could not argue against human bondage on the basis of its alleged immorality; Judge Thompson had made that clear. They now intended to make the case a national concern and then seek changes through the legal system that would undermine slavery and promote their ideals.

But whereas Theodore Sedgwick and others were convinced that they had to seek the blacks' freedom on the narrow ground of a violation of Spanish laws and treaties, Christian abolitionists like Lewis Tappan wanted more. They hoped to convince the court—and the American people—that the *Amistad* blacks were native Africans, kidnapped from their homeland and deserving freedom on the basis of universal, God-given rights. Not even the president of the United States would then have the power to intervene. In their legal encounter in the circuit court, they had had only a slight chance to win because the law regarding a writ of habeas corpus was vague at best. In the second round, that in the district court, the chances were even slimmer, for legislation supporting slavery in the United States was fairly specific. Furthermore, the district judge was Andrew T. Judson, an anti-abolitionist known for his racist views. The abolitionists' only hope was to keep the *Amistad* matter focused on the irreconcilable conflict between natural rights and positive law. Such an approach entailed a further exposition of the evils of slavery and the slave trade, as well as an all-out effort to demonstrate the humanity of the *Amistad* captives.

I

For Lewis Tappan the *Amistad* mutiny was a "Providential occurrence." Lawyers and jurists would publicly argue the great questions of liberty and property; Americans could see the Africans in the free state they had enjoyed before white men had corrupted them; and it would become possible to turn the increasing hostility toward the slave trade to the recognition that one could not abolish the trade without also ending slavery—"the *market* that invites the *supply*." Tappan intended to keep the *Amistad* case before the American public, for, as he explained to a fellow abolitionist, the Reverend Leonard Bacon of New Haven, Judge Thompson's denial of human justice to the blacks was a "simple truth" that would have "lasting effect." Tappan added, "I have long thought that the heart of the nation would not be effectually touched except through the power of sympathy—either for martyred abolitionists—or murdered slaves—but did not anticipate such a mysterious Providence as has occurred." The outcome of the recent trial should cause debates "that will bring up the whole subject matter of slave as well as the slave trade."[1]

Indeed, one way the *Amistad* affair attracted national attention was by involving nationally known figures. John Quincy Adams had agreed to provide informal legal advice to defense counsel. Though not an abolitionist, Adams staunchly opposed slavery as inhumane and contrary to the principles underlying the Declaration of Independence. Adams admitted in his memoirs that the *Amistad* case occupied much of his time and all his "good feelings." He was perplexed by the "multitude of questions" aroused by the matter. Ellis Gray Loring, the Boston attorney and abolitionist follower of William Lloyd Garrison, had sought Adams's feelings about the case and soon received permission to forward his ideas to Tappan, who turned them over to the blacks' defense attorneys.[2]

Adams carefully studied the legal and moral issues before replying to Loring's inquiries in early October 1839. He recommended that the defense consider several questions in presenting its case before the district court. What was Gedney's authority for seizing the vessel, cargo, and passengers and for taking them to New London? How could American officials justify holding the blacks for piracy and murder? What were the legal grounds for holding the children as witnesses? Were they too young to offer testimony? If the youths were slaves, were they competent to testify in matters relating to piracy and murder? By what authority did the court hold the blacks at the same time on criminal charges and as claimed property? If they belonged to Ruiz and Montes, did not the laws of slavery require forfeiture of property when slaves committed piracy and murder?[3]

If the judge had no right to commit the blacks to prison, Adams continued, were they not by writ of habeas corpus returnable before a judge of the state of Connecticut? Though Thompson cited the *Palmer* case of 1818 in declaring that the circuit court had no jurisdiction over crimes committed on a foreign vessel on the high seas, Adams noted that two years after that Supreme Court decision Congress authorized punishment for piracy, thereby approving jurisdiction. Thompson made an unfortunate reference to the *Antelope* decision in asserting that slaves were property and had to be returned to owners; Chief Justice John Marshall had made it clear that the Supreme Court was divided over the question and had established no principle. Moreover, the blacks on the *Antelope* were unquestionably slaves, whereas those on the *Amistad* were "free men in possession of the ship itself" who held the two Spaniards as property. Adams concluded that the blacks' "only practical protection" for personal liberty was a writ of habeas corpus.[4]

Loring doubted that all of Adams's observations would hold up in court. He agreed that Gedney's actions were wrong, noting that Sedgwick had called them unauthorized and illegal. But Gedney would probably attempt to justify his acts by the congressional law of March 1819 that permitted salvage in cases where the president authorized naval commanders to seize any vessel "the crew whereof shall be armed & which shall have attempted or committed any piratical aggression." One may argue that Thompson had no legal right to confine the blacks to jail after ruling that the circuit court lacked jurisdiction; but the prosecution would doubtless have countered that the Spaniards had under oath accused them of the offenses. Loring thought that slave codes permitted incarceration of slaves as both property and suspected criminals. If the courts found slaves guilty of a crime, he believed, the right to ownership would be suspended only while they were in jail. Once released, the slaves would revert to the master. Finally, Loring was certain that a state judge could release a person under a writ of habeas corpus, even though that person was in jail for violating a federal law. This was a controversial question, Loring admitted, but he thought that legal authorities held this view.[5]

As Loring viewed the case, the defense had to show that the color of the *Amistad* captives had determined the verdict. "Can any one believe," he asked, "that Judge Thompson would have remanded white men to prison, there to lie for months, or years perhaps, till the question of their freedom had been regularly adjudicated by the court of the highest appeal?" The only remedy was a "wholesale & quickened state of public opinion."[6]

On November 19, the day district court convened, Adams expanded his thoughts about the *Amistad* case in another letter to Loring. Adams emphasized that Gedney's seizure of the vessel was the "foundation of all the other questions of the case." From that illegal act on, the blacks were victims of false imprisonment. The congressional act of 1819 did not justify Gedney's action, for it applied to piracy by a crew upon another vessel, and could have no bearing upon a rebellion led by "*passenger* slaves." Furthermore, Thompson had justified his decision by the *Palmer* case—that American courts had no jurisdiction over piracy of a foreign vessel—and this was "directly adverse" to Gedney's claim to authority. Thompson's decision, Adams declared, constituted abdication of a right necessary to any nation: jurisdiction over pirates, regardless of national origin. The *Amistad* case should also have come to trial because Thompson had no duty to "prejudge a case of life and death." The blacks were not slaves at the time of capture, Adams insisted; they had freed themselves by "self-emancipation." Pinckney's Treaty of 1795 made no reference to fugitive or self-emancipated slaves, and one could never demand the surrender of rebellious slaves on the basis of some general provision relating to the return of property. If slaves were property, Adams asserted, they were property of a "peculiar character" and had to be "specially named." The *Amistad* blacks had exercised their "natural right to liberty by conspiracy, insurrection, homicide and the capture of the ship."[7]

The abolitionists had found an important ally in their emphasis on natural rights, but recent newspaper stories reminded them that they still faced widespread racial prejudice. As one Southern newspaper insisted and several Northern papers agreed, color was "incompatible with freedom." Cinqué, especially, was not above reproach—even if the stories were untrue. The New York *Evening Star,* in a brief article entitled "Cat out of the Bag," reported Tappan's alleged admission that Cinqué "owed a debt in Africa and GAVE A MAN for half of it, and not being able to satisfy the balance of the claim, was violently seized himself." With satisfaction, the New Orleans *Times Picayune* maliciously declared that the "black piratical murderer" was a "slave dealer and a slave seller himself." A correspondent to the New York *Morning Herald* spoke derisively of the "poor Africans," "who have nothing to do, but eat, drink, and turn somersaults—a far more happy life than they ever enjoyed in Africa." The paper published an engraving allegedly showing a "faithful representation" of a scene in the Hartford jail: Cinqué kissing a young white girl handed him by her mother, while another black was turning a somersault; white visitors who were "fashionable, pious, learned, and gay people of Connecticut," all listening to "lectures and instructions in African philosophy and civilization"; the blacks "scratching themselves and laughing at the 'white mans' with great glee." In the corner of the engraving, the paper noted, was a "very excellent likeness" of Tappan with his white hat off, "looking upon the hero Cinqué enjoying the sweet lips of the white little girl, and drinking in the new philosophy with great sanctimoniousness." Only time, according to the New York *Advertiser & Express,* would show "what mischievous consequences may follow their ridiculous fraternizing with the barbarians who would, probably, eat them, if they could catch them in their native country!"[8]

II

With a month to pass before district court proceedings began, Tappan arranged to have the *Amistad* blacks bring civil suits against Ruiz and Montes for assault and battery and for false imprisonment. Such suits would force the courts to define the captives as either persons having legal rights or as slaves not entitled to bring civil suits against their masters. Moreover, they entailed jury trials, which would further publicize the cause. They also would shift the proceedings from Connecticut (where slavery was legal until 1848) to New York (a free state), where the blacks had a better chance to win. If they won, Judge Judson, a Democrat, might rule against the Van Buren administration's wish to return the blacks to Spanish authorities. The chances of winning were small, as Tappan realized, but the very act of bringing the suits would cause a public sensation.

The suits might have been prompted by the publication of the two Spaniards' "Narrative" of the mutiny in which they attempted to exonerate themselves of charges that they had cruelly abused the blacks on the *Amistad*. Tappan dismissed it as a "lame account" that needed correctives by the publication of the captives' own story. Ruiz and Montes contradicted themselves, he declared. How could they have engaged in conversations with the African captives? Civil suits against the Spaniards would permit the blacks to present their side in court. To Joseph Sturge, his friend and fellow abolitionist in England, Tappan explained that the purpose of the suits was to determine whether a man, "although he is black," could find justice in the American court system.[9]

To counter the Spaniards' narrative, the abolitionist George E. Day published two long letters to the editors of the New York *Journal of Commerce* (owned by the Tappan brothers), which presented the blacks' version of the mutiny. Day had been a professor at the New York Institution for the Deaf and Dumb, and he had established a limited communication with the blacks through sign language. His letters probably embellished things, but they achieved their purpose of arousing considerable public sympathy. Day claimed that Cinqué recalled that in Havana nearly all of the blacks were in tears, including himself, "because they had come from the same country, and were now to be parted forever." Separate accounts by Cinqué, Grabeau, and others agreed that the blacks on the *Amistad* had undergone cruel treatment throughout the voyage—having been driven to hunger and thirst by inadequate provisions and, after repeated beatings and floggings, having had vinegar and gunpowder rubbed into their wounds. Cinqué claimed that he had led the others in revolt because the cook said they would be eaten upon reaching land. Grabeau declared that this had "made their hearts burn." Their only objective, Cinqué asserted, was freedom, and "if he tells a lie, God sees him by day and by night."[10]

To further discredit the Spaniards' account, Tappan informed the Reverend Bacon in New Haven that he wanted affidavits from the captives calling for the arrest of Ruiz and Montes. Such a move, Tappan hoped, would draw more attention to the case by causing a furor among both the proslavery press and Southern slaveowners. Ruiz had recently left Hartford, and Tappan wanted Dwight P. Janes in New London to have both men arrested if they appeared. Staples, according to Tappan, thought that Baldwin should have Ruiz arrested in New Haven. In any event, Tappan wrote Baldwin, it was better to have the men arrested in Connecticut than in New York; this suggests that he was less interested in winning the case than in confronting proslavery elements for the sake of publicity.[11]

But both Spaniards had already arrived in New York City, where on October 17 Tappan himself carried the writs to the sheriff and volunteered to accompany his deputy in pointing out the accused. The two men encountered Ruiz and Montes at their hotel, where the deputy sheriff arrested the Spaniards on two civil suits in state court for assault and battery and for false imprisonment. To complicate the matter, Tappan had arranged for one of the suits to come from the New York court of common pleas and the other from the state's superior court. Cinqué and another of the captives, Fuliwa, had given the affidavits in New Haven, demanding joint damage claims totaling $3,000. After bail was set at $1,000 each, both Spaniards were taken to the city prison. The real objective of the abolitionists, according to the New York *Commercial Advertiser*, was to force another public discussion of the legal questions.[12]

The arrests caused the national sensation that Tappan had envisioned. He happily wrote Sturge that the *Amistad* case was "exciting the attention of the American people." Sturge later claimed that, "more than all," the abolitionists' purpose was to keep the blacks "constantly before the public, not only for their own sakes, but that a portion of the sympathy and right feeling which was elicited in their favor might be reflected towards the native slave population of the country, whose claim to freedom [rested] upon the same ground of natural and indefeasible right." Theodore Dwight Weld assured Gerrit Smith that the *Amistad* case had done "wonders" for the abolitionist cause. "God's Providence is the Monarch Emancipator!"[13] If Tappan had meant the arrests of Ruiz and Montes to maintain public interest in the case, he could have devised no better scheme.

News of the arrests angered anti-abolitionists in the North as well as defenders of slavery in the South. The conservative New Yorker Philip Hone noted in his diary the great excitement caused by this "outrageous proceeding." Under the "specious cloak of an abstract opposition to slavery," the abolitionist fanatics could start a civil war. Several Northern newspapers were irate. According to one, the "savages" of the *Amistad* were "merely the tools of the abolitionists in this gross act of inhumanity and outrage." It was ridiculous, added another, that pirates and robbers could have their victims thrown into jail. Others remarked that the abolitionists, as "self-constituted agents" of the blacks, were guilty of a "continued perversion of truth," and had made their protégés "quite obstinate and unmanageable." Two foreigners had sought court protection after narrowly escaping death and were instead thrown into jail on the "suborned affidavit of an uneducated ignorant heathen." In a statement foreshadowing controversies soon to erupt over sojourner and fugitive slaves, the New York *Advertiser & Express* declared, "The next step we shall hear of will be the arrest and imprisonment of Southern gentlemen traveling in the Northern States at the suit of their own servants." The Southern press naturally joined the chorus. In an article entitled "STRANGE PROCEDURE," the New Orleans *Times Picayune* accused the abolitionists of "going to all lengths to screen the black murderers from the consequences of their crimes." The Richmond *Enquirer* declared that the abolitionists should be in "lunatic asylums." Did they plan to "make the blacks our masters?"[14]

The Spanish reaction to the arrests was also instant and heated. The Spanish paper in New York, *Noticioso de Ambos Mundos,* asked how these "unfortunate, friendless Spaniards" could be imprisoned. It was shameful that the abolitionists should "discredit the cause of freedom" by supporting "notorious murderers" and "savages." The new Spanish minister to the United States, Pedro Alcántara de Argaiz, hotly protested the arrests as a "scandalous deed," claiming that a foreign court had no jurisdiction in matters out of its province and repeating his predecessor's argument that the president should surrender the blacks to Spanish authorities. The depositions, Argaiz remarked, were "so identical as to appear to have been dictated by one and the same individual." The blacks have admitted to "their state of slavery by confessing that they have been sold." When and where did a slave have "civil rights"? Pinckney's Treaty, Argaiz pointed out, stipulated that in cases of seizure for "*offenses committed* by any citizen or subject of the one party *within the jurisdiction* of the other, the same shall be made and prosecuted ... according to the regular course of proceedings usual in such cases." New York courts should never have listened to the blacks' complaints, for the alleged offenses had not occurred within their jurisdiction. In an ironic twist, Argaiz urged the executive to use a writ of habeas corpus to secure freedom and indemnification for Ruiz and Montes.[15]

The Van Buren administration was again in an uncomfortable situation. Eastern newspapers agreed with the Spanish minister that the president should surrender the blacks because American ships might likewise need aid if forced into Cuban waters. And yet the abolitionists had aroused so much public sympathy for the blacks that this once obvious remedy was no longer so obvious. Van Buren could not make a move that would condemn the *Amistad* blacks to certain execution in Cuba and turn reform-minded Americans against a White House that seemed inhumane. In reply to Argaiz's note, Forsyth made a major concession to the abolitionists' argument that they, of course, could not have known. The suits against Ruiz and Montes, he noted, came from "certain colored men, natives of Africa," who in a "simple case of resort by individuals against others" sought recompense in courts "equally open to all without distinction." The president could not intervene in this judicial matter.[16]

The Van Buren administration was attempting to squirm out of the tight position the abolitionists had forced it into. In doing so, Forsyth had adopted two irreconcilable legal positions at the same time, and yet both furthered the secretary's purpose of keeping the matter under executive control. Whereas he had earlier leaned toward returning the blacks as property in accord with Pinckney's Treaty, he now privately referred to the *Amistad* captives as Africans and not as slaves, implying that the White House had conceded the abolitionists' major claim that the blacks were persons victimized by the slave trade. If this change in policy appeared consistent only with political expediency, it explains Holabird's surprising switch in tactics during the circuit court hearing of the preceding September. The stance offered the district judge the option of authorizing the president to return the blacks to Africa, in line with the congressional act of 1819. Furthermore, while Forsyth had admitted that the blacks were individuals having the right to bring civil suits in American courts, he also pointed out that Ruiz and Montes could seek indemnification in those same courts.[17]

Forsyth's intention seems unmistakable: he sought to relieve the president of responsibility in the case. But this objective was becoming increasingly elusive. Had the secretary of state agreed that Van Buren could interpose his authority in New York, as Argaiz wanted, the action would have raised an outcry from states' rightists in both the Northern and Southern wings of the Democratic party. More important, the action would have exceeded the powers of the executive. There appeared to be only one way out of this quandary. If the president conceded the matter to the state courts, he could escape blame for the outcome and, at the same time, dignify the move by referring to provisions in the Constitution. Moreover, the chances were that Judson, a loyal supporter of the administration, might resolve the entire problem by ruling that the president should surrender the blacks as property to Spanish authorities, in accord with Pinckney's Treaty. It appears safe to say that when the Van Buren administration weighed the alternatives, its most important consideration was reelection.

III

The White House was deeply concerned about the proceedings in New York and resorted to questionable tactics designed to further a court decision favorable to Ruiz and Montes. Although Forsyth told Argaiz that the executive could not intervene in civil suits, he committed that office to actions that constituted a violation of its powers. In a note (a copy of which he gave Argaiz), he informed the United States attorney for the southern district of New York, Benjamin F. Butler, that to assure the release of the two Spaniards and to win an indemnity, Butler's office should be "useful" to Ruiz and Montes and offer "advice" and "aid, if necessary."[18] The Van Buren administration had renounced interference with the judicial process, and yet it had offered the Spaniards assistance needed to win the case. No help, of course, went to the blacks, and this raises questions about legal ethics as well as about the legality itself. The two parties did not receive equal constitutional guarantees of fair legal treatment. How could there be justice if the presidency helped one side and not the other?

Amid growing excitement Judge Inglis of the New York Court of Common Pleas held preliminary hearings in his chambers on October 22. Neither plaintiffs nor defendants were present, and attorneys for both sides were extraordinarily careful about presenting their cases before a judge equally cautious about hearing the charges. Counsel for Ruiz and Montes—a young, hot-tempered lawyer of Spanish extraction, John Purroy—declared that his clients could not put up bail of $1,000 each and would go to jail. Ruiz, Purroy insisted, had not known and *still* did not know that Cinqué was African by birth. Ruiz and Montes had loaded their fifty-three blacks onto the *Amistad* before dark, not during the night to avoid British cruisers, as the opposition had alleged. The blacks had not been in manacles on board and had had sufficient provisions. Ruiz thought that Tappan had brought the suit against him and had done so without the plaintiff's approval or knowledge. At one point Purroy lashed out at Tappan, who was present at the hearing, calling him a "Judas" and "arch fiend." Seth Staples responded by castigating the lawyer, noting that the "Spirit of Slavery" had so darkened the atmosphere that its "direful influence" had "debauched" this court and the entire nation. After Inglis brought the proceedings back to order, Theodore Sedgwick, also representing the blacks, argued that the jury process was the only way to decide whether his clients were free or slave. The *least* Ruiz and Montes could claim was that they had bought contraband goods and aided the slave trade.[19]

Within a week Inglis convened a second session in his chambers, during which he noted the importance of slavery to the case. He explained that by general rule he could not judge the merits of a cause in chambers and that therefore he could not decide whether the plaintiff was a slave belonging to Ruiz. In a statement that infuriated abolitionists, Inglis explained that should he rule Cinqué a slave, the plaintiff's case would collapse, for a slave could not bring civil action against his master. Inglis knew that slavery was the central issue in the controversy, but he assumed that at this introductory stage of the proceeding the plaintiff had a right to bring action for personal injury, without making reference to the relationship of master and slave.[20]

Inglis was ready to give his opinion in this hearing. The only questions before the court, he said, were whether the plaintiff could show that the defendants had violated his personal rights, and, if so, whether bail at $1,000 was too high. Inglis decreed that the court could not hold Montes for assault, because he had been a bystander when the cook on the *Amistad* hit Cinqué. Ruiz, however, had given "apparent consent" to the trespass and was therefore a "co-trespasser." He claimed to be Cinqué's owner and yet had done nothing to stop the cook from striking the plaintiff. But the affidavits did not establish that Ruiz either put Cinqué on the *Amistad* or imprisoned him. They also did not link Ruiz with the claimed kidnapping in Africa; nor did they affirm "atrocity or oppression" beyond the alleged imprisonment. The judge could not believe that a jury would award sufficient damages to the plaintiff to justify a bail so high. Inglis freed Montes on common, or nominal, bail, which actually released him on his own recognizance, and reduced Ruiz's bail to $250.[21]

Ruiz's attorney planned an immediate appeal to prevent future litigation. Nearly forty other blacks from the *Amistad,* Purroy feared, could bring similar suits against his client.[22]

Inglis's ruling won approval in the state's higher courts. The superior court upheld the decision against Ruiz and stipulated that no one could begin a similar process against either of the Spaniards until a jury had decided the present case of *Cinqué* v. *Ruiz.* In the other suit, *Fulah* [Fuliwa] v. *Ruiz,* the New York Supreme Court used the same grounds for a decision that Inglis had used. Bail was also $250, affirming the court's jurisdiction and the plaintiff's right to a jury decision on the question of his freedom and the amount of injury sustained.[23]

Minister Argaiz expressed incredulity at the ruling. The whole world, he declared, knew that a court could not deal with "crimes or delinquencies committed in other countries, or other jurisdictions, and under other laws." Furthermore, no court would admit "petitions or accusations of slaves against their masters." Was there no federal power to "interpose its authority to put down the irregularity of these proceedings?" Surely the United States government had the power to halt Ruiz's "suffering" and "unjust and unlawful imprisonment." Argaiz warned that if the secretary of state was unable to execute the treaty of 1795, the treaty likewise did not bind Spain.[24]

The abolitionists, meanwhile, did not let the matter rest. Despite the superior court's decision, another *Amistad* captive, Tonni, brought the same charges before the circuit court, which set bail at $800. The case threatened to become farcical because Ruiz was still in jail on Cinqué's charge. The abolitionists insisted that this was not a new proceeding; it was the continuation of a process already begun. The Richmond *Enquirer* complained that the "ultra-abolitionists" had gone too far. Raising the specter of future arguments over fugitive slaves, it asked whether this meant that "if a master from the South claimed his slave in New York, the abolitionists would be able to secure an affidavit from the slave that asserted his freedom and claimed damages for his detention—thus placing the master before a state judge to put up bail or go to prison, and with the entire case resting in a prejudiced and fanatical jury." If the abolitionists' purpose was to stir the South's fears, they were successful. For the moment, though, the *Emancipator* rejoiced that the abolitionists had won a "great point" in showing that blacks could bring civil suits.[25]

For the Van Buren administration, the outlook seemed grim—
especially since Butler himself did not appear to be doing enough
in New York. He had offered his services to Ruiz's defense counsel.
He visited Ruiz in jail, trying to secure more facts in the case.
From Purroy he acquired a copy of the papers and a statement of
proceedings. After checking into the law of Cuba with Purroy and
then contacting a Spanish lawyer who had been for many years a
judge in Havana, Butler could find no new arguments for Ruiz's
release. Although American courts lacked jurisdiction over criminal offenses by foreigners within the territory of a foreign state,
under the principle of reciprocity they had jurisdiction over civil
suits between foreigners inside the United States that arose under
contracts made in a foreign state, as long as Americans could also
institute similar civil actions in that foreign state. The former judge
in Cuba affirmed that Cuban courts would allow such civil suits
there. Butler believed that the only recourse was to go ahead with
the trial, confident that a jury would acquit Ruiz. If the court rendered an adverse decision, he would advise the proper steps for
appeal, even to the United States Supreme Court.[26]

The atmosphere intensified as charges appeared in the New
York *Evening Journal* that the Van Buren administration had
made an arrangement whereby Ruiz would flee the country after
procuring bail. Butler defended the White House. He admitted that
both he and Ruiz's attorney, Purroy, had advised Ruiz to post bail
and free himself—but *not* to escape. Ruiz, however, had refused to
do so, claiming it was the duty of the United States government to
secure his release. It was a "national matter," he insisted. Butler
emphasized to Ruiz that he, as a district attorney in New York,
had no power to provide or secure bail for him and that his only
action could be to offer advice and aid. But Ruiz preferred to
remain in jail, continuing to argue that he was part of a larger
issue—one between his government and that of the United
States—and that his incarceration was a small price to pay for
principle.[27] His decision for confinement eased accusations of collusion between the White House and Ruiz, but it did not relieve
the embarrassment occasioned by the constitutional workings of
federal-state relations and of the separation of powers between the
executive and judicial branches of government.

Excitement over the arrests ultimately came to nothing, however, because Montes had meanwhile left the country for Cuba,
and although Ruiz remained in jail for nearly four months, he
finally paid bail and joined his companion after realizing that his

case was not going to become an international issue. Though he had been depicted as languishing in jail, Ruiz had been in a highly relaxed confinement that allowed him any provisions he could buy and considerable freedom to come and go from his quarters. Because Ruiz appeared confident that the United States would surrender him on application of the Spanish minister, the *Emancipator* denounced his decision to forgo bail as a *"ruse* to excite sympathy, and prejudice the community against the Africans and their defenders." Tappan later sarcastically remarked to an abolitionist friend in England that Ruiz had wanted only to embroil the United States and Spain in controversy—and "merely for stealing half a hundred men and women."[28]

Relations with Spain further deteriorated as Argaiz repeatedly tried to persuade the Van Buren administration to intervene and secure Ruiz's release. Ruiz and Montes, he charged in an unexplained and curious statement, were "victims of an intrigue, as accurately shown by Mr. Forsyth, in the conference which he had with the undersigned on the 21st of October last." The arrests, Argaiz asserted, had exacerbated the entire *Amistad* question. Both political and racial considerations, he believed, were involved in the White House stand. Had not Forsyth told him (with a Spanish associate of Argaiz's present) that the president's "hands were tied" and that he could not release Montes and Ruiz "without causing a public outcry" among Americans sympathetic to the *Amistad* captives and hurting his chances for reelection? Argaiz was also "well persuaded" that had the *Amistad*'s blacks been white, the United States "would have observed the rules by which it should be conducted under the constitutional institutions of the country, and would have limited itself to the ascertainment of the facts of the murders." In a statement laden with sarcasm, Argaiz declared that he did not "comprehend the privilege enjoyed by negroes" in the United States.[29]

Tappan had succeeded in his major objective of drawing national attention to the *Amistad* matter by having Ruiz and Montes arrested; however, little of the reaction was favorable. The New York *Evening Star* claimed that Ruiz's four-month imprisonment had taken the United States back to the days of the Spanish Inquisition. The New Orleans *Times Picayune* called for controls on "TAPPANISM." A letter signed "Vindex" in the New York *Advertiser & Express* defended the two Spaniards on the ground that they had done what American planters in Cuba did every day: they purchased slaves in the public market for use on island estates. The abolitionists sought not justice for the blacks, Vindex asserted, but more exposure of the *Amistad* case. Less than a week afterward, "Fiat Justitia" replied to Vindex that both seller and purchaser were guilty; according to the proverb, "the *receiver* is as bad as the *thief.*" Ruiz had committed a "gross injustice" by "attempting to reduce to perpetual servitude these innocent young men."[30]

The Ruiz-Montes episode demonstrated the tenuousness of the abolitionists' position. Tappan had provided critics with evidence for their charges that the abolitionists were fanatics willing to do anything to further their cause. If he had hoped that the allowance of a civil suit against the Spaniards would confirm that blacks were persons, he had been mistaken. More important, he had encouraged the popular view that the abolitionists, despite their claims of wanting to build a nation based on just laws, seemed determined to bring chaos that would destroy the present government. Tappan's strategy had perhaps cost the abolitionists—and the blacks themselves—more public favor than he would have admitted. And yet, on another level, he had succeeded in placing pressure on the Van Buren administration. The abolitionists' activist strategy was risky because it relied heavily on public opinion, which was always subject to changing emotions and fluctuation. The delicacy of their reformist approach becomes evident when one realizes that, if newspapers were a reliable index of opinion, public sympathy for the captives considerably dissipated during the Ruiz-Montes controversy. Whatever the final verdict on this series of events, the *Amistad* captives could not escape their appointed time before District Judge Andrew T. Judson.

6

"Neither Slave . . ."

The circuit court decision of September had left the *Amistad* captives with an amorphous status similar to that held by many free blacks in the United States: they were neither slave nor free. Thompson's ruling was the proper one. He could not have freed the blacks on grounds of natural rights, for that would have negated all law. The blacks' attorneys had raised serious doubt about the Spaniards' property claims, and yet prejudices based on race and color had combined with the Van Buren administration's political aspirations to confuse matters. The abolitionists intended to focus on several issues, all touching the central racial problems in the United States. Did free blacks have citizenship? Were slaves simply property, devoid of rights? Did American courts have jurisdiction over the case? Can one claim salvage on human beings? In raising these questions, the abolitionists stirred arguments that further complicated an already complex situation. Now, in admiralty proceedings in Hartford, they prepared for the second phase of a sustained battle in America's courts.

I

For several reasons the approaching district court trial did not promise much for the *Amistad* Committee and the rest of the abolitionists. First and foremost, the law was not on their side. No matter how hard they had tried to convince the public that American law was sharply out of line with natural rights, they had not been successful. Second, a long history of racial prejudice in the United States would become increasingly evident as the *Amistad* case progressed through the legal system. A third consideration was custom and tradition. Slavery had existed in North America since the seventeenth century and was sanctioned by the United States Constitution. The abolitionists found it no easy task to persuade Americans that slavery was suddenly immoral and unchristian. Fourth, political realities did not allow the blacks to go free. And fifth, the White House had to be careful not to prove Spanish violations of their anti-slave-trade treaties and thus provide the British with an excuse to intervene in Cuba. These points help explain why the abolitionists were particularly concerned about the district court trial.

But there was another ingredient: the presiding judge in the trial would be Andrew T. Judson, who had earned a reputation for being racially prejudiced while professing to oppose slavery. In a court case a few years earlier in Connecticut, he had led the opposition to Prudence Crandall, a young white woman who had opened a girls' academy in the rural village of Canterbury and soon admitted only blacks, most of whom came from outside the community. During the ensuing two-year struggle, Judson, a town selectman who lived in a new house adjacent to the school, warned that the teacher intended to promote an amalgamation of the races. Judson became famous overnight—in no small measure because William Lloyd Garrison wrote a story in the Boston *Liberator* entitled "Heathenism Outdone," in which he included Judson's name in bold black letters in a list of the five townspeople who led the movement against Crandall.[1] Many observers believed that Judson had received his appointment as district judge because of his role in the Crandall affair.[2] In the longer term, the Crandall case probably furthered the abolitionists' cause by showing the inseparability of racism, slavery, and civil rights.[3] But in 1839 the abolitionists were more concerned about the immediate problem of Judson's impact on the *Amistad* affair.[4] Lewis Tappan shuddered at the prospect that someone who had taken such a stand during the Crandall espisode was now in the position of authority in the *Amistad* case.[5]

It was a matter of public record that Judson, an officer and lifetime member of the American Colonization Society, a Jacksonian Democrat, a former congressman, and now district judge, had presided over the town proceedings that eventually led to the collapse of Crandall's school. Addressing Canterbury's townspeople at one point in the controversy, he had warned that the school would become "an auxiliary in the work of *immediate abolition"* and that once this door was open New England would become "the Liberia of America." According to a town resolution, the school was a *"theater"* for Crandall to "promulgate" the "disgusting doctrines of amalgamation." A committee of ten circulated a petition denouncing "the evil consequences of bringing from other States and other towns, people of color for any purpose, and more especially for the purpose of disseminating the principles and doctrines opposed to the benevolent colonizing system." Under great pressure, the state assembly passed the "Connecticut Black Law" in May 1833, by which black people not living in the city were barred from private schools without the permission of town leaders and which provided for the expulsion of those already there.[6]

Crandall was arrested. Her defense counsel, financed by Lewis and Arthur Tappan, included William W. Ellsworth, now one of the attorneys in the district court trial in Hartford. Counsel for the state included Judson and two others.

Before the jury Judson explained that he saw no problem in having blacks attend district schools, for he did not oppose education for blacks, and he certainly did not support slavery. But he then presented an argument that infuriated abolitionists. The Constitution condoned slavery, Judson declared, and each state had the right to decide whether it wanted the institution. Therefore, all antislavery groups were Garrisonians because they were resisting the Constitution and calling for dissolution of the Union. Judson solemnly warned that the abolitionists' purpose in supporting education for blacks was to prepare them to instigate slave insurrections in the South. And finally, he argued that slavery was not an issue in the North. The United States is "a nation of *white men*," Judson told the jury, "and every American should indulge that *pride* and *honor*, which is falsely called prejudice, and teach it to his children. Nothing else will preserve the *American name*, or the *American character*. Who of you would like to see the glory of this nation stripped away, and given to another race of men?" He concluded with a warning: "The *professed object* is to educate the blacks, but the real object is to make the people yield their assent by degrees, to this universal amalgamation of the two races, and have the African race placed on the footing of perfect equality with the Americans."[7]

Besides Judson's role in it, the Crandall episode was also germane to the *Amistad* case because it focused on the question of whether free blacks were citizens of the United States. Crandall's attorneys had contended that the state law of 1833 was a violation of the Constitution's assurance to citizens of one state that they

had the same rights in other states as citizens *in* those states. Thus,
counsel continued, Article IV, Section 2, of the Constitution protected Crandall's pupils by guaranteeing "citizens of each state . . .
all privileges and immunities of citizens in the several States." But
Judson insisted that "colored persons" were not citizens, although
he refused to define what their status was. He argued that blacks
brought into the country could not be naturalized and could never
enjoy a citizen's privileges and immunities; but he did not deal
with the concomitant question of the position of blacks born in the
United States. Abolitionists insisted that privileges and immunities related to natural rights and that government's major purpose
was to guarantee these rights.[8] Ellsworth poignantly observed that
for Judson the "criterion of citizenship" was "complexion"; for
Ellsworth it was "birth and naturalization." According to one of
Ellsworth's associates, the term *citizen* is "under a republican government, what the term *subject* is under a monarchy; it embraces
high and low—rich and poor—male and female—white and colored—a general term which includes the whole republican family."
The American Revolution changed subjects of Great Britain into
citizens of the United States. All persons were citizens by nature of
the new republican nation, he insisted. The Declaration of Independence made no distinctions based on color.[9]

Crandall's defense had presented an eloquent argument, clearly
ahead of its time, but the court refused to deal with the constitutional question of citizenship, preferring to pass it on to others. Her
counsel then appealed the case on the grounds that free blacks were
American citizens and that the law of 1833 was discriminatory and
not in line with the United States Constitution. Crandall was twice
tried and convicted before the state's supreme court of errors
reversed the decisions on a technicality relating to information presented in the trial.[10]

The Crandall case brought attention to a key issue that remained
unsettled until ratification of the Fourteenth Amendment following the Civil War: whether free blacks were citizens. The definition
of citizenship during the antebellum period was unclear, although
there was general agreement that it rested on reciprocal responsibilities of protection and obedience between state and individual.
The problem was that no one had clarified how one secured citizenship, nor had anyone defined a citizen. In the United States the
matter had become especially complex because under the system
of federalism the same person might be a citizen both of the nation
and of the state. But citizenship at one level did not automatically

confer citizenship at the other. And it was unclear what rights a person might enjoy at either level if he claimed citizenship at one or both. Abolitionists nonetheless argued that either citizenship in a state carried with it citizenship of the nation or it meant that the same rights claimed in one state earned the same rights in any other state. Their point was that blacks were citizens and could not be victims of racial discrimination in any state in the Union. Not surprisingly, the Connecticut court of errors left this matter unsettled.[11]

The abolitionists' anxiety over Judson and the location of the trial was understandable, for in many ways the state of Connecticut was similar to the South in racial attitudes on the eve of the *Amistad* affair. Although people in the state opposed slavery and did not favor its spread into western territories, this did not mean that they welcomed blacks.[12] Indeed, of the New England states, Connecticut was perhaps the most hostile to the abolitionists.[13] Separatism prevailed in the public schools, and in 1830 an antislavery advocate encountered a rock-throwing audience in one of the towns and had to be hustled from the area by the constables.[14]

Moreover, antiblack sentiment in Connecticut had not diminished by the time of the *Amistad* affair. Hartford itself had recently been the scene of a race riot. By the late 1830s a pattern seemed to have developed in Connecticut: residents of the state preferred the status quo on racial matters. While not calling for more limitations on blacks, they were not seeking more rights either.[15]

II

Great interest had developed in the Hartford community as Judge Judson convened district court proceedings at 10:00 A.M. on November 19. Both Ruiz and Montes were absent, the former still in the New York jail, the latter en route to Cuba. Seven of the Africans had been brought in from New Haven the evening before, and on the morning of the trial several antislavery men arrived from New York—among them Dr. Richard R. Madden, a staunch British abolitionist who had been on the Anglo-Spanish mixed commission to halt the slave trade to Cuba and who was now leaving his position on the island as superintendent of liberated Africans. After hearing of the *Amistad* trial, Madden had offered to testify about slave conditions in Cuba and to examine the African captives to determine whether they were slaves or native Africans. Excitement had grown about two weeks earlier when news spread that en route to England he intended to meet with Tappan in New York and visit the blacks in New Haven.[16] Madden appeared to be a potential key witness of the blacks' defense counsel. The atmosphere seemed conducive to an epoch-making battle over slavery, the slave trade, and the rights of man.

Judson doubtless realized that the abolitionists intended to bring these controversial matters before the court. He probably also had searched for an escape from his precarious position, for he knew what the Van Buren administration in Washington wanted—he was, after all, a loyal Jacksonian Democrat—but he also was aware of popular sympathy for the *Amistad* captives. Furthermore, Judson realized that his decision would be subject to review by the circuit court and perhaps by the United States Supreme Court. An ambitious man's career could be hurt by a higher court's reversal. Politically, socially, and legally, Judson had to walk a narrow line that would award something to all parties and at the same time allow him to escape blame for the outcome, whatever that was.

The abolitionists had one last legal procedure designed to prevent the case from coming to trial. Roger S. Baldwin made a plea in abatement, which, as in the circuit court proceedings, called for dismissal of the case on jurisdictional grounds. Lieutenant Gedney had seized the blacks in New York and, Baldwin argued, had illegally taken them to Connecticut. Since New York was a free state, Gedney's action constituted a wrongful attempt to reduce them to slavery. Salvage claims were unjustified, Baldwin contended, and no Connecticut court had jurisdiction over the blacks; they had never been slaves and should go free. No trial should take place before Judson and the district court. The blacks were entitled to trial by jury in New York.[17]

Baldwin's attempt to bring an end to court proceedings led to a long exchange with General Isham, acting on behalf of Gedney and Meade. Isham declared that Baldwin should handle his defense and stop interfering with questions relating to salvage: Gedney and Meade had a right to salvage for saving property. Baldwin thought this claim "most extraordinary." The blacks were included in the libel as property, and the libelants appeared in court to seek salvage on the basis that the blacks were property; and yet the blacks were not allowed to make a denial in court. What was the consequence? If the court determined that the blacks were not property, they had to go free. No one could argue that they had committed a crime in winning liberty. Should the court prohibit the blacks' appearance, it would violate their personal rights by denying them a chance to show that they were not property. The court had to permit them to explain the "injustice and cruelty" of their arrest. Otherwise the blacks would have no redress. The entire proceeding against them rested on Gedney's libel. If the court would not allow a plea in abatement, the proceeding could not legally go on.[18]

After considerable discussion, Judson permitted counsel to argue the issue of a plea in abatement, but curiously he warned the attorneys against inquiring into the merits of the question. The potential conflict between property claims and rights of liberty was not the issue at this time, he insisted; the only point the parties could discuss was the schooner's location when it had been seized. If Gedney had acted wrongfully in New York, as Baldwin claimed, the judge would have to dismiss the case. If Gedney had acted on the open seas, the case was before the proper court. Judson noted that he had arranged a firsthand investigation of the matter in October and that the participants' information was available.[19]

Testimony on the *Amistad*'s location dominated the afternoon proceedings of November 19. The two principal issues were the vessel's location when Gedney seized it and the number of blacks on shore at the time. The defense argued that Gedney should have taken them to the nearest admiralty court—which would have been in the free state of New York. Without making the allegation explicit, Baldwin implied that Gedney had known that chances for salvage on the blacks would have been minimal in New York.[20]

The abolitionists intended to undercut all the libelants' claims to salvage and hoped that out of the competing arguments the exact location of the *Amistad* might become clear. One group of claimants, led by Henry Green, sought salvage on the basis of an argument that worked to the abolitionists' advantage: that the schooner and most of its occupants had been inside New York's territorial jurisdiction when discovered. If the court awarded salvage to Green and associates, the abolitionists could argue with considerable force that Gedney had acted illegally in taking the vessel and cargo from the state. The other group, led by Gedney, declared that the *Amistad* and most of the blacks were on the high seas and that he and his officers had acted acceptably in proceeding to Connecticut. If the court had awarded salvage rights, Baldwin recognized, it would have tacitly approved the right of a person to move slaves from a free state in order to seek a trial in a more favorable setting. Such a decision would have had an impact on one of the major controversies on the eve of the Civil War: whether hunters of fugitive slaves could claim the same right upon capturing their prey. The abolitionists did not raise this matter in Hartford, but they had grasped the immediate importance of the salvage question: John Quincy Adams had that very day emphasized to Ellis Gray Loring that all succeeding questions hinged on it.[21] Although Judson had prohibited discussion of matters touching upon the merits of the case, the allowance of salvage to Gedney would effectively reduce the abolitionists' chances of winning the case.

Testimony by Green and his four friends made clear that in an effort to secure salvage rights to the *Amistad* and its cargo, they had been willing to resort to any measures to evade the American brig they knew was off Long Island. Intending to take the *Amistad* and its cargo to a prize court, Green had attempted to deceive the blacks into thinking that the American navy would return them to slavery and that their safest course was to accompany him. When Gedney approached the schooner, Green testified, it was less than five hundred feet from shore and at least twenty blacks were on the beach. Green and his companions already had the situation under control. Indeed, he and his associates had helped in the capture by detaining the blacks until Gedney's men arrived on shore. Furthermore, at one time the blacks had a considerable amount of gold that was part of the present claim for salvage. Green swore that Burnah, who spoke a little English, was the black who had told him that four hundred doubloons were in the trunks and that plenty more were on the *Amistad*.[22]

If the abolitionists hoped that Green's testimony would hold up in court, that hope began to disappear as his companions tried to confirm his story. One of them, Peletiah Fordham, drew an outburst of laughter in the crowded courtroom when he testified about the trunks brought ashore by the blacks. Cinqué, he explained, "lifted one trunk, and I heard the money rattle." Showing less than mastery of the English language, Fordham asserted, "Me and another nigger lifted the other trunk, and then I heard some more money." After the judge banged his gavel to restore order, Fordham, now thoroughly confused, further damaged his testimony by accidentally reversing his expression: "So we determined to have the vessel at all hazards—forcibly if we can, peaceably if we must."[23]

The testimony of Green and his associates was instantly challenged by their rival salvage claimants. Gedney and Meade, both neatly and authoritatively dressed in naval uniforms that starkly contrasted with the drab apparel worn by Green and his companions, insisted that the *Amistad* had been at least a half mile from shore and that only eight or nine blacks had been ashore. They had acted legally because both the vessel and the majority of its occupants were on the high seas. The captain's slave Antonio testified that he had been ashore at the time of capture and that only eight blacks had been there. After the seizure, five of them had been taken to the *Washington* in the *Amistad's* boat and three in the boat belonging to the American brig itself. The United States district attorney, William S. Holabird, introduced Burnah, who in broken English further discredited Green's story. Moreover, Cinqué and five other blacks confirmed Burnah's account. A newspaper correspondent at the trial claimed that the story of Gedney and Meade was "perfectly consistent" and that it was affirmed by those men who, upon Judson's directive, had gone out in the cutter to determine the exact location of the *Amistad*.[24]

Perhaps sensing the unlikelihood of its having the case removed from Connecticut, the defense turned to its primary objective—to prove that the blacks were not slaves. Staples and Baldwin repeated the argument delivered before the circuit court the preceding September. The blacks were natives of Africa who had been born free but kidnapped in Africa and put on a vessel "unlawfully engaged in the slave trade" by "certain persons to them unknown." Both Spanish claimants, the attorneys insisted, were aware of the blacks' status as free persons and were guilty of "confederating" with those illegally engaged in the slave trade and "intending to deprive them of their liberty." Ruiz and Montes had each made a "pretended purchase" of the blacks on the *Amistad* from persons who had no right to them. The purchases were "null and void" and gave the claimants no title. Liberty was an ongoing process, the defense argued; anyone who denied it at any point in a man's life was as guilty as the one who first interfered with that freedom. Ruiz and Montes had loaded the blacks onto the *Amistad* to be "enslaved for life." Cinqué had led a mutiny motivated by "love of liberty natural to all men" and by a drive to go back home to families. He and the others had sought only to return to Africa or find asylum in some place where slavery was forbidden.[25]

The defense asserted that the blacks of the *Amistad* had accomplished their sole objective of securing liberty when they reached the free state of New York. Arriving at Culloden Point, they anchored less than a mile offshore and inside the state's territorial waters. Cinqué and his friends were therefore subject only to New York's laws and protection. But when a small number went ashore for provisions, they were "forcibly & unlawfully taken" at the command of Ruiz and Montes, whose only intention was to secure them as slaves. Gedney claimed salvage for what he termed a "meritorious act," when in reality there was no danger and he had wrongfully taken the blacks from New York to Connecticut. They were free upon arrival in New York; they should go free now.[26]

After several hours of argument, Judson adjourned the proceedings until the following day. The defense had recognized that its case was not going well and that the blacks had no chance without testimony from their chief interpreter, James Covey. The black cook from the British vessel, then in New York, was born a Mende; after conversing with the captives in New Haven, he had concluded that they were all native Africans. But Covey had become too ill to travel to Hartford. Baldwin appealed for a postponement in the proceedings until Covey could testify. Judson appeared reluctant to grant the request until the libelants' counsel, Isham and W. F. Brainard, explained that they were unable to remain in the city, because of prior engagements. Judson announced that district court proceedings would resume on January 7, 1840—in New Haven. In the meantime Judson agreed to take the testimony of Madden that afternoon at two in his chambers in the City Hotel.[27]

At first Judson's decision to change the location of the trial seemed unusual—except that this perhaps suited his political purposes. Possibly he had discerned that public sympathy for the blacks' liberty was stronger in New Haven than in Hartford. If Judson wished to remain popular in Connecticut, New Haven might be a better arena for any decision that bucked the administration in Washington.

III

Dr. Richard R. Madden's testimony, it was assumed by Judson and others, would strongly support the blacks' claim to freedom. In addition to providing a firsthand account of conditions in Cuba, Madden, by his mere presence, would suggest that the British government itself was on the side of those who sympathized with the *Amistad* captives. His interest in the case had grown from the moment he first heard of the mutiny. During his preparation in Havana for departure to England, he learned that the trial of the blacks for murder and piracy was about to begin. Confident that they were not Cuban slaves but *bozales* recently imported into the island and illegally held as slaves, he traveled a thousand miles out of his way to testify on their behalf. Some of his superiors had opposed this move, but he thought it his duty and believed that the secretary of state for the colonies would approve. He was correct. In a letter of January 1840, R. Vernon Smith of the British Colonial Office praised his zeal.[28]

To abolitionists in the United States, Madden's background made him an ideal figure to give testimony in the case. In 1835 he had been appointed to safeguard freed Africans and to serve as arbitrator in the mixed-commission court in Havana. Established after Spain had agreed to terminate the slave trade between Africa and the West Indies in 1820, one court sat in British territory at Sierra Leone and the other in Spanish territory at Havana. Madden served as superintendent of liberated Africans in Cuba from 1836 to 1839. Shortly afterward he was appointed judge arbitrator in the court in Havana. When he first arrived in Havana, Madden recorded in his memoirs, that city was the capital of Spain's colonies and the "chief commercial center" of the West Indies slave trade—"the extinction of which" was his mission. He fought virtually alone against Cuban slave traders, "then supported by the Spanish authorities." All laws were openly violated, he noted: "Justice is bought and sold in Cuba with as much scandalous publicity as the Bozal slaves are bought and sold in the barricones."[29]

Madden was a fervent foe of slavery. Only when he traveled, he continued in his memoirs, did he fathom the horror of slavery in Cuba. "I have already said," he wrote, "and I repeat the words, so terrible were these atrocities, so murderous the system of slavery, so transcendent the evils I witnessed, over all I have ever heard or seen of the rigour of slavery elsewhere, that at first I could hardly believe the evidence of my senses." While in Cuba, he wrote two poems describing the system. Madden's exposure of the evils of slavery and the slave trade led to conflict with Spanish authorities that was comparable to the British consul David Turnbull's experiences, discussed earlier. Turnbull claimed that no man could have been "more sincerely or more entirely devoted" to his duties than Madden. He was well known in the world of literature and noted for his "moral fitness" and "kindness to the African race." For all the reasons Turnbull cited in praising Madden, Spanish officials joined slave-trading interests on the island in hating him. Spanish authorities demanded Madden's recall, but Foreign Minister Lord Palmerston in London refused and instead expressed satisfaction with his work.[30]

Madden was already fairly well known in the United States before his arrival in early November 1839. During a previous visit, he had discussed the question of abolition with President Andrew Jackson. It had worked in the British West Indies, Madden told his seemingly interested host. He added, "The sooner, General, you adopt a similar measure in the United States the better. It would be a fitting finale of a great career like yours to connect it with such an act of emancipation." The president, standing before the fire in his study, broke out in laughter, turning to guests on both sides of the room and declaring, "This gentleman has just come from the West Indies, where the British have been emancipating their slaves. He recommends me to make myself famous by following their example." To his private secretary, Jackson said, "Come here, . . . put the paper in the fire, bring in a barrel of gunpowder, and when I am placed on it give the red poker to the Doctor [Madden], and he will make me famous in the twinkling of an eye."[31]

Madden had arrived with good credentials, according to abolitionists in the United States. In a letter to Tappan and other abolitionists, William Lloyd Garrison introduced Madden and praised his work in Havana. Garrison also noted Madden's literary attainments, including an "excellent work" on slavery in the West Indies. Several "abolition friends" had met him and were pleased. Madden was in the country, Garrison explained, "especially to do all that can be done to prevent the African prisoners of the *Amistad* being sent back to Cuba." He hoped that the "friends of bleeding humanity" would receive Madden as an "angel of mercy."[32]

The accolades heaped on Madden meant he would automatically be unpopular among anti-abolitionists and other Americans who hated trouble-making outsiders. Critics dismissed him as a hotheaded Irish abolitionist who had supported liberty for slaves in Jamaica and was so prejudiced that many of his reports contained errors favorable to his case. Had the American consul in Havana, Nicholas Trist, read Garrison's letter, he would have vehemently disagreed with its praise. Madden, one might note, was among Trist's most bitter critics during the unsettled controversy over whether the consul participated in the island's slave trade for personal profit. To Secretary of State Forsyth, Trist wrote that Madden had long been retained in Havana as a "supernumerary," a "wretched mixture of the bigot and fanatic, blended with the worldly-minded man." In a letter to a friend, Trist insisted that Madden was filled with "malice, envy and all uncharitableness."

He added, "*Truth* [was] not in him." An anonymous correspondent of the abolitionist William Ellery Channing also attacked Madden, asserting that he was "either a zealot or a hypocrite"—but "more likely both."[33]

The New York *Commercial Advertiser* noted that Madden was the sole passenger on the schooner *Texas* (the same vessel that had recently taken Montes back to Cuba) as it arrived in New York on November 5 from Havana. He joined Tappan, and the two men traveled to New Haven to visit the *Amistad* captives. Afterward Madden confirmed his willingness to testify before the district court in Hartford.[34]

In Judson's chambers during the afternoon of November 20, the clerk recorded Madden's testimony before the small group of interested parties in the *Amistad* case. After testifying, Madden asked the clerk for a copy to show his government. But when the clerk began the long process of copying, Judson interrupted and called it irregular to have copies of testimony made before he had decided the question of admissibility in court. Consequently, Madden made arrangements for a copy to come from his memoranda and the notes of a reporter. But then one of the daily papers of New York somehow secured and published what it called an abstract of Madden's testimony. Since the abstract was a poor summation, Judson decreed it necessary to publish the entire testimony after all.[35]

Madden's testimony caused considerable excitement because it upheld the abolitionists' arguments that the *Amistad* blacks had been imported from Africa recently. The captives were not *ladinos*, or acclimated blacks brought to Cuba before 1820, and they were not *creoles*, or blacks born on the island. The *Amistad* blacks, Madden declared, were "bona fide Bozal Negroes quite newly imported from Africa." Ruiz and Montes bought them in barracoons, or slave markets, which were fitted exclusively for receiving and selling *bozales* in the illicit slave trade. Ruiz made his purchase on the account of his uncle, Saturnio Carrias, who was a merchant in Puerto Príncipe and who intended the blacks "for sale at that place." All the blacks of the *Amistad* had come from Don Pedro Martínez, whose slaver had brought them from Africa. Martínez and Company, Madden noted, was one of the largest illegal slave traders in Havana—a "notorious house."[36]

Madden was also convinced that both licenses for the transportation of the blacks, Montes's dated June 22 and Ruiz's June 26, 1839, were frauds. He had seen all the blacks except the four children, and he had seen the two permits, or *trespassos*; the term *ladino* did not describe the captives in New Haven. Montes's *trespasso* was "wholly inapplicable" because the African children were too young to have been acclimated and long settled on the island. Yet, Madden explained, all slave merchants had to do to acquire a *trespasso* was make an application and pay fees to island authorities. Applicants wishing to move *bozales* simply called them *ladinos*. Madden declared that neither the captain general nor his officers inspected the blacks, and no one had to take an oath. Such "*fraud*," Madden emphasized, could not take place without the slave traders' "connivance" and "collusion" with Cuban authorities, who in turn received a bounty on blacks imported from Africa.[37]

Madden noted that it was "generally reported and believed" in Havana that the *Amistad* blacks fitted the pattern of the slave trade on the island. A man named Riera ran a barracoon called *la misericordia*, or "mercy," which Madden had recently visited with a person who was well acquainted with the slave market. The "factor," or "major domo" of the master, told Madden that he knew the *Amistad's* blacks and that a man from Puerto Príncipe had bought them there. The factor made the remark "*Que lastima*" ("What a pity"). Surprised, Madden asked for an explanation. The factor thought that the blacks would be executed for murder and piracy in the United States and regretted the "loss of so many valuable Bozals."[38]

Madden believed that he was qualified to make a judgment on the *Amistad* blacks. As a resident of Havana for over three years, he had served one year as British commissioner in the mixed court, which adjudicated cases of blacks captured in slave ships by Spanish and British cruisers. And as superintendent of liberated Africans, he had had under his charge many hundreds of *bozales* after their court emancipation. Madden had helped register them and was experienced in determining ages. In New Haven he spoke to one black in Arabic by reciting a Mohammedan form of prayer, and a man seated beside that black immediately answered in Arabic, "*Allah akbar*" ("God is great"), and gave an oriental salutation. Of the captives Madden saw, Cinqué and the others appeared to be less than twenty-six years of age. Among the adults, three seemed to be nineteen or younger, which meant that they, like the four children, were too young to have been imported into Cuba before the Anglo-Spanish treaty against the slave trade went into effect in 1820.[39]

At the completion of the testimony, District Attorney Holabird cross-examined Madden, hoping to discredit his story. Were not lawful slaves of Cuba, when put up for sale, also placed in the barracoons? They were not, Madden answered emphatically. Lawful slaves were not generally for sale, and, in any case, the barracoons were "for Bozal negroes only" and were part of the illegal slave trade—a process begun in Africa. Was not the native language of Africans retained for a long time on certain plantations? Holabird asked. Madden thought that the reverse was true. It had been a "matter of astonishment" to him that blacks on the plantations so quickly dropped their languages for Spanish. This observation, he explained, came from his "very intimate knowledge" of the blacks' condition—a knowledge derived from frequent visits to plantations and into the Cuban interior.[40]

Not only was Madden not discredited, but his other testimony reinforced his description of the illegality of Cuban practices. Spanish authorities, he said, never interfered with "illegally captured and illegally enslaved" blacks. In exchange, they received a $10 bounty, or impost per head, which was called a "voluntary contribution" but was in reality a tax with no legal sanction. Within the last three years, nearly twenty-five thousand slaves had been introduced wrongfully into Cuba. The mixed commission was virtually powerless because its jurisdiction did not extend into cases involving blacks who had already reached Cuban shores. The court could deal only with treaty violations brought before it by captors of slave ships. The captain general alone had jurisdiction over crimes in Spanish territory.[41]

Madden's performance was impressive and convincing. Abolitionists rejoiced at the confirmation of every allegation they had made about the slave situation in Cuba.[42] No longer could the Van Buren administration hope for an outcome that would hide the issues in the case by ridding the country of the blacks before they became a public concern. Their return to Cuba, Madden's testimony made clear, doubtless meant certain death, for, as the Spanish minister in the United States warned Forsyth in early September 1839, slave dealers could not condone mutiny on the *Amistad* without inviting other slaves to rebel. Spanish authorities in Madrid and in Havana recognized that the justice rendered Cinqué and his companions would have to stand as an awesome example of the fate awaiting potential mutineers and insurrectionists.

Madden's firsthand observations had exposed the inhumanity inherent in returning the *Amistad* captives to Cuba. And yet most Americans, charitable as they claimed to be, were not willing to make their country an asylum for black insurrectionists. Madden's testimony had focused the issues involved in the *Amistad* mutiny. It was now up to the contestants on all sides of the questions to argue their cases before Judge Judson when district court reconvened on January 7, 1840.

7

" . . . Nor Free"

If the first phase of district court proceedings had moved the blacks closer to freedom, they still had a long way to go. The trial's postponement gave all sides time to assess their positions. Whereas the defense had been relieved to have an additional period for Covey's recovery, the other parties must have been concerned that the abolitionists would use the interval to promote their case in the press. Domestic and foreign pressures dictated that the Van Buren administration take some sort of action. The election campaign was near, and the Spanish government was increasing its demands for the blacks' return. The delay in court proceedings might provide the White House an opportunity to reverse the course of events and assure the blacks' status as slaves, returnable to Spain under Pinckney's Treaty.

I

During the interim the Spanish minister in Washington, Pedro Alcántara de Argaiz, resumed his protests against America's handling of the *Amistad* affair; but now his argument made a subtle and important shift in emphasis. Forsyth had recently assured Argaiz of a favorable outcome in the trial by sending him a copy of Attorney General Felix Grundy's opinion on the case. But the legal arguments that seemed so sound in the statement had not stood up in Hartford, and when the district judge postponed the trial until January, the Spanish minister repeated his earlier complaints. But instead of dwelling on the treaty of 1795, Argaiz declared that the "public vengeance had not been satisfied" and that his government did "not demand the delivery of slaves but of assassins." Perhaps the Spanish government had joined District Attorney Holabird in recognizing the diminishing prospects of securing the blacks' return as slaves.[1]

Forsyth assured Argaiz that the delay in fulfilling the treaty had resulted from causes "beyond the control" of the executive. Argaiz, the secretary continued, did not understand the "true character of the question" and the "rules by which, under the constitutional institutions of the country," the outcome had to take place. The judiciary was an independent part of the American government, and the president could not interfere with its proceedings. But, Forsyth promised Argaiz, final settlement of the case would emanate from "no other source than the Government of the United States."[2]

It became obvious that the Van Buren administration expected a favorable decision from the district court and that its principal task in regard to Spain was to keep the *Amistad* affair from becoming diplomatically disruptive. The White House's preference was for Judson, as a loyal and ambitious party member, to rule that Pinckney's Treaty bound the United States to return the ship, cargo, and slaves to Spain as property. Treaties were part of the supreme law of the land, and Judson certainly knew that. At the same time, however, the treaty of 1795 had permitted Holabird to leave the door open during circuit court proceedings for use of the congressional act of 1819 in returning the blacks to Africa. For every conceivable reason, it appeared, Judson would close the matter in a way acceptable to the administration. In the meantime Forsyth had to ease Argaiz's concern.

To assure a speedy end to the *Amistad* affair, the White House agreed to a suggestion from the Spanish minister—that immediately after Judson's decision the United States provide a ship to transport the blacks to Cuba. Indeed, the president and his secretary of state were so confident of the outcome of the trial that they made special arrangements with the Department of the Navy temporarily to divert the USS *Grampus*, under the command of Lieutenant John S. Paine, from its anti-slave-trade patrol along the West African coast in order to carry the blacks to Havana. If Forsyth proved correct in asserting that the district court would order the return of the *Amistad*, its cargo, and the blacks, Argaiz wanted to follow his advice, as Argaiz wrote, to "take charge of them as soon as the court . . . pronounced its sentence or resolution." The *Amistad* was in no condition to make a voyage to Havana, and if the United States provided a ship, the Spanish government would

regard this as an "act of generosity" and a "most particular favor."
The president approved the suggestion because, he claimed, the
Amistad captives had insisted that they were not slaves and that
their return would allow them to prove this in Cuban courts.[3]

The Van Buren administration had dropped its rigid claim that
the *Amistad* blacks were slaves, returnable to Spain under the
treaty of 1795. Holabird had first suggested this change in direction
when he admitted in circuit court that the blacks were native Africans. Now, the White House tacitly conceded that the blacks might
be free, and the administration was willing to give them the opportunity to prove their case in court—albeit a Cuban court. But
appearances were deceiving. Arguments in the district court had
caused a shift in tactics, not a change in policy. The objective was
still to rid the administration of the problem before the presidential election of 1840. By adopting either stance—referring to the
blacks as slaves or as native Africans—the White House intended
to help them leave the country. Whether they went as property to
Spain under Pinckney's Treaty or as accused assassins to Cuba,
they would be outside the United States.

At this point the White House took a major step in an obstruc-
tionist strategy that soon grew into executive interference with the
constitutional rights of due process. Forsyth expected the district
court to uphold the administration, and he knew that if that happened the abolitionists would push for an appeal—or perhaps even
break the captives out of jail. The administration's plan for a quick
removal of the *Amistad* blacks to Cuba by an American naval vessel was designed to prevent this. Forsyth instructed Holabird to
work with the United States marshal and the naval officer in implementing the plan. The vessel was "to be in readiness to receive
the negroes from the custody of the marshal as soon as their delivery shall have been ordered by the court." If the court should
decide "as is anticipated," the president's order was "to be carried
into execution, unless an appeal shall actually have been interposed." The most critical part of the directive, however, was the
following: "You are not to take it for granted that [the appeal] will
be interposed." In the event that the decision went the other way,
Forsyth added, Holabird himself was to move an appeal.[4]

Questions immediately arise about the ethics, if not the legality
and constitutionality, of such a scheme. Forsyth's directives from
the president clearly authorized the district attorney to subvert the
judicial system by taking the blacks out of the country without
allowing time for their counsel to exercise legal and constitutional

rights of appeal. Surely this ill-considered approach by the White House resulted more from anxiety over the approaching election than from illegal intentions. But, in either case, the result would be the same: as in the Ruiz episode in New York, the White House was willing to overstep its authority. This time, however, the move was more serious. President Van Buren was condoning executive interference with the due process guarantees of the Constitution.[5]

The secret arrangements for this action reveal how careless the administration was in developing such a mission. On January 2, 1840, the Department of State sent a memorandum to Secretary of the Navy James K. Paulding, ordering him to have an American ship anchored off the port of New Haven by January 10, ready to take the blacks to Cuba. On the "real condition" of the blacks, Forsyth wrote Holabird, the president had directed Gedney and Meade to accompany the blacks to testify in whatever proceedings might take place in Cuba. These orders were top secret—"not to be communicated to any one." Paulding instructed Lieutenant Paine to have the *Grampus* in New Haven no later than January 9.[6]

Paine, however, warned of probable snags in the expedition. Because of cold weather, he explained to Paulding, he had been unable to have the schooner fitted for sea and could not be certain of being in New Haven on time. Iced-over waterways might make New Haven inaccessible, raising questions about the practicability of moving the blacks from that point. Also, space limitations made it impossible to accommodate the blacks below, along with one watch of the ship's crew. They would have to be "deck passengers" and kept in irons. Thus they would suffer a great deal under the best of circumstances. Paine did not want to think about the havoc a storm would bring. No vessel the size of the *Grampus* could properly fit all of its own officers and crew at one time below deck; only a frigate could do that. Paine recognized that an "important and delicate duty" had fallen on him, and he tried to make adjustments. If the commanding officer in the area did not object, he would allow only enough mates on board to work the vessel— about forty—and proceed to Havana. Upon completion of the mission, he would return to Norfolk and fill up the crew from the receiving ship and go to Africa. The procedure should cost only a few days and would allow him to replenish provisions.[7]

Time was the most important factor, for the American vessel had to whisk the blacks away immediately after the court's decision. Paulding responded to Paine's concerns on January 6, repeating that it was vital for Paine to be off New Haven no later than January 10. He could return to Norfolk for supplies and repairs after completing the mission. The secretary of state wanted Paine to contact Holabird immediately upon arrival in New Haven about receiving the earliest possible news of the court's decision and carrying out the assignment. The president had ordered the marshal to place the blacks in Paine's hands as soon as the court made its decision. Paulding, meanwhile, sent Gedney a packet containing a letter from the Spanish minister introducing the two American officers to the captain general in Cuba. The matter had become so urgent that Paulding refused a letter of resignation from an officer on the *Grampus* because the vessel was under orders for "special and delicate service."[8]

Despite obvious risks to life, the White House had hurriedly approved a plan designed to fulfill its political objectives. Both the ship and the crew, not to mention the blacks, would be in danger because of the ice around New Haven and the possibility of bad weather en route to Cuba. More important, the blacks would be exposed to the elements by having to sleep on deck. The plan had the elements of a potential tragedy with domestic as well as foreign repercussions.

For a brief moment the details appeared to come together. Paine arrived in New Haven during the night of January 9 and entered the harbor the following morning, exactly on time. After informing Marshal Willcox of his orders to take custody of the blacks after the trial, Paine persuaded him that because of the ice it would be more feasible to pick them up at New London. As the *Grampus* proceeded to New London, Captain Andrew Mather of the revenue cutter *Walcott* offered to help execute the president's order. Willcox accepted the offer.[9]

At this point complications developed. Paine noticed an error in the president's warrant contained in the State Department letter. It stated that the *Amistad* case was pending before the *circuit* court rather than before the district court. In a remarkable oversight, the administration in Washington had made a mistake in the warrant that could provide a legal ground for blocking the removal to Cuba. Under Holabird's advisement, the marshal immediately sent an express to Washington to have the warrant corrected. Nor was this all. The navy's area commander had not received Paulding's approval of Paine's reduction of the crew; he ordered Paine to have a full contingent of men. Paine had already "dreaded" the administration's plan. Now it seemed to be falling apart, and Paine knew that the blacks would be the victims. Upon arriving in New London, he intended to charter a small vessel that would carry half of the blacks and some of Paine's men along with Gedney or Meade and one of Paine's officers. The remainder of the blacks would be on the *Grampus*, which would convoy the other vessel to Havana. Paine's most important consideration was "humanity." But he also did not want to open the administration to charges of cruelty and thus to strengthen the abolitionists—the "faction" that, as an American, he "could wish to see destroyed."[10]

Problems continued to mount. Paine arrived in New London on January 13, six hours later than expected, because of the ice. He immediately became concerned that the paperwork connected with the court decision (preparing a copy of the proceedings to take with him to Cuba) would take several days and delay departure. The impression abroad seemed to be, Paine commented, that the *Grampus* was there to take the blacks to Africa, an opinion he did "not think proper to contradict." Indeed, Lewis Tappan was among only a few who believed that the schooner was there to take the blacks to Cuba.[11]

But, shortly after Paine's arrival in New London, matters brightened again when orders came from Paulding that settled Paine's central concern: he could temporarily cut his crew to accommodate the blacks and, after completing the mission in Havana, return to Norfolk for repairs and supplies. To fill the need for officers, Gedney and Meade would provide their services. Paulding included the following instruction: "You will be careful to afford the Slaves every convenience and comfort in your power. As well from motives of humanity as to remove all just grounds of accusation both as regards the Government and yourself on an occasion so peculiarly delicate and which is liable to be so much misrepresented."[12]

The presence of the *Grampus* in New London harbor heightened the abolitionists' suspicions that the Van Buren administration intended to interfere. A recent issue of the *Emancipator* contained a serious indictment of the White House. The abolitionist paper claimed that a person of "great moral worth" and "officially connected" with these matters had recently talked with a "Spanish gentleman of standing, whose opportunities of knowing the state of this question [were] quite peculiar and official." The Spaniard declared that the White House was prepared to compensate Ruiz for the value of his property if he would drop the case; but the government in Madrid was not interested. Argaiz contended that the nations must comply with the treaty of 1795, which required the United States to return the blacks. Abolitionists wondered whether the president was willing to employ virtual bribery to secure a favorable conclusion.[13]

To abolitionists, another sign of trouble came from the *National Intelligencer* in Washington, which they regarded as the administration's supporter. An article signed "Justice" agreed with the president that his duty was to return the blacks as property to the Spanish claimants. Baldwin immediately sent a letter to the editors of the paper, arguing that the blacks had been kidnapped and that the paper's position seemed to be an effort to influence a pending court decision by calling for executive interference with the constitutional functions of the judiciary. Matters involving ownership of property, Baldwin insisted, fell under the purview of the judiciary, not the executive. Pinckney's Treaty declared that issues relating to the return of property came under the courts of either nation. Before there could be a delivery of merchandise rescued from pirates or robbers, two facts had to be clear: that those in possession of the property *were* pirates or robbers, which must be confessed or judicially determined; and that the claimant was the true owner. Though the property might come from a Spanish port and might be accompanied by papers that were prima facie evidence of Spanish ownership, no lawyer could argue against an American's right to seek to prove title in the courts by showing that the papers were fraudulently secured or, as in the *Amistad* case, were used to cover persons or property fraudulently substituted for that described in the license.[14]

Only the courts could resolve these questions, Baldwin insisted. If the executive dealt with them, the claimant had no right of appeal, because that office lacked judicial powers. This would be dangerous enough if the matter concerned only property rights. "How much more important is it," Baldwin wrote, "that such powers should not be assumed by the Executive, when questions of personal liberty, and perhaps even of life and death, are involved in the issue." The *Antelope* case was relevant only because it involved the obligation of the courts to rectify the situation by returning matters to what they had been at the time of capture. But in that case, Baldwin emphasized, the Supreme Court was equally divided over the obligation to restore property. The *Amistad* blacks, however, were never slaves and hence never property. They were kidnapped and taken to Cuba in violation of Spanish laws. The schooner's papers described them not merely as slaves but as *"ladino slaves,"* a term not applicable to African blacks imported since 1820. There was no description or designation except by Spanish names that the blacks themselves did not recognize. The license was a *"cover"* by Ruiz and Montes to ship *bozales,* as Ruiz and Montes knew. When seized by Gedney, the Africans were *"de facto* as well as *de jure* free."[15]

Baldwin declared that in focusing on the property issue, Americans had failed to recognize that the real significance of the *Amistad* case lay in the primacy of natural rights. The question before the court was "whether men and children who were born free, & who have never been held as slaves for a moment, except as the victims of piracy and fraud, shall when they have escaped from bondage and sought an asylum in our country, *be reduced to slavery* by the active interference of the Executive, or of the Judicial tribunals of our country." Even if Spanish municipal law permitted the enslavement of free people illegally imported, Baldwin continued, the question of liberty or property had, as the United States government recently told Lord Palmerston, to be "determined by some other test." The Africans had "never voluntarily submitted themselves" to either Spanish or Cuban municipal law. The blacks were "equally free, by the laws of Spain—and of the United States, as well as by the laws of Nature."[16]

Tappan was also becoming increasingly wary of the administration in Washington. To John Scoble, Tappan noted that Gedney had suddenly seemed willing to drop his libel if the process interfered with the United States's effort to deliver the blacks to Spanish officials. If all parties withdrew their libels, Tappan feared, the district court would simply turn over the blacks to the president of the United States. But, fortunately, Green refused to drop his claim, and, as Tappan observed to Ellis Gray Loring, this would "keep the cause in the court." The White House could not remove the blacks from the court's jurisdiction unless by "some monstrous act of usurpation." "We hardly think our Government will attempt it," Tappan told Scoble. But, he added, we should be prepared for it. "I hope your Govt. will interpose."[17]

Tappan was concerned that the blacks' defense counsel had had great difficulty in securing testimony. In mid-December he wrote to Joseph Sturge that they got "no facilities" from the government in Washington. Despite their requests for State Department help in providing authentic copies of Anglo-Spanish treaties relating to the case, the defense attorneys had gotten no cooperation from Forsyth, who was, after all, a slaveholder. Moreover, British members of the mixed commission in Havana were reluctant to ask the Spanish governor in Cuba for certified copies of the treaties. They feared that such a request would be an "extra-judicial act," subject to censure by their own government in London as well as by the one in Cuba. Yet the defense had to have copies for the trial, and Tappan asked Sturge to try to get them in London.[18]

The abolitionists' fears were justified. No one could deny the political priorities of the Van Buren administration, and the wide array of rumors about its undercover policies were not far off the mark. But the issues had become so complex that to many persons unacquainted with the law the simplest and most obvious remedy was to accept the administration's argument relating to Pinckney's Treaty and to let the president deal directly with Spain in resolving the matter. Executive interference with judicial proceedings in New York, followed by a willingness to violate due process in New Haven, had not drawn public attention for two reasons: in the Ruiz episode White House correspondence was secret, and in the case of the *Grampus* the abolitionists could not have been aware of the administration's intentions to interfere with the defendants' right of appeal.

Other administration policies were questionable as well. The White House may have been sincere in wanting to cooperate with Spain by sending district court records to Cuba, but that act of apparent generosity carried serious overtones of impropriety. Since the return of the blacks to Spanish authorities was to follow a court decision favorable to the administration, this would have constituted a tacit admission that the blacks were assassins, as Argaiz now contended. The inclusion of the trial proceedings that led to this finding would not have done much for the blacks' case in the hostile surroundings of Cuba. Furthermore, testimony by Gedney and Meade would have been injurious to the blacks' cause; the two naval officers could not change what they had said in Connecticut without jeopardizing their salvage claims and opening themselves to charges of perjury. White House advisers had doubtless not thought out the ramifications of the initial decision to silence the *Amistad* case for political reasons.

II

District court proceedings resumed in New Haven on January 7, amid an atmosphere of great excitement. Students from Yale Law School, members of the Theological Seminary, and distinguished residents of the community all squeezed into the narrow confines, especially eager to witness a precedent in federal court: testimony from the blacks themselves. At numerous points in the trial, Judge Judson had to rap the assembly to order, particularly after Baldwin drew cheers with his dramatic defenses of liberty. Tappan attended the trial and prepared written accounts of each day's proceedings, which were published in full in the *Emancipator.* In the last days of the week-long session, spectators refused to leave the courtroom during the long recesses for fear of losing their seats.

Judson, of course, presided, austere and solemn, doubtless concerned about his own political tightrope. For the blacks, Staples and Sedgwick again joined Baldwin, and by now they had their arguments virtually memorized. Isham and Brainard took their places to argue for Gedney and Meade, and Ellsworth prepared to continue his losing battle for Green and friends. One change in personnel was the appearance of William P. Cleveland of New London on behalf of two Spanish owners of the cargo on the *Amistad.*[19]

Another change, a move that confirmed the abolitionists' fears of collusion between their government and that in Madrid, came with Holabird's announcement that the Spanish minister had "merged" the claims of Ruiz and Montes with that of the United States. He, as district attorney, would present them as one.[20] For Tappan and others, the thought of combating two national governments in alliance probably confirmed the righteousness of their cause.

Defense counsel for the blacks once again entered a plea on jurisdiction, this one striking to the heart of the case by denying that the blacks were property. After repeating the arguments of the November session, the attorneys called two witnesses from New London: Sullivan Haley and Dwight P. Janes, the latter being the abolitionist who had first informed Tappan of the *Amistad* affair. Both men had been on the *Washington* when Judge Judson ordered an inquiry into the *Amistad* upon its arrival in New London the past August.[21]

Almost immediately tensions began to rise. When it became clear that Haley and Janes intended to testify that Ruiz and Montes had admitted that the blacks had come from Africa recently, Holabird objected, saying that the two Spaniards had no counsel and no longer had anything to do with the matter. He, as district attorney, was appearing on behalf of the Spanish minister. Baldwin and Staples sharply asked what right the district attorney had to be at the trial. For practical purposes, Holabird replied, he was the counsel for Ruiz and Montes; the president had directed him to represent the Spanish minister by "executive courtesy." Isham's remarks on this matter undoubtedly confirmed the abolitionists' concern that Gedney was closing ranks with the Van Buren administration. Isham insisted that the district attorney had come to "preserve the faith of this government inviolate"—to make sure the blacks were returned to the Spanish government if found slaves or to Africa or elsewhere if not slaves and the matter became a state question. Someone had to present the claims of Ruiz and Montes, Isham concluded; they were libelants.[22]

Judson moved quickly to settle the issue. He ruled that since the sole question before the court was that of property, it would accept the two Spaniards' claims.[23]

That matter resolved, Haley and Janes testified against Ruiz's claim to the *Amistad* blacks as property in slaves. While on the *Washington*, Haley declared, he had in the ship's cabin overheard a conversation in which Janes asked Ruiz about the blacks. Ruiz said that Antonio alone could speak Spanish and that the rest of the blacks were "just from Africa." Only one could speak a few words of English, which he probably had learned on the African coast. When a question arose about how Haley and Janes understood Spanish, Haley replied that Ruiz spoke good English. Isham interrupted to ask, "Did you not know that he was educated in Connecticut?" To blunt the impact of Isham's remark, Baldwin quickly rejoined, "He ought to have known better if he was educated in Connecticut." Janes confirmed Haley's story. Under Baldwin's questioning, Janes explained that he had followed Ruiz into the cabin and had asked whether any of the blacks could speak English. "A few words," Ruiz replied. Spanish? "*No*, they were just from Africa."[24]

Additional testimony came from James Covey and Charles Pratt, the two Africans who had talked with the *Amistad* captives in their own language during the autumn of 1839 and who were confident that all of them had come from Africa recently. Covey, about twenty years old and now recovered from the illness that had forced postponement of the trial, testified that he had been born in Mende in Africa and had learned English in Sierra Leone. Nearly eight years ago he had been "stolen by a black man" and taken as a slave to Lomboko, where he was placed on a slaver sailing for Havana. A British cruiser captured the slaver, however, and Covey later decided to enlist as a sailor on the *Buzzard*, a British man-of-war. He had been in New Haven for four months, where he stayed with "Mr. Bishop." The man had asked for no money. Although Covey did not know who was paying his board, it is likely that Tappan had made the arrangements. In exchange for the British naval captain's agreeing to let Covey testify, Tappan had promised his safety until his return. After Covey talked with Cinqué and other captives in New Haven, he concluded that all were from Africa and that all but three of them were Mende. Two or three spoke different languages, but all had Mende names, all talked of rivers familiar to Covey, and all agreed on where they had sailed from when leaving Africa. Pratt's account confirmed Covey's. Pratt was an African, twenty-five years of age, born in Sierra Leone. He was the captain's cook on the *Buzzard*. He had learned the Mende language while there with his father doing trade. Like Covey, Pratt was convinced that the captives had come from Africa recently.[25]

During the morning of January 8, Professor Josiah W. Gibbs of Yale College appeared for the defense, giving a long, intricate explanation of the importance of language that probably suggested to the audience that any excitement in the trial would come later. Repeatedly referring to a large pile of notes he clutched in his hands, Gibbs elaborately explained why the terms *ladinos* and *bozales* were crucial to the case. But before he could describe his procedure in inquiring into the language of the captives, Gedney's counsel raised a question, and perhaps because of what Tappan later termed the pressure of "public sentiment," Judson stunned the courtroom by declaring that he "was fully convinced that the men were recently from Africa, and it was idle to deny it."[26]

In one sentence, Judson took the position Holabird had suggested in circuit court the preceding September and ruled in favor of the most important argument made by the abolitionists: the blacks were not slaves and therefore were not property. This ruling dissolved the claims of Ruiz and Montes and denied the United States government its stated obligation to return the blacks to the Spanish minister as property under Pinckney's Treaty. Several questions immediately arose. Could the president comply with the Spanish government's demand for the surrender of the blacks as assassins? If the captives had been kidnapped, did they have the right to gain liberty by any means possible? Could they be held accountable in Cuban courts for seeking to escape an attempt to reduce them to slavery? Had not Judson suddenly taken the abolitionists' side in the *Amistad* question? If the blacks had the right to liberty, the only decision Judson could make was to order their return to Africa—their homeland. Would the implication be that color was *not* incompatible with freedom?

While these questions perhaps crossed the minds of perceptive observers, Gibbs resumed his testimony, which by this time seemed anticlimactic. He explained what he knew about the African language, and how he had learned Mende from Covey. After collecting a vocabulary, Gibbs conversed with twenty or thirty of the captives. In reality he had earlier presented an irrefutable argument in the press for the captives' origins in Africa, when he showed how each of the black's names denoted an object, place, or thing in the Mende language. The Spaniards could not have given them their names; they did not know the Mende language and could not even pronounce the words. Moreover, Gibbs explained, if the Spaniards had taken African names "at haphazard and given them to Africans indiscriminately, it would, in the multiplicity of African dialects, have been a miracle for the Mende names to fall so exactly on Mende people." Besides, had the Spaniards taken the names from the Mende and then passed them back, they would have "corrupted" the words in both "form and sound." The blacks, Gibbs concluded in court, could not speak Spanish, but spoke several African dialects. They were "native Africans & recently from Africa."[27]

After this lull in excitement, the moment most of the crowd had waited for came when Cinqué was at last called to the stand. A wave of anticipation swept the room as the leader of the mutiny rose from his seat, wrapped in a blanket but showing that he was taller than his companions, distinguished and erect in bearing, almost suggesting the pride of majesty. Covey accompanied him to the stand as interpreter. Before the court, Cinqué attested that he believed in God and understood that if he broke the oath to tell the truth he would be punished.[28]

As Cinqué delivered his testimony, the large audience listened with what one observer described as "breathless attention." Cinqué explained that he had been at work on a road in Mende when captured by four men. Perhaps attempting to undermine any justification for his capture, he contradicted his earlier claim that he had been taken for a debt. Leaving behind three children and a wife, he was taken to Lomboko, where he was sold and transported to Havana. During the long voyage he was chained, hands and feet together, and "packed" on the slaver. To illustrate, Cinqué sat on the floor of the courtroom and held his hands and feet together to show how he had been manacled. All the *Amistad* captives arrived in Havana on the same ship except the four children, who were already in the city but likewise were recent imports from Africa. The three girls, Cinqué noted, were Mende. He first saw Pepe (a nickname for José, Ruiz's first name) in Havana at the "prison house." Accompanied by the man who brought the blacks from Africa, Pepe felt them to see whether they were healthy. Cinqué's testimony had added impact when he demonstrated how Ruiz had conducted the inspection.[29]

Cinqué emphasized that on the *Amistad* he and the other blacks had had inadequate provisions and been subjected to cruel treatment ordered by Ruiz. The captives were chained on the vessel and allotted only one plantain, two potatoes, and half a cup of water per day. During the coastal voyage, the sailors whipped four men, including Burnah, under Pepe's orders and in his presence. Even the captain participated. No, Cinqué replied to an inquiry; Montes (who owned only the four children) did not engage in the whipping. No one struck Cinqué except the cook, who slapped him with a plantain. Was it in play, counsel asked. "Oh no, no," Cinqué emphatically replied.[30]

Cinqué recounted their arrival in New York. He was onshore with a large number of blacks when seized by Gedney; he named ten of them but could not recall the others. Yes, he told Green that he could have the *Amistad* if he took them to Sierra Leone. Was there gold on the schooner? Cinqué explained that after the mutiny, he had found a box below, which he broke up for firewood. The box contained some money, which he and the other blacks wrapped and tied around their bodies and later used partly in paying for supplies. The rest they gave to the white men in the boat. *Clothes* were in the trunks taken ashore. In a statement that contradicted his earlier story, Cinqué declared that the trunks had contained no money.[31]

That afternoon, two other blacks, Grabeau and Fuliwa, confirmed Cinqué's testimony. During cross-examination, Grabeau said that he had been seized in the road and taken to Lomboko, where he first met Cinqué. He did not know the name of the ship on which they departed for Havana. No doubloons were in the trunk, Grabeau attested. He was seeking water ashore with Cinqué when Gedney seized the *Amistad*. Grabeau claimed that Green had agreed to take them to Sierra Leone. Fuliwa said that he had also been onshore when Gedney arrived. Yes, Pepe ordered a sailor to whip him and others for stealing water. The cook said that they would be eaten after their heads had been cut off. The blacks killed the cook first, while he was lying in a boat. They had not wanted to kill the captain, but when he killed one of them they turned on him.[32]

The defense recognized that the prosecution intended to discredit the testimonies of Cinqué and the other blacks and prepared for the attack. Marshal Willcox was among the first to disagree with the blacks' testimony. In relating what Covey had told him about the blacks, Willcox declared that Cinqué had admitted to owing a man two pounds (holding up his two fingers) and to meeting his debt by selling the man two blacks. But one of them ran away, and apparently Cinqué was unable to pay the debt and was seized and sold to pay it. To counter the marshal's story, the defense called George E. Day, a teacher at Yale College who had helped instruct the blacks. He claimed that he was in the room at the time referred to by Willcox and that there was much confusion. One of the men present had tried to leave the impression that Cinqué had been a slaveholder, but Day never understood Cinqué to say that he had ever sold a man as a slave. Covey assured Day three weeks afterward that Cinqué never told him such a story.[33]

On the morning of the third day of the trial, the district attorney asked for a postponement because of the sickness of one of the witnesses—the Spanish consul Antonio G. Vega of Boston. Holabird declared that Vega could invalidate Madden's testimony by proving that the slave traffic was legal in Cuba. Vega had also filed a libel for the return to Cuba of Antonio, the slave belonging to the captain and owner of the *Amistad*, Ramón Ferrer. Antonio was a subject of Spain, Holabird asserted, and wanted to return to Cuba as a slave belonging to the captain's representatives. Vega also demanded immediate restoration of the *Amistad*, its cargo, and the slaves under Pinckney's Treaty. The United States government, Holabird explained, would comply with the court if it ruled the treaty applicable to the case.[34]

Baldwin did not want another postponement; he doubtless believed that the case was going the way of the defense and that a delay would hurt matters. He proposed calling the marshal to the stand to prove that, in New London, Vega had said that the slaves were from Africa and could not be held legally in Cuba. This would make Vega's testimony immaterial and a postponement unnecessary. Baldwin remarked that the district attorney had been aware of Vega's illness the day before and had not then objected to continuing the trial—probably because he had the purpose of "fishing out" the other side's evidence. Judson sharply rebuked Baldwin for his implication. Baldwin, the judge declared, used "very improper language" in imputing "a course to the Attorney of which he has not been guilty." Besides, Judson noted, had the motion come the day before, he would have refused a postponement until all testimony was in. Baldwin withdrew the words after claiming that he had not used them in the way the court understood them.[35]

Baldwin tried to show that Cinqué had not been a slave trader. When Covey entered the jail, Baldwin explained, there was great excitement and confusion as the blacks realized that a fellow Mende had arrived. The noise had probably caused the marshal to claim mistakenly that what Covey had told him then was different from what was repeated in court. Gibbs testified that Covey had said nothing about Cinqué's having traded in slaves. Willcox thought he was sure that what he had testified before came from Cinqué, not from Grabeau, although he admitted that there was confusion in the room. Colonel Stanton Pendleton, the jailer, said that when Cinqué was asked how he was taken, he replied that he had owed a debt and paid it with two Africans and promises of clothes. But one of the Africans escaped, and since Cinqué could not pay for him, he was taken in lieu of the debt.[36]

To add another side to the story, Antonio underwent a long examination with a Brazilian as interpreter. Cinqué and the others boarded the *Amistad* at night, Antonio testified, six days after its arrival in Havana. There was plenty of food and drink on the vessel. No African was killed—contrary to what the Africans said about the captain's killing one of them in the scuffle. Cinqué, Antonio declared, killed the captain by a machete blow to the forehead; the cook had already been dead about a quarter of an hour. The mutineers threw the captain overboard, but only after Cinqué took his watch. Antonio could not understand why the cook told them that they would be eaten. Cinqué, Burnah, and Grabeau took command after the revolt. When Cinqué threatened the lives of Ruiz, Montes, and Antonio himself, Burnah stopped him, only to have Cinqué angrily turn his knife on him. Antonio explained that Cinqué had tied him to the anchor but that Burnah had turned him loose. Cinqué also whipped Burnah for stealing water. According to Antonio, Burnah talked a lot with Montes, and since Cinqué knew Burnah wanted to return to Havana, he was afraid that Burnah and Montes would do so. When some of the blacks threatened to kill Montes, Burnah declared, "No, no; kill man no good."[37]

In the cross-examination of Antonio, it became apparent that his testimony actually hurt the prosecution's case because he contra-

dicted his previous stories. During the inquiry immediately following the *Amistad*'s arrival in New London, Antonio had told Judson
that Cinqué had led the way in killing the captain. During a private
examination in New Haven, he had declared that Cinqué "did not
kill anybody." Then, before the circuit court in Hartford, Antonio
claimed that he did not know who killed the captain. Also in Hartford, he had said that the blacks boarded the *Amistad* at 4:00 P.M.
Now, in district court, he reversed everything.[38] Antonio clearly
intended to say what seemed advantageous to him at the moment;
with the American and Spanish governments apparently aligned,
he provided testimony they most wanted to hear. His efforts, however, had promoted the case for the defense.

On January 10, the fourth day of the trial, Holabird attempted
to discredit Madden's testimony by reading Vega's statement. The
Spanish consul had lived in Cuba for several years and was well
acquainted with its laws on slavery. He claimed "there was no law,
that was considered in force in the island of Cuba, that prohibited
the bringing in [of] African slaves." The mixed commission had
no jurisdiction except in captures at sea, meaning that "newly
imported African negroes were constantly brought to the Island."
After their arrival, they were "bona fide transferred from one
owner to another without any interference by the local authorities
or the mixed commission." Spanish law condoned slavery, making
these blacks "lawful property." Contrary to Madden's testimony,
the slaves maintained their native language on the plantations for
years. All kinds of slaves were sold at the barracoons, which were
public markets. The *Amistad*'s papers were "genuine, and . . . in
the usual form." Indeed, Vega declared, it was not necessary to
engage in fraud to secure such papers from government officials.
None of the papers carried the signature of Martínez and Company, as Madden claimed. Martínez did not even hold the office
where one of them originated.[39]

The irony is that Vega's statement actually confirmed Madden's
testimony: though laws against the slave trade were on the books,
officials in Madrid and in Havana did not attempt to enforce them.
First, the Spanish law of 1817, reinforced by royal decree of 1838,
prohibited the African slave trade and declared that illegally
imported slaves became automatically free upon reaching any
Spanish dominion. The problem was that, as both Vega and Madden recognized, hardly anyone on the island considered this law
in force. Second, Madden had emphasized what was clear to all
observers: the major flaw in the mixed commission was that its

jurisdiction ceased once slavers made it to Cuban shores. There were no Spanish laws prohibiting *slavery* in Cuba, which meant that blacks who had been slaves before 1820 (along with their descendants) remained slaves. Such a system guaranteed trouble— *if* the island's authorities enforced the laws and freed illegally imported slaves. Not surprisingly, the captain general and other officials recognized the potential disaster in creating a large class of frcc blacks living alongside black slaves, and they refused to enforce the laws. Vega was correct that papers on the *Amistad* were "genuine" and "in the usual form"; but this was not to say that the papers were legal, and it by no means excused the system operating in Cuba. For government officials to ignore the wrong did not remove its existence. In reality, Vega affirmed Madden's observations and pronounced judgment on these same officials when he emphasized that it was not necessary to engage in fraud to procure such papers. Madden testified to the illegalities that permeated the entire system. Vega, in refusing to admit to illegalities, confirmed them.

The case was moving toward a conclusion as the attorneys reiterated their arguments, trying to bring the major points into focus. While the *Grampus* lay ominously in New London harbor, the court proceedings continued into the evening and consumed nearly all of the following Saturday. For the most part, one could predict what each attorney would say before he spoke. At one point, however, Isham expressed pent-up anger that Gedney and his associates had been accused of wanting salvage for "human flesh," and added that they had been subjected to unjustified "insinuations and taunts." In a statement that contradicted the claim he had filed in circuit court during September 1839, he declared that if observers would read the claims for salvage, they would find that his clients sought salvage only for the *Amistad* and its cargo. Indeed, he was now sorry that Gedney had come across the schooner; "overwhelming sympathy" for the blacks had caused the "sufferings" of Ruiz and Montes to be "altogether lost sight of." His clients had no desire to see the blacks in bondage. In a statement that raises questions about how Isham could differentiate between the ship's "cargo" and the blacks on board, he declared that they were property according to Spanish laws and customs and that the United States government should surrender them to the Spanish minister.[40] If the blacks were property, Gedney's claim to salvage, or so it would seem, would include all merchandise on board the *Amistad*. The institution of slavery had certainly led contemporaries to adopt convoluted legal and moral positions.

Afterward Judson adjourned the session, noting that he hoped to have a decision on Monday.[41]

III

Monday morning, January 13, before the packed courtroom, Judson opened the proceedings by first denying the defense counsel's attempt to secure a plea in abatement: the district court had jurisdiction because Gedney's seizure of the *Amistad* had taken place on the high seas. According to the New York *Commercial Advertiser*, Judson decreed that the vessel had been found where the tide "ebbs and flows," less than half a mile off Culloden Point. The law stated that if a claimant seized a ship on the high seas, adjudication could take place in any district court but must come to trial where he first brought it in. The court accepted the definition of "high seas" found in Daniel Webster's argument of 1818 before the Supreme Court in *U.S.* v. *Bevans*: the "open ocean, where the dominion of the winds and the waves prevails without check or control." Ports and harbors were "places of refuge" protected from the open ocean by "inclosures and projections of the land." The seizure did not occur in any harbor, port, bay, or river. "There is scarcely an indentation on the coast between Montauk and Culloden Point," observed the New York newspaper. The distance from shore was not crucial. Despite the assertion that the blacks were ashore at the time of seizure and could not be subject to admiralty court jurisdiction, the judge ruled that since their "specific" and "temporary object" had been to seek water and provisions, they were still "attached" to the *Amistad*. The court had jurisdiction.[42]

Now turning to the salvage question, Judson dismissed the claims presented by Green and his companions. Their argument, he explained, had rested on the erroneous assertion that they had taken possession of the *Amistad*. The claimants had indeed traded with some blacks found ashore and had agreed to "take the vessel to *their* place." But this was *Green*'s understanding, Judson emphasized, not that of the blacks; they wanted to go to Sierra Leone. The white men's "*actions*" showed that they realized the blacks wanted only to go to Sierra Leone. Green and his friends were never on the *Amistad*, and they had not rendered a "meritorious service." There was no basis for salvage.[43]

Judson, however, decided in favor of Gedney and associates as well as of the two Spanish owners of the cargo on the *Amistad*. On the bases of "meritorious" and "highly praiseworthy" services, he awarded salvage to Gedney on vessel and cargo, the latter referring only to the inanimate objects aboard. The *Amistad* was "at the mercy of the winds and waves," and it was in the hands of blacks who knew nothing of navigation and were on the point of leaving for Africa without hope of getting there safely. For saving the goods from total loss, Gedney and his associates would receive a "reasonable rate" of one-third the appraised value of vessel and cargo. Judson upheld the cargo claims presented by the two Spaniards at the same rate. The *Amistad* and its goods were to be restored to the Spanish government, subject to lien for salvage and costs.[44]

Judson proceeded with his ruling on the blacks. They "were born free," he asserted, "and ever since have been and still of right are free and not slaves." Judson's gaunt and drawn face betrayed inner tension as he handed down a verdict foreshadowed by his statement before the court on January 8—a verdict the White House could not have liked and probably did not expect. The captives had "never domiciled" in Cuba or in Spanish territory, but were "severally kidnapped" in violation of "their own rights and of the laws of Spain." In Cuba they were "unlawfully sold as slaves." They had revolted out of "desire of winning their liberty and of returning to their families and kindred." At the time of their importation into Cuba, Judson noted with increasing certitude and calm, a Spanish law of December 1817 prohibited such practice. On the question of murder and piracy, he ruled that the homicide took place on a schooner that belonged to a Spaniard, sailed under a Spanish flag, and was commanded by a Spanish subject. No American court could have jurisdiction in the case. Only Spanish law could deal with it.[45]

Judson had dismissed the property claims by Ruiz and Montes, as well as those presented by the United States district attorney on behalf of the Spanish minister. For Ruiz and Montes to demand restoration of property, the judge continued, they had to have lawful title to that property. If property and title proved to be in Spanish subjects, Pinckney's Treaty was applicable, and the property had to be surrendered. The burden of proof lay with the Spaniards. But what evidence had they sent? "A deed—a bill of sale—a transfer? No. It is a permit—a license—a pass"—signed by the captain general of Cuba. The blacks, Judson emphasized, were *bozales*, not *ladinos*. "Here then is the point," he said, "the point upon which this great controversy *must* turn!" The laws of Spain were vital to the case and in court were "matters of fact." The Spanish law of 1817 forbade the importation of blacks from Africa. The *Amistad* blacks entered Cuba in violation of this law and had to go free by that same law. Judson had no doubt about the law. It explained why the Spanish consul asserted that if the blacks were returned to Cuba, some of the leaders were subject to punishment, but that none could become slaves. The objective of returning the blacks to Cuba, Judson noted, would be to have *bozales* come to trial to determine whether they were slaves under Spanish law. Since Spanish law made it clear that the blacks were *not bozales*, Judson explained, it would serve no purpose to send them back to Cuba: "If by *their* own laws, they cannot enslave them, then it follows of necessity, they cannot be demanded." Finally, on the charge of murder, Judson likewise refused to return the captives to Cuba, because they had revolted against illegal bondage only out of "desire of winning their liberty and returning to their families and kindred."[46]

How could one explain the apparent failure of Ruiz and Montes to realize that the blacks were *bozales*? Judson declared that the captain general's pass contained, "on its face, an untruth," because it did not "truly describe" the blacks who were shipped. Thus the alleged seller had no title. Judson explained that in Cuba it was the custom—a "practice against law"—to buy such blacks and ship them as *ladinos* or *creoles*. But one had to assume that subjects of a foreign government knew their own nation's laws; they could not come to the United States asking it to violate the rights of others, "in justification of the breach of their own laws." Poor execution of a law, either in Spain or the United States, Judson asserted, "is no evidence that the law does not exist." Ruiz's only remedy was to find the man who took the $20,000 from him. Had he and Montes been more vigilant, Judson remarked with pent-up irritation, "this Court might have been relieved from this heavy responsibility, which has been pressing it down for these four months."[47]

In response to the question everyone wanted to ask, Judson ruled that, in accord with the congressional law of March 1819, he would place the captives under charge of the president of the United States, who would arrange their passage home to Africa. Judson explained his decision. The law declared that "it shall not be lawful to *import or bring*, IN ANY MANNER WHATEVER [Judson's emphases], into the U. States or territories thereof, any negro, mulatto or person of color, with intent to hold any such negro as a slave, or to hold to service or labor any such person." If such importation occurred, the same law authorized the president to remove from the United States to Africa "all such negroes, mulattoes, or persons of color, as may be delivered and brought within their jurisdiction." The court, Judson indicated, had to determine whether in leaving Cuba the blacks had been brought into the United States with the intent to "*hold to service*" or "*to hold as slaves.*" It seemed clear that Ruiz and Montes had put the blacks onto the *Amistad* to hold as slaves and to service and that their plans had continued to the time of the mutiny. Perhaps these intentions were "suspended" when they lost control over the blacks, Judson allowed, but evidence showed that as soon as Gedney appeared, the Spaniards resumed their original aims. The act of 1819, Judson pointed out, made it unlawful "to import or bring in any manner whatsoever, into the U.S. from any foreign country any negro, with intent to hold him as a slave." The "broad language" of the act made it illegal to bring in a negro with the purpose to "hold to service, any where, and in any place." The blacks were returnable by the president under the law.[48]

Judson had stretched the law of 1819 nearly beyond recognition. Ruiz and Montes never intended to import the blacks into the United States, which made it irrelevant to discuss whether their purpose was enslavement or service. Furthermore, when the *Amistad* arrived in New York, it was under command of the blacks; their objective, of course, was to *escape* any efforts to hold them as slaves or for service. Judson's other comments about the intended humanity of the law of 1819 only partly explained his purpose: as he would repeatedly emphasize afterward, he was concerned about satisfying the blacks' wishes to return home. This may have been so. But Judson was also concerned about placating the White House. He had not decreed the blacks' return to Cuba, as the administration wanted, but he might console the president, and the American public, by choosing the second option suggested by Holabird in circuit court—that of authorizing Van Buren to send them to Africa. Indeed, the move might enhance the president's image— and on the eve of a presidential campaign. Perhaps for these reasons, Judson thought his strained interpretation of the law of 1819 would either go unnoticed or at least not meet serious objection.[49]

Practical considerations also affected Judson's ruling. Had he accepted the prosecution's argument that the blacks were slaves, he would have faced, he realized, the problem that neither federal nor Connecticut state laws authorized their sale or granting of title.

Furthermore, as he had pointed out before the start of circuit court proceedings in September 1839, Connecticut law said nothing about determining the values of slaves, which meant that there was no basis for allowing an appraisal and appointing appraisers, or for making an estimate. Nor could Judson accept an appraisal made elsewhere. A court decree, he reminded listeners, assumed having the power to enforce it.[50]

Judson's decision astounded the defense attorneys, for he had accepted their argument that the *Amistad* blacks were free—albeit with the stipulation that they were to return to Africa under presidential supervision. The rumor was that the abolitionists had been so certain about a verdict surrendering the captives to Spain that they had arranged for a vessel belonging to the underground railroad to be in New Haven harbor to spirit the blacks to Canada after the court ruling. Years afterward the New Haven *Journal & Courier* asserted that members of the *Amistad* Committee had either made those escape arrangements or had worked with Nathaniel Jocelyn, brother of the committee member Simeon Jocelyn.[51] Such dramatic steps proved unnecessary in light of the court decision.

There was another part of the decision, scarcely noticed at the time. Judson ruled for the delivery of Antonio to his owners in Cuba, which, as the New York *Commercial Advertiser* observed, was an illustration of his reasoning *not* to return the others on the vessel. In the circuit court case of *La Jeune Eugénie*, Judson showed, Justice Joseph Story in 1822 authorized a surrender of slaves because the French claimants established their legal right of ownership to property. And by the *Antelope* decision of 1825, he added, Chief Justice John Marshall of the Supreme Court declared that the slave trade was in harmony with international law and that the claimant in the case only had to prove title to his property. At the time of Captain Ferrer's death, Antonio was his legal slave—a *creole*. Judson therefore decreed that he was returnable as property under Pinckney's Treaty.[52] The Van Buren administration had won a major victory in establishing that foreign slaves could expect no asylum in the United States. Yet this part of Judson's decision attracted little attention amid the excitement over the other issues.

To conclude that the abolitionists had won the case would be misleading. They had hoped for a decision setting the blacks unequivocally free; the announcement of freedom had stipulated the blacks' return to Africa. That the blacks *preferred* to go home was not the point; to demonstrate the indivisibility of freedom, the abolitionists wanted that decision to belong exclusively to the blacks.[53] In no way had the judge conceded that blacks were persons enjoying the same rights as white people. Furthermore, the decision to authorize the president to send the blacks to Africa under the law of 1819 left the erroneous impression that they had been imported into the United States for either "service or labor." The captives were in command of both the vessel and the Spaniards when they arrived off Long Island; there was no justification for implying that they were slaves illegally brought into the United States. The abolitionists also feared that the blacks might not reach Africa—they did not trust Van Buren—and even if they did, the threat still existed that another slave trader would take advantage of their plight to kidnap them again. In addition, Judson's decision had not disturbed the institution of slavery. Its principles were intact. Judson had made no suggestion that slaves possessed rights as persons; rather, he conceded that Antonio was property, returnable to owners under the treaty of 1795. Finally, the judge's decision had no bearing on the question of citizenship for free blacks: he had not defined their freedom as indivisible.

For abolitionists the outcome in New Haven was nonetheless a small step forward in a long struggle that would consume much more time and many more court cases. Though the Boston *Liberator* expressed great pleasure over the captives' imminent freedom, few abolitionists agreed with the New York *Commercial Advertiser* that the decision was "lucid, able and most righteous," and that it did "honor" to Judson by comprising "a judgment of mercy to the unfortunate and the oppressed." Nor would many of them have accepted the comment by the New York *Evening Post* that Judson's opinion had demonstrated the absence of conflict between America's laws and the "great principles of justice." The Reverend Henry G. Ludlow of New Haven was an exception. Though an abolitionist, he praised Judson's "masterly manner" and "enlightened head and a warm heart" and declared that the decision had "immortalized his name." Sedgwick, however, wrote Baldwin with great satisfaction that the district judge was a "singed cat" and believed that they "should make no attempt to disturb" the decision. Staples agreed and thought that they should oppose an appeal.[54]

Sedgwick assumed that Tappan was fully satisfied with the court decision, but this was not accurate. Tappan admitted that he was willing to drop the *Amistad* matter; the blacks had suffered enough and deserved to go home. He realized that Judson had twisted the congressional act of 1819 in justifying his decision, but he also recognized that the judge had been in an awkward position and had to find an escape that offered some satisfaction to all parties. In attempting to "steer between" slavery and freedom, Tappan noted, Judson had succeeded. Tappan was not prepared to push an appeal—as long as the other parties were also willing to drop the case. But, he warned, if the prosecution filed an appeal, he and the other abolitionists would rejoin the battle even if it ultimately went before the United States Supreme Court.[55]

Amid their immediate elation over Judson's decision, the abolitionists suddenly learned that their battle over the *Amistad* was not over: the United States district attorney had filed an appeal. The *Grampus* had departed New London, its Cuban mission aborted, but orders were under way to Holabird from President Van Buren, with the full approbation of the Spanish minister, to move an appeal to the next circuit court meeting in April 1840 on two counts: that part of the district court decision relating to the blacks, and that relating to the granting of salvage on vessel and cargo. And this was not all. The Spanish owners of the cargo on the schooner appealed Judson's award of salvage on their goods.[56] These moves virtually guaranteed an appeal to the Supreme Court, for Judge Smith Thompson, the one who had denied the writ of habeas corpus in the original trial in Hartford, was the circuit court judge who would sit with the district judge, Judson again, in considering the appeals. The overwhelming probability was that they would approve the district court decision and thus bring on an appeal to the Supreme Court under Chief Justice Roger B. Taney. Five members of the Court, including the chief justice himself, were Southerners who had at one time or another owned slaves. Tappan and Baldwin asked for the captives' release on bail, but Judson, perhaps fearing an effort to steal them away to Canada, must have felt relieved when the abolitionists dropped their request upon his ruling that, to set the amount, authorities must first appraise the value of the blacks on the Cuban market. To accept this stipulation was tantamount to defining the captives' status as slaves. Prospects for a favorable outcome seemed worse now than in the dark days following Thompson's initial ruling of September 1839.

8

The Politics of Democracy

In the period following the district court trial, the abolitionists' distrust of the administration in Washington deepened as rumors spread that the president planned to interfere. Van Buren, according to his critics, was concerned only with the coming political campaign of 1840 and would resort to any measure to make sure the *Amistad* affair did not embarrass his chances for reelection. There were growing charges of executive pressure on judges, of collusion between the United States and Spain to return the blacks to Cuba, and of State Department tampering with documents relating to the case. The validity of the accusations remains questionable, but from a historical perspective, and certainly to those Americans directly involved in the matter, the events and suspicions often coincided, leaving a pattern of executive behavior that approached and sometimes crossed the bounds of legality.

I

Abolitionists were convinced that the executive office would interfere with the *Amistad* case, especially after Judson's decision. Lewis Tappan believed that Van Buren had already done so by directing the United States district attorney to represent the Spanish minister. Seth Staples had heard of "no movements" concerning the blacks since his arrival in New York, but on the morning of his departure from New London he saw an American sloop of war in the harbor. Indeed, Staples had seen the *Grampus,* whose commander had been there to take the blacks to Cuba but had then received orders after the adverse court decision to resume slave-patrol duties off the west African coast. Moreover, a "gentleman" had told Staples that the president's son, John Van Buren, had expressed "great dissatisfaction" with the district court decision in that the matter had a "great & important political bearing of which Judson had taken no notice." John used "strong terms of disapprobation" in referring to Judson's opinion.[1]

Suspicion would not abate. The Hartford *Patriot and Democrat,* a Whig paper, claimed that before the district court convened in New Haven, the president had sent a letter to the judge, urging him to transport the blacks in a government vessel to Havana, where they would be sold as slaves. It also claimed that the *Grampus* had orders to be on hand to receive them. Such a letter, according to the paper, was a "flagrant interference of the Executive with the Judiciary." The New Haven *Herald* did not know whether the story was accurate, but it noted that the *Grampus* had been in the harbor on a "mysterious errand." If the accusations were true, the paper remarked, this was executive interference with the judiciary that savored of Turkish democracy.[2] Whether Van Buren sent a letter remains uncertain, but the presence of an American naval vessel in the dangerous, ice-laden waters off Connecticut, especially of one diverted from important duties in Africa, was proof of administration involvement. The New York *Commercial Advertiser* doubted the story, declaring that Van Buren was "too old a fox" to commit himself to that kind of venture.[3] Yet it seemed reasonable to believe that Judson was under heavy indirect and possibly even direct pressure from the White House to render a politically favorable decision.

Months afterward, in June 1840, the New York *Express* fed the rumors of executive involvement in the case. Reports had circulated that despite Judson's decision, the president intended to deliver the blacks to Spanish officials in Cuba. Evidence in "documents," the paper charged without referring to any in particular, showed that Van Buren wanted to do this, even though it meant "certain death" for the blacks. The paper remarked that any man who would interfere with the course of justice was not fit for the presidency of a "free republic."[4]

By late June the abolitionists had seen to it that the charges of presidential interference reached London. Before the British and Foreign Anti-Slavery Society, the Reverend Cyrus P. Grosvenor of Massachusetts offered a resolution expressing "regret and astonishment" at his government's action. The "interference of the National Executive" was promoting the oppression of the blacks by seeking to deliver them to "unjust claimants, and thus reducing them to absolute and perpetual slavery." Grosvenor wanted the British government to "remonstrate with that of the United States" on the matter. Henry B. Stanton of New York City remarked before the convention that the British minister in the United States, Henry S. Fox, could be doing more in the case.[5]

Though the abolitionists wanted the British government to take an active role in the *Amistad* affair, this was not likely to occur. The case was not a subject for Anglo-American affairs; on the international front, it belonged to the United States and Spain. For this reason, the *Amistad* was not mentioned in either the diplomatic instructions of the Department of State or the dispatches from American ministers to England during the entire period. British interest in suppressing the slave trade, of course, could justify official statements of concern over how the outcome might affect the illegal traffic; but the case could not reach the diplomatic level unless something occurred that directly affected the relationship between the United States and England. Given the numerous existing problems between the Atlantic nations, neither wanted to see another one develop.[6]

And yet, Americans were concerned about British aims in Cuba. As Secretary of State Forsyth explained to the American chargé in Madrid, Aaron Vail, the United States was interested in the island's welfare. Trade, geographical proximity, slavery—these and other factors made Cuba increasingly important to American security, and made Forsyth worry about British "designs" on the island. Forsyth instructed Vail to use "tact and delicacy" in warning the Spanish government against providing "pretexts" for British actions in Cuba. Despite the Anglo-Spanish treaty of 1817 prohibiting the African slave trade, the traffic went on "notorious and undisguised." If England objected to the lack of enforcement of the treaty, Forsyth noted, it might make territorial claims on Cuba or try other means to gain influence. The United States, the secretary insisted, had a "fixed resolution" against British involvement in Cuba. He warned Vail not to put in writing any communications to the Spanish ministry on this matter, but to handle it through "informal and confidential conversations" with government officials. If Vail detected any Spanish willingness to give Cuba to the British or to any power, either temporarily or permanently, he was to warn Madrid that the United States would oppose such a move "at all hazard"—including a resort to "military and naval resources." Forsyth wanted the Spanish government to avoid giving England any "real motive" for the "remotest pretense for interference" in Cuban affairs. Madrid should therefore adhere to a "scrupulous performance" of treaty obligations.[7]

Whether England would have intervened in Cuba because of the *Amistad* affair is a matter for speculation, but it appears that ministry officials seriously considered the possibility of placing some sort of diplomatic or naval pressure on Spain. The *Times* of London, which spoke for the British government, referred to the mutiny as "justifiable homicide" and argued that the blacks had become free upon entering Spanish territory. The slave-trade treaty, the paper complained, was "scandalously evaded, and not covertly, but clearly with knowledge and through connivance of the authorities, in the transatlantic dominions of Spain." The British and Foreign Anti-Slavery Society in London exerted pressure on the government to intercede on behalf of the blacks. Madden informed British minister Fox in Washington that Vega had argued that the Anglo-Spanish treaties against the slave trade contradicted the laws of the Indies sanctioning the traffic and were harmful to the Cuban people's interests. The treaties with England, according to Vega's interpretation, "were of no avail, & being of no effect they were invalid."[8]

Fox reinforced growing suspicions in London by notifying Foreign Secretary Lord Palmerston that the charges against Spanish officials were true. The *Amistad* blacks had been "illicitly imported" into Havana, and the Spaniards had held them "feloniously and piratically" in bondage on the schooner. Though they should be free in a "moral sense," the case was complicated in the eyes of the law. Fox did not consider it "proper" or practical to interfere at this point, for he thought that public favor in the United States would bring their freedom. But if he detected a "design" on the part of the Van Buren administration to interfere with the judicial process, he would make a "formal protest" that such an act was a violation of the laws of Spain and of the Anglo-Spanish treaties against the slave trade. Palmerston agreed with Fox and directed him only to use his "good offices" in securing the blacks' liberty. But Palmerston meanwhile instructed the British minister in Madrid to urge the Spanish government to order Cuban authorities to grant the blacks their "undeniable title" to liberty if the United States complied with the Spanish minister's demands. Palmerston also wanted island officials to enforce the law against Ruiz and Montes for violating the slave-trade laws by buying newly imported blacks in Havana. Had Palmerston's diplomatic efforts failed, he would have had the choice of either resorting to economic pressure or backing down. The latter alternative, of course, would have been out of the question. In a policy illustrating the influence of the abolitionists in England, Palmerston kept the British and Foreign Anti-Slavery Society informed of these actions.[9]

If Forsyth was correct in believing that the British might cite Spain's failure to enforce the treaties as a pretext for intervention in Cuba, Palmerston had taken the first step in that direction. By the autumn of 1840, Britain had increased its requests that the government in Madrid prosecute Ruiz and Montes in Cuba. Indeed, parliamentary papers published that same year in England show that the government in London demanded the blacks' freedom in the event that the American courts decreed their surrender to Spain.[10] Had this public demand gone unanswered in Madrid and the blacks faced trial and probable execution, the British government, it seems likely, would have resorted to more-stringent measures—perhaps even a naval blockade.

Ironically, the Van Buren administration had contributed to this situation. British intervention in Cuba was more likely if the Supreme Court awarded the blacks to the Spanish minister for delivery to Cuba; if island authorities refused to free them or to arrange to execute them, public reaction in England might force its government to intervene. Had the White House accepted the district court decision and facilitated the blacks' transportation to Africa, the action would have confirmed their status as free men and showed Spain's violation of treaties, but their lives would have been spared and the threat of British intervention in Cuba would have markedly declined. The administration's appeal to the Supreme Court had kept alive the chances for British intervention.

II

During the spring Minister Argaiz in Washington resumed his protests. He had earlier called Judson's decision a "scandalous resolution" not deserving comment. Only Spanish courts had jurisdiction in the *Amistad* case, he now argued, and Judson had not ruled on the basis of international law and precedents between Spain and the United States. Instead, he had decided on the basis of cargo. There was no treaty or convention between the nations that authorized inquiries into the nature of the blacks' condition aboard. If they were *bozales,* the Spaniards broke Spanish law and were not subject to American law. The following month Argaiz referred to a report by the Senate Committee on Foreign Relations (cited earlier) in repeating his argument that vessels on a lawful voyage remained under their home government's jurisdiction. John C. Calhoun's resolution, unanimously approved by the Senate in mid-April, declared that a ship on the high seas, in peacetime and on a "lawful voyage," was, by the law of nations, under the sole jurisdiction of its own country. If any uncontrollable factor forced the vessel into a foreign port, the resolution continued, it and all items aboard remained under the law of nations. This was part of the "principles of equity," Argaiz observed.[11]

Forsyth soon responded that the president had not changed his position in regard to returning the schooner and its cargo to Spain. But the secretary of state reminded Argaiz that while the case was pending, his department could take no steps contrary to the verdict of the lower courts.[12]

Abolitionists realized that an appeal to the circuit court was tantamount to an appeal to the Supreme Court and that, to avoid further suffering for the blacks, it would be better to accept the district court's decision. In late January 1840 Tappan intended to convince the president that returning the blacks to Africa would be wise. He remarked to Baldwin, "I was attempting a negotiation with the President & promised to relieve the courts & the Executive from further trouble if he would send the Africans to Sierra Leone." But the same day Tappan wrote this letter, he received a letter from a friend in Washington who told him that the president had already directed an appeal to the circuit court. According to Tappan's informant, the president seemed "altogether willing" to accept the decision of the district judge but feared that "it would not do" to approve the "erroneous principles" contained in that decree.[13]

Van Buren's reference to legality may have been genuine, and it was clearly legitimate, but it seems safe to conclude that politics had again made the difference. Whether the "erroneous principles" were a reference to Judson's misuse of the law of 1819 or to other matters relating to slavery and the treaty with Spain, the president was within his rights in lodging an appeal. In late March the secretary of the navy asked whether it was proper to use funds allotted to the 1819 act against the slave trade in meeting the expenses of removing the *Amistad* blacks, and the attorney general, Henry D. Gilpin, replied that the act did *not* apply. Furthermore, although Judson's decision would rid the country of the *Amistad* captives, the bitter reality was that their return to Africa constituted American approval of mutiny as an escape from slavery. It is impossible to be sure of the guiding principle in Van Buren's thinking, for his *Autobiography* does not mention the *Amistad* affair and his private papers provide little help. But it seems a reasonable conclusion that Van Buren wanted to satisfy the South and proslavery elements in his political party and that circumstances and his general attitude toward a North-South coalition of planters and plain Republicans, as he called them, shaped his policy toward the *Amistad.* It is certain that the case had become a national issue, as the abolitionists had wanted, and that if the president sent the blacks home without punishment for what Southerners and other Americans considered piracy and murder, this would have been tacit approval of slave insurrection.[14] The politically advantageous approach—again dignified by a White House explanation that it sought only to obey the law—was to turn to the Supreme Court, whose Southern preponderance offered more than a faint hope of negating the lower courts' decision.

Once the White House made known its appeal to the circuit court, the blacks' defense attorneys introduced a motion in early April calling for dismissal of the appeal. The United States, Staples and Baldwin insisted, did not claim "any interest in the said appellees respectively, or either of them," and had no right under the law of nations, the Constitution, or American laws to institute claims to property in behalf of the Spanish government. The United States could not enforce the claims of subjects of other countries.[15]

In early May, Judge Thompson, sitting on circuit court with District Judge Judson, refused the defense attorneys' motion and affirmed the district court decision *"pro forma"*: the *Amistad* case would go before the Supreme Court during its January term of 1841. Tappan had not been confident of dismissal. He later wrote John Scoble in London that Thompson had advised counsel to keep its arguments short to prevent any delay in forwarding the case to the higher court. Tappan noted with consolation, however, that had Thompson dismissed the appeal, the district attorney would have appealed that decision to the Supreme Court. If the Court decided that Thompson's decision was wrong, it would remand the case for further examination. The ensuing process would take perhaps two years. The *Amistad* matter now stood between two governments, Thompson explained, a proper subject for the highest tribunal in the land.[16]

The abolitionists finally recognized the futility of fighting the government's appeal to the Supreme Court and worked toward better conditions for the captives in the interim. Staples expressed concern about the summer confinement of the blacks, and he asked Thompson whether the children, at least, should be out on bail. But the judge replied, "They are not now before me at all. The appeal is not before the Circuit Court." If any different arrangement proved necessary, Thompson said, it had to result from an agreement between the Spanish minister and the United States government. He could not permit bail, because it was a "singular case" beset with great difficulties. Thompson did allow, however, that the blacks were in the law's custody and that the court could put them in a more comfortable place if the defense could establish that they had been "cruelly treated." But this was not enough for Staples. If they were Frenchmen, he asked, would the judge permit bail? "Certainly," Thompson replied, "they would be released under the habeas corpus." But the laws of the United States did not allow the Africans to "stand in that point of view." *Color* was the difference, he seemed to imply. In a statement illustrating the unenviable position Thompson was in, he underlined the point that American law took precedence over questions of morality: "I say again, as I have said a hundred times, that however repugnant slavery may be, sitting here as a Judge, I must recognize that the laws of this country do admit the right of property in men."[17]

After Thompson refused to release the blacks on bail, defense counsel asked the court to relocate the children in private homes. According to counsel, the four youths had expressed an interest in this change. Respectable families in New Haven, the attorneys explained, were willing to take them and instruct them in education, morals, and manners. But the judge was satisfied with the jailer's assurance that the children were not undergoing hardship. It would not "hurt them to remain as they were till January next."[18]

III

Baldwin had meanwhile become more suspicious of the White House's intentions after receiving no cooperation in his effort to secure documents relating to the case. When he had first cited Spanish laws and treaties in arguing that his clients were not slaves, the United States district attorney demanded that the court admit only authenticated copies of the documents. Baldwin had asked the White House for copies from State Department files, but Forsyth replied that the papers were missing, leading Baldwin to believe that the administration was engaged in a concerted effort to undercut the defense by denying essential evidence. The controversy over documents soon took a more serious turn when nonabolitionists joined Baldwin and friends in believing that the Van Buren administration had altered documents to substantiate its case.[19]

Baldwin had written Representative William L. Storrs of Connecticut, outlining the defense counsels' difficulty in getting authentic copies of documents that the attorney general had wanted during the district court proceedings—the treaty of 1817 and the royal decree of 1838. Thinking that the same situation could arise in circuit court, Baldwin had written Forsyth for documents from State Department files on the issue during the Adams-Onís negotiations of 1819. To Baldwin's surprise, Forsyth replied that neither the copy of the treaty sent by Lord Castlereagh nor that sent by Luis de Onís was in the files. Baldwin wrote the president, asking him either to direct the district attorney to admit the documents referred to as authentic evidence or to accept the Spanish government's offer to put relevant documents into the State Department files. But even though Baldwin had written this letter early in April, the district attorney stated in circuit court on April 29 that he had received no instructions from the president. Moreover, Baldwin was aware of no effort to have documents placed in State Department files. Baldwin explained to Storrs that the only way to secure the documents was to enlist the aid of the House of Representatives. Baldwin said that he would consider it a "favor" if Storrs showed this letter to John Quincy Adams, who had been secretary of state during the negotiations with Onís. Baldwin hoped that Adams would inquire whether these documents, "which it [seemed had] been withdrawn from the Department of State," might not be among the files of other departments in Washington.[20]

In late April, Tappan wrote Baldwin that it was "very singular" that documents relating to foreign affairs were not on file in the office of the secretary of state. Baldwin, Sedgwick, and Staples had recently inquired about seeing the Anglo-Spanish Treaty of 1817, hoping to prove that Spain had prohibited the slave trade. Forsyth had replied to all three attorneys that no copy was on file. Tappan wrote his brother Benjamin, a United States senator from Ohio, asking him to see the president about the matter. Three days later Tappan wrote Baldwin again, saying that his brother saw the president, who wrote on the back of Lewis's letter an order to the secretary of state to provide copies of the desired documents—if Forsyth considered them genuine. But the secretary was gone from his office and would not be back for a couple of days. Tappan inferred from his brother's letter that the president's "dignity was a little hurt" by Baldwin's writing directly to him and not through the secretary of state or a "friend of the administration."[21]

While that controversy smoldered, Baldwin opened a new question when he informed Adams of an "important error" in the translation of a Spanish document contained in the papers on the *Amistad* recently sent by the president to the House of Representatives. He reminded Adams that the document described the blacks shipped by Ruiz and Montes as being *ladinos* and as having "names by which these Africans were never known, & which none of them recognize." And yet the district court had found the blacks to be *bozales* and the passports inaccurate. Now, in the translation sent to the House, Baldwin declared that *ladinos* was rendered *"sound negroes,"* which gave the word an "entirely different" meaning. It may have been an honest mistake in translation but was surely convenient for the administration's case. Put before the Supreme Court in this fashion, he noted, the issue concerning the blacks would become whether they had been sound or healthy when boarding the *Amistad*—not whether they were recent imports from Africa. On May 10 Adams confided to his diary that there had indeed been a "scandalous mistranslation" of the Spanish documents. Baldwin had been correct in drawing it to his attention, and Tappan had that day sent a letter repeating the charge. Within a short time, Adams pursued the matter further in Congress when he read a resolution against the detention and imprisonment of the *Amistad* blacks.[22]

In mid-June the matter reached the public when the New York *Express* accused the White House of having altered documents in the *Amistad* case. The original passport claimed that *ladinos* were to be shipped, and yet the district court had established that *bozales* were on board the schooner. In a packet of documents sent by the president to Congress, House Document 185, the word *negroes* was not in the original passport found in the district clerk's office. Instead of *negroes ladinos,* the words *sound negroes* had appeared—hiding the fact that *bozales* were shipped. "Who ever heard of such frauds perpetrated in governmental documents, transmitted to Congress by a President of the United States?" the *Express* asked. "There was no accident in this manner—it was a cunningly devised fraud."[23]

Adams's involvement in the case deepened when in early December the State Department's translator, Robert Greenhow, complained to him that Judge William Jay had accused him of an erroneous translation in Document 185 dealing with the *Amistad.* Jay had charged Greenhow with inserting the word *negroes* in the Spanish certificate, and Greenhow countered by insisting that the word *sound* in the printed document was not in the manuscript translation that he produced and sent to the House. Greenhow asked Adams to clear him of the charges.[24]

The following day, December 10, Adams brought the matter before the House and introduced a motion to establish a five-man committee to investigate whether Document 185 had been "falsified." He explained that he had found discrepancies between the manuscript of the document and its printed version. In the manuscript the word *ladino* had been inserted in the translations of both permits. Also, in the printed document the word *sound* had been substituted. In the document of April 15, 1840, he explained, there were two sets of papers: one certificate granted in Havana in the form of passports for forty-nine *negroes ladinos,* and a second for the three girls and calling them *negras ladinas.* But in the new document submitted by the president to the House, it read forty-nine "sound negroes." That was the translation presented to the House by its printer. "Sound negroes," Adams declared, was a "fraudulent translation."[25]

Adams referred to a paper in his hand containing Judge Jay's review of government proceedings in regard to Ruiz and Montes. Jay claimed that after the "Havana fraud," there was a new one— an "extraordinary falsification of papers, perpetrated, probably, in the Department of State." A passport for Africans imported prior to 1820 was, by "State necromancy, converted into a *bill of health* for forty-nine negroes." The legal presumption now, Jay declared, was that the term *ladino* meant an African slave imported before the slave trade was illegal. These permits were the only evidence that the *Amistad* blacks were slaves and could be the only justification for a government decision to surrender them. It was obviously important to twist the translation to conceal the central fraud of the Havana official. If the blacks were claimed as *ladinos,* Jay pointed out, there was sufficient evidence that they were *bozales.* But if the claim was to *"sound negroes,"* or healthy negroes, there was no proof that they had been unhealthy at the time the island officials issued the permits.[26]

Adams himself was appointed head of the congressional inquiry into what he feared was still another part of a conspiracy against the blacks. In his diary, he wrote of "deep anguish of heart" caused by the "abominable conspiracy, Executive and Judicial, of this Government, against the lives of those wretched men." He intended to carry the matter as far as facts would allow.[27]

But it soon became obvious that if the White House were culpable, the Adams committee would be unable to prove it. A short time before Christmas the proofreader for the printing house of Blair and Rives, John H. Trenholm, testified that *he* had ordered the compositor to make the change. He explained that when comparing the proof sheet with the manuscript, he had been unable to make out the word *ladino.* He thought that it was an English word and that *sound* seemed to fit best in terms of spacing and context. He did not know that *ladino* and *ladina* applied to black slaves, and he thought that their meaning was "sound." Moreover, he added, it was common practice for the proofreader to make necessary grammatical alterations. When asked whether he was aware of the administration's interest in the subject of the documents, Trenholm replied that he knew only what he had read in the newspapers. Thomas S. Geddes, the compositor at the printing house, testified that by Trenholm's direction he had substituted *sound* for *ladino* and *ladina.* Yet Greenhow, the State Department translator, insisted that *sound* could in no way be the correct translation.[28]

In preparing the committee's report, Adams encountered more obstacles in his attempt to prove fraud. To show his disapproval of proofreaders' altering public documents without authorization, he had wanted to include a statement that the proofreader had committed the falsification. But two Democratic members of the committee, James McKay from North Carolina and William Medill from Ohio, opposed any statements of censure. The only duty of the committee, they declared, was to present the facts. Adams felt frustrated with the restrictions and wrote a report declaring that the proofreader had committed a falsification, but he did not include a statement of censure. The committee, however, wanted statements absolving the proofreader of "bad intention," the house printers of responsibility, and the Van Buren administration of "all knowledge or participation in the wrong." After a lengthy, acrimonious session, the committee adjourned without indicating whether it approved the report. But on January 4 there passed in the House of Representatives a motion for printing the report as Adams had written it.[29]

Adams remained perplexed by the episode. He was convinced that the White House had interfered in the *Amistad* case before, and he was not sure of its innocence now. He realized that errors could be made in the copying of documents, and yet he found it difficult to believe that coincidence explained a mistranslation of words that altered the entire thrust of the documents in the administration's favor. It was too convenient. He vowed, however, to be more careful about "his own suspicions in the imputation of motives."[30]

<h1 style="text-align:center">IV</h1>

Throughout, the abolitionists had become increasingly concerned about their fourth and final confrontation with the Van Buren administration. Tappan had tried to bolster the abolitionists' hopes by referring to correspondence published in Washington and by remarking, "Even some of the friends of Mr. Van Buren say [the trial] is 'outrageous.'" Tappan said he was confident that public opinion would support "strong measures" for the blacks' "deliverance." And yet he revealed doubts when he wrote to John Scoble that the White House was "decidedly against these Africans" and would resort to any means to return them to Cuba. Baldwin wrote to Forsyth citing Thomas Jefferson as a precedent that the United States government had no power except by treaty to deliver anyone for punishment who had sought asylum in the country. Moreover, under the treaty of 1795 the executive could not surrender the blacks as property. According to the Constitution, Baldwin noted, "All cases in law or Equity, arising under the laws of the U.S. and *Treaties* made by their authority" belong to the judiciary. Surely the president would "not feel himself at liberty to interfere with" the "appropriate jurisdiction" of the court. The abolitionist Amos Townsend, Jr., expressed his concern to Tappan that the Supreme Court would prove unable to resist "the opinions & minds of men in power." To turn over the blacks to *"murderers,"* he added, would be a "violation of all right principles human & divine."[31]

Abolitionists feared that as the election of 1840 neared, the Van Buren administration would become more determined to secure a favorable outcome of the *Amistad* case. In late October the *National Anti-Slavery Standard* of New York criticized the president for politicizing the case. Van Buren wanted it to languish in the courts until after the election. In that way he would remain uncommitted in a question "so delicate in southern sensibilities."

It was a "base game," according to the paper. The blacks would be "disposed of" in the way most "popular and expedient" for the administration. "No other men, but Africans or colored men, would have been detained an hour."[32]

The abolitionists tried to keep the plight of the captives before the American public. The *Amistad* Committee asked the Reverend Leonard Bacon to deliver an address on the subject at New York's Broadway Tabernacle in May. Tappan wanted eight to ten of the "most intelligent" Africans there to read and sing. The purposes of the meeting were to raise money for the support and education of the blacks and "to awaken an interest in the community" in their returning home with "the gospel in their hands & hearts." The Connecticut *Observer* noted that the blacks were now in Westville, about two miles from New Haven, where they were reading and writing English, studying the New Testament, and becoming "civilized" and, it was hoped, "Christian men." Perhaps, the paper added, God had brought the *Amistad* blacks to the United States for Christians to make them His "most honored ambassadors to the dark continent of Africa." For those who could not travel to New Haven, Peale's Museum in New York had re-created the captives in wax, along with scenes of the mutiny. Boston's Amory Hall went a step farther: it had wax figures on display—with hair from the captives' heads.[33]

Not all the publicity was favorable. In New Haven there was exhibited a painting 135 feet long and entitled *The Massacre on Board the "Amistad."* The artist showed the captain with cuts on head and breast, down on one knee with head drooping and left arm hanging, while Konoma, or "the Cannibal," held the dying man's right wrist and with his other hand aimed a dagger at his heart. An abolitionist letter called the charge of cannibalism "supremely ridiculous," saying that Konoma had pointed his teeth *"to make the ladies love him."* The writer, probably Tappan, added that Konoma was the most "inoffensive, harmless, quiet, cowardly, submissive" of all these "creatures." Cinqué was "perhaps the most prominent character" in the painting. Armed with a cane knife, he was trying to free himself from other blacks who were preventing him from killing Ruiz and Montes. Fuliwa was near Cinqué, shown with a "countenance expressive of deep malignity—the index one would think of a heart joyous in deeds of darkness—looking with hellish satisfaction on the scene." Again, the letter claimed that Fuliwa was a "kind hearted man" who hated meanness, wrong, & blood" and wanted others to "do right." The painting was "most unjust."[34]

In mid-May the abolitionists' suspicions seemed confirmed: the *Liberator* reprinted an article from the New Haven *Herald* entitled "Extraordinary Proceedings," which revealed White House involvement in both the Ruiz episode in New York and the *Grampus* affair in Connecticut. Quoting from documents that the Van Buren administration released to the House of Representatives, the writer charged that the American public would "learn with astonishment" that, despite the district court ruling of January 1840 declaring the *Amistad* captives to be free blacks kidnapped in Africa, the president of the United States, "REPRESENTING THE AMERICAN PEOPLE," was offering aid to the alleged slaveowners. The United States was pledged to support the Treaty of Ghent promoting abolition of the slave trade, and yet the White House was "*volunteering* its aid in behalf of the slave traders, and using its power and influence to rivet still closer the chains of their victims!" Furthermore, the article continued, the Van Buren administration dispatched the *Grampus* to New Haven, under presidential orders, "in *anticipation*" of a court decree permitting Lieutenant John S. Paine to transport the blacks to Cuba.[35] At this point, one may note, the writer accused the executive of illegal involvement in both instances. He was not yet aware of the president's willingness to go one step farther and obstruct the constitutional right of appeal.

Tappan was convinced more than ever that the White House would interfere in the case. To Baldwin he wrote, "The Executive has been tricky I fear." Though Van Buren had allegedly written the district attorney to acknowledge the validity of the documents copied in court reports—"provided they were genuine"—Holabird had assured Tappan that he had received no instructions from the president. Just that day, September 9, Tappan had received letters from both the acting secretary of state and Forsyth; they said that the president had ordered instructions to go to Holabird, but without stating what the instructions were. Though Forsyth referred to his letter to Holabird of April 30, Tappan commented, "I do not believe it amounts to much."[36]

Tappan's observation was accurate. Though the president saw no reason to deny the defense counsels' request, Forsyth reminded Holabird that the documents in question were not "relevant or competent evidence." In the attorney general's opinion, the matter belonged in the courts of Spain. Only if the American Supreme Court decided that such evidence was proper could Holabird follow the president's suggestions to recognize it as genuine.[37] Thus the administration was prepared to admit the documents as authentic but was confident that the Court would rule that it lacked jurisdiction. The documents would not be important, the Court would turn over the business to Spain, and the president would be absolved of accusations of interference with judicial proceedings.

The abolitionists believed that the blacks were in great danger of being returned by the White House to Cuba and, in a suggestion that clearly was unlawful, began considering the possibility of removing them from the country should the Supreme Court decision deny them their freedom. James G. Birney, once a slaveholder and now an abolitionist and a lawyer, pointed out that the blacks should stay together as the trial neared. "If it is the design to bail them out," he wrote, "in order to secure their freedom by forfeiting the bonds, in case the Court shall decide against their freedom, this also it might be well to do." Townsend agreed. If the "design" was "to bail them out in order to secure their persons & then let them be among the missing," he likewise favored keeping them together.[38] Thus, while the abolitionists were incensed at the suspicion that Van Buren was flaunting the law, they were prepared to engage in similar activity.

Tappan notified Baldwin in mid-October that he was trying to persuade Judge Thompson to allow the "bailing" of the blacks. He had no indication that Thompson would agree; it would put him in an "awkward position." The judge had refused the *Amistad* Committee's offer to board the children without charge because the government's cost of keeping them was small. Consequently, the committee had offered to take all the blacks on the same terms. In about two weeks, however, Tappan again wrote Baldwin, complaining, "Judge Thompson takes no notice of our last petition!" About a week later Tappan informed Baldwin that the judge had notified him of his refusal to put the blacks in the custody of the committee partly because he believed that it was not authorized to make such an application. On Baldwin's recommendation, Tappan dropped the bailing idea.[39]

That same month the full story of executive involvement in the *Grampus* affair became public when both the *Emancipator* and the *Liberator* published documents showing that the president had ordered the vessel's commander to take the blacks to Cuba *"before an appeal could be interposed."* Under presidential order, American authorities in Connecticut were to put the blacks on the *Grampus* "unless an appeal shall have actually been interposed." Correspondence between the secretaries of state and navy, along with that between the secretary of state and the United States district attorney, proved that the executive intended to subvert the right of appeal.[40]

The abolitionists had made serious charges against the president in the Ruiz and *Grampus* episodes; and yet the accusations had little impact on the American public. This was primarily because many Americans saw the abolitionists as a vocal but small minority of fiery-eyed fanatics whose goal was to destroy the Union either by racial amalgamation or by racial war. But there was possibly another reason. Van Buren, as president of the United States, was the supreme law-enforcement officer in the country and was doubtless assumed by the public to be above committing any illegal or unethical action. Furthermore, even had the Whigs picked up the issue, in an election year the easiest approach to such accusations would have been to dismiss them as politically motivated. For the abolitionists to have a chance at persuading other Americans to accept their arguments, they had to find support from nonabolitionists.

In view of the coming battle before the Supreme Court, the abolitionists wanted a nationally known figure to lead the defense. Of the three attorneys, only Baldwin had proved highly satisfactory. Indeed, the *Amistad* Committee would soon terminate Staples's services; Tappan complained that he did not explore deeply enough the morality and legality of the case. Though Sedgwick would stay on, Tappan did not believe that he could "argue a case well." Yet there was a problem with Baldwin: he lacked the national prominence that the struggle now needed. With this thought in mind, Tappan in May informed Daniel Webster, the renowned legal figure and veteran of many appearances before the Supreme Court, that the *Amistad* Committee wanted him to lead the blacks' defense before the Supreme Court. But Webster declined, explaining to Tappan that he did not wish "to continue or extend his practice in that Court." Besides, he added, the men already retained were "very Eminent" and needed no assistance. In mid-October, Tappan wrote Baldwin that the committee would write Rufus Choate of Boston, whom it had considered at the outset of the case. Within a week, however, Baldwin replied that even though Choate was an "able man," his health was not good, and he did not attend the Supreme Court regularly. Tappan had meanwhile asked Choate in Boston to serve as associate counsel for the blacks; but Choate declined because of other commitments and the shortness of the notice.[41]

It should have come as no surprise that Webster and Choate declined to defend the *Amistad* captives. Webster may have meant what he said to Tappan, but other factors undoubtedly influenced his decision. He was from Massachusetts, a state that certainly opposed slavery, but he was only moderately antislavery and had enormous respect for the law—even if it sanctioned slaves as property. At the time of the *Amistad* affair, he was also tied up in another slavery case before the Supreme Court—that of *Groves* v. *Slaughter*. Furthermore, he had no use for abolitionists and little sympathy with their effort to capitalize on the case. Finally, Webster was interested in the presidency, and an alliance with abolitionists was not the way to higher office. As for Choate, he opposed the abolitionists as dangerous to the Union and wanted to keep the slavery issue quiet.[42]

The abolitionists now turned to John Quincy Adams. While in Boston to see Choate, Tappan asked "friends of the cause" whether Adams would serve as senior counsel. It appeared unlikely that he would accept, for the Massachusetts congressman was in his seventies, nearly deaf, and had not argued a case for over three decades. Yet he was a fervent supporter of fundamental liberties—for blacks as well as for whites—and he hated slavery. Had he not bitterly opposed the "gag rule" prohibiting all House discussion of slavery? Tappan joined Ellis Gray Loring, Adams's longtime friend, in the nine-mile ride from Boston to see the elderly statesman at his home in Quincy. Adams at first seemed opposed to accepting the position, but he finally consented to work as senior counsel with Baldwin and Sedgwick. He also agreed to make the closing argument before the Supreme Court.[43]

According to Adams's memoirs, Loring and Tappan had "earnestly entreated" him to aid the defense. Adams tried to excuse himself on the basis of "age and inefficiency," his duties in the House, and his "inexperience" for the past thirty years as a trial lawyer. But they prevailed upon him "so much" in a case involving "life and death" that he gave in. After all, he was already indirectly involved as adviser. Direct involvement in the case seemed only a matter of time. Tappan left Adams his scrapbooks containing printed materials he had collected on the case. Loring assured Adams that Baldwin would provide a complete brief.[44]

Tappan had to be careful not to alienate Baldwin in informing him that Adams was replacing him as senior counsel. He explained to Baldwin that Adams felt "deeply" about the *Amistad* case and would devote his "best powers" to it. Adams's "station, age, character," Tappan noted, would "give an importance" to his involvement in the cause. To safeguard against ill feelings, Tappan praised Baldwin as the one who had "borne the burden & heat of the argument," and he noted that Adams was pleased to be associated with the person he considered the "principal advocate" in the matter. Adams wrote Baldwin in November that he had agreed to serve at the "urgent request" of Tappan and Loring. His reluctance, he declared, rested "entirely and exclusively" upon recognition of his own "incompetency to do justice" to the blacks. In every other way, Adams explained, he had "no higher object of ambition" than to be counsel for those "unfortunate men." If Baldwin was disgruntled about Adams's involvement in the case, he did not show it. He told Adams of his "great satisfaction" over his joining the fight and would send him the materials on the case.[45]

Adams made immediate preparations for the monumental task before him. He left Boston on November 16 for Hartford and was in New Haven the following day to talk with Baldwin. In Baldwin's office they discussed the case for two hours. Adams joined him in visiting the blacks in Westville. The thirty-six males were in one chamber about thirty feet by twenty feet. All but one were under thirty years of age, Adams wrote in his memoirs, and none seemed taller than five and a half feet. Cinqué and Grabeau, the "two chief conspirators," had "very remarkable countenances." Adams did not see the three girls; they were now living with the family of Colonel Stanton Pendleton, the jailer. He later told Tappan that the visit had given him "much pleasure." But he was unhappy with the clothing, bedding, and other items furnished the blacks.[46]

In late November, Adams met with Attorney General Gilpin in his office in Washington and urged him to suggest to the president that the parties dismiss the case by "consent without argument." This would be "expedient" for "obvious reasons," Adams emphasized. But Gilpin told Adams that no dismissal could take place without an argument before the Supreme Court, because the Spanish minister had demanded the return of the blacks and because the circuit court had earlier refused a motion to dismiss. Adams must have known that this last-ditch effort would fail and that he faced a January rendezvous before the Supreme Court.

Joseph Cinqué (The New Haven Colony Historical Society)

The *Amistad* off Culloden Point, Long Island, 1839 (The New Haven Colony Historical Society)

Grabeau (or Grabo) (Beinecke Rare Book Room and Manuscript Library, Yale University)

Kale (Beinecke Rare Book Room and Manuscript Library, Yale University)

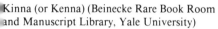

Kinna (or Kenna) (Beinecke Rare Book Room and Manuscript Library, Yale University)

Margru (or Margue) (Beinecke Rare Book Room and Manuscript Library, Yale University)

Banna (or Bana) (Beinecke Rare Book Room and Manuscript Library, Yale University)

Roger S. Baldwin (Baldwin Family Papers, Yale University Library)

Arthur Tappan (Amistad Research Center)

Lewis Tappan (Amistad Research Center)

Martin Van Buren (Library of Congress)

John Forsyth (Special Collections Division, University of Georgia Libraries)

Felix Grundy (Library of Congress)

Smith Thompson (Library of Congress)

"Trial of the Captive Slaves," New Haven, Connecticut, 1840, by Hale Woodruff (1939). From "The *Amistad* Murals," Savery Library, Talladega College. (The New Haven Colony Historical Society)

John Quincy Adams
(Library of Congress)

Roger B. Taney (Library of Congress)

Henry D. Gilpin (Library of Congress)

Joseph Story (Library of Congress)

Daniel Webster (Library of Congress)

"Return of the Natives," arrival in Africa, 1842, by Hale Woodruff (1939). From "The *Amistad* Murals," Savery Library, Talladega College. (The New Haven Colony Historical Society)

9

"Oh How Shall I Do Justice . . . ?"

John Quincy Adams agonized many hours while preparing his defense of the *Amistad* blacks before the Supreme Court. He recognized his limitations—age, long absence from the courtroom, numerous responsibilities as a House representative—and yet he and his family had always upheld fundamental principles of liberty, even when popular opinion argued otherwise. His father had taken up the cause of the British soldiers who fired the first shots of the "Boston Massacre" during the Revolution and had succeeded in securing reduced charges in the emotion-laden atmosphere of Massachusetts. How could he, John Quincy, refuse an opportunity to go before the highest court in the land and proclaim the principles of justice contained in the Declaration of Independence?

Adams may well have sensed that his appearance before the Court had taken on an aura of inevitability. If so, this did not ease the pressures. Former president of the United States, one-time secretary of state, minister to Russia, outspoken critic of slavery though not an abolitionist, caustic assessor of others—Adams knew that many Americans were waiting for him to stumble and perhaps to fall. He also knew that he ran risks in leading what amounted to an attack on the Van Buren administration. What was important, however, was the principles underlying the case and the lives of the captives themselves. "Oh," Adams wrote in his memoirs, "how shall I do justice to this case and to these men?"[1]

I

President Van Buren had lost his run for reelection. At least one historian believes that the *Amistad* case may have been a factor, and another considers it likely that Van Buren's proslavery policies cost him six Northern states that he had captured in 1836.[2] The electoral margin was large—the Whig William Henry Harrison took 234 votes to Van Buren's 60—but the popular vote in several states was so close that, according to the Washington *Globe,* a change of only about 8,000 popular votes would have awarded Van Buren 90 more electoral votes and hence the election.[3] Van Buren had upheld slavery on the grounds of states' rights, attempting to prevent a split in the Democratic coalition; ironically, he had succeeded in placating the South while driving away the North. Moreover, the abolitionists and others who voted for the Liberty party candidate, James G. Birney, may have tipped the balance in New York and denied Van Buren his home state. In any event, the outcome of the election was attributable primarily to factors other than slavery—to the financial and economic conditions brought by the panic of 1837 and the ensuing depression.[4]

Even though Van Buren no longer had reelection in mind, his administration's position in regard to the *Amistad* remained constant, giving rise to questions about the legitimacy of the abolitionists' charge of political expediency. It nevertheless seems safe to assume that the guiding principle had always been politics. Perhaps now, formerly secondary considerations had taken priority and persuaded the White House to stay on the same course. The Democrats had been defeated, but they were still committed to a policy on the *Amistad* affair that received support from Americans who were concerned about competing British interests in Cuba and from Southerners who were worried that such examples would stimulate slave unrest. Moreover, the president may have been determined to complete a task his administration had started. For both foreign and domestic reasons, the White House maintained its stand.

The abolitionists and Adams had reason for optimism. Lewis Tappan happily wrote Baldwin on Christmas Eve that the approaching trial was "exciting great interest" in Washington. The New York *Commercial Advertiser* probably expressed the views of many Americans when it called the possible surrender of the blacks to Cuba an "outrageous violation" of "justice and human rights." And in that same city, a play entitled *The Black Schooner or the Private Slaver "Amistad"* ran several evenings before packed houses at four theaters and took in over $5,000. More than growing public interest and concern underlay Adams's optimism, for he had learned of new evidence that might strengthen his case. George

Wilson of New London informed him on Christmas Day that John Jay Hyde, editor of the New London *Gazette* and a "gentleman of respectability and veracity," had won the trust of Ruiz and Montes while they were in that city in 1839, and that Hyde was now willing to attest that the Spaniards had told him the blacks had not been out of Africa six weeks when put on the *Amistad.* He had been summoned to district court but did not attend. He would appear before the Supreme Court if his expenses were paid. Four days later Wilson again wrote Adams that Hyde had explained his absence at the district court by saying that "his fees were not legally rendered" and that he did not want his testimony to lead to perjury charges against these men. Wilson suggested that the district court proceedings must have been illegal, for authorities had not compelled such an important witness to appear.[5]

Adams felt enormous pressure in preparing his argument. Baldwin had sent his brief as promised; but it contained little that was new to Adams, for in his correspondence with Loring at the outset of the case, Adams himself had recommended many of the legal principles later used by Baldwin in Hartford and New Haven.[6] Baldwin's brief was long and entangled but provided Adams with material for his central argument on behalf of natural rights and principles of natural law proclaimed in the Declaration of Independence. Adams returned to the point he considered crucial to the case: Gedney had no right to seize the *Amistad.* Regardless of whether the blacks were in New York territory or aboard ship on the high seas, Gedney lacked authority. As Baldwin emphasized in his brief, Gedney had no warrant and the blacks committed no crime making them liable in American courts. Yet Adams feared that he would not be permitted to raise this question or that for some reason it would be "suppressed." As the days swiftly passed, Adams tried to find time to study the case, but his duties in the House of Representatives consumed precious time, leaving him deeply concerned about being "utterly unprepared." As late as January 20 he complained that he could not devote "five minutes" to preparation. Ten days later he wrote in his memoirs that his left eye was inflamed and that he might not be able to present the argument. The mounting pressure, he declared, only aggravated the disability.[7]

Adams worried most about the blacks. Two of the captives, Kale and Kinna, had written him in English, confirming that they were from Mende and did not speak Spanish. They also claimed to be unhappy, although often laughing and saying they had plenty to eat. Kale explained the apparent contradiction. Their jailer, Colonel Stanton Pendleton, had warned that whites were afraid of them when they appeared angry. So, Kale said, they laughed. He and Kinna assured Adams that they had killed the captain because he killed one of them; they had killed the cook because he said that they would eat the Mende people. Kale and Kinna wanted Adams to tell the "Great Court" their story. Cinqué, who had also learned to write in English, had likewise told of bad treatment in the Westville jail. To Baldwin, his "Dear friend," Cinqué complained that Pendleton had put chains on their hands and whipped them. Pendleton said that Tappan and others had lied to the Mende people and that they would never return home. He claimed that "all good things" in their possession had come from him—meat, clothes, everything. Pendleton, Cinqué observed, was a "bad man" who did not think of God and whose soul would be "lost . . . to hell." Speaking for the other captives, he asked Baldwin to tell Pendleton not to beat them again. Cinqué felt "sorry for him [Pendleton]" because he did "not think of God." "We forgive him," he said, "and he curse us and he whip us."[8]

Adams's personal notes on the case made it evident that a major thrust of his argument would be an indictment of Forsyth. In the secretary's "extreme zeal" to comply with the Spanish government's wishes, he "mistook the nature of the demand" and informed the district attorney in Connecticut that the Spanish minister had called for the return of the *Amistad,* its cargo, *and* the blacks as Spanish property under Pinckney's Treaty of 1795. But, Adams believed, the minister's demand was for *persons* as assassins and not for property in slaves. Indeed, the minister had come into conflict with Ruiz and Montes by demanding that the blacks remain in the United States as prisoners until they could return to Havana to stand trial and "glut the *vengeance* of Cuba's slave traders—not as Slaves but as Assassins." In a statement corroborated by the documents, Adams asserted that the minister demanded them as Spanish subjects, accused of capital crimes and triable only in courts of their own country. He insisted that American courts could not consider a salvage claim on the blacks as property. Upon Forsyth's "misstatement" of this demand, Adams insisted, the American government issued the warrant for the seizure of the blacks. Adams was willing to attribute the secretary's mistake to "inadvertence." But this did not change the fact that the district attorney filed a libel and claim based on these instructions and thus practiced a *"deception"* on the court.[9]

Adams also prepared to charge the president with interfering in the judicial process and in practicing deceptions. The district attorney had followed Van Buren's instructions, no doubt unaware of the Spanish minister's real demand. Holabird's libel and claim, Adams declared with indignation, had placed an issue before the court that focused on freedom or slavery for a large number of black people without even having their names on the document. The court heard the claim as presented by the United States at the demand of the Spanish minister, when in reality it was "against his protest." Argaiz "bitterly complained" that the "public *vengeance* of the African Slave traders in Cuba had not been *satisfied.*" That could come only by the *"blood"* of the blacks, Adams declared, "not as *Slaves* but as *assassins.*" If the minister's demand had been clear, the district court could not have considered returning the blacks as assassins. "[I]f the Secretary of State knew what he was about," Adams asserted, "what motive could he possibly have for this imposition upon the Court, but to get the men into possession of the Executive to keep them in custody inexorable and convey them to the place of execution in Cuba!"[10]

Adams wrote in his notes that the Van Buren administration had through "many most obsequious and exceptionable acts, manifested its own disposition and eagerness to comply" with the Spanish demand. One indication was the secretary of state's "constant and studious avoidance" of denying the Spanish demands as "utterly inadmissible, inconsistent and absurd." A second was the attempt to mislead the district court by directing the district attorney to present the Spanish minister's demand as one for the return of slaves under the treaty. And while the secretary was doing this, he was also relying on the attorney general's opinion that the president should order the marshal to turn over the blacks to whomever the Spanish minister designated. A third factor was the secretary of state's directive to the district attorney *"to take care."* Adams angrily remarked, "What a flap at the Courts!" Fourth, the secretary had made secret verbal contacts with Argaiz, which were "obscurely but very intelligibly referred to by the latter in his written correspondence." A fifth sign was the steps taken to seize the blacks and carry them to Cuba. All these considerations, Adams lamented, demonstrated that the only concern of the Van Buren administration was to satisfy the Spanish.[11]

Adams was ready to accuse the White House of bias against the blacks. From the time Gedney seized the *Amistad,* Adams believed, every executive action rested on the *"assumption"* that the captives were "slaves" and *"murderers"* who had to be delivered to the Spanish minister for their masters. Yet Argaiz never sought the blacks' delivery as property; he wanted the United States to keep them in custody until their return to Cuba as assassins. The secretary of state "fabricated" the minister's demand as one for slaves and kept the real demand for murderers from the district attorney for one reason: to prevent the truth from going before the court and showing that despite the administration's claim that it was abiding by the treaty of 1795, it was in reality prepared to condone judicial murder to quiet the case. Adams concluded that the Van Buren administration wanted the best of both worlds: "The Attorney General was for surrendering the Africans as Slaves—he was for surrendering them as Assassins." In either case, Adams believed the executive office guilty of interference in the judicial process.[12]

There is no question that Adams was correct in claiming that the Spanish minister had demanded the blacks as criminals to stand trial in Cuban courts; the problem comes in proving that the Van Buren administration intentionally misread the Spanish position as a call for property. If Forsyth erred, he should have known better. Though not as experienced as Adams in diplomacy, he did not need special expertise to determine the Spanish government's central demand. In the Spanish minister's notes of September 6 and November 26, 1839, he had made his wishes clear. In the latter note, Argaiz complained that because the United States had not implemented the treaty of 1795, "the public vengeance has not been satisfied; for be it recollected that *the Legation of Spain does not demand the delivery of slaves but of Assassins*" (emphasis added).[13] It seems fair to conclude that Forsyth deliberately misinterpreted the Spanish claim so that the administration could defend the move as a treaty obligation. To surrender the captives as accused assassins would be tantamount to participating in a mass judicial execution. Adams recognized how far from justice the political aims of the Van Buren administration had taken it. He hoped to prove this in court.

II

In mid-January the Spanish minister sent a note to Forsyth that suggested Adams was wrong in his assessment of Spain's demands: Argaiz claimed the blacks both as property of Spanish subjects and as assassins to stand trial in Spanish courts. He based the first claim on the treaty of 1795, the second on reciprocity between nations. In his support, Argaiz enclosed two articles from the Spanish newspaper published in New York, *Noticioso de Ambos Mundos.* The first disagreed with a recent assessment by Judge William Jay, in which he argued that on the basis of the law of nations and not of the treaty of 1795 (as fugitives and not as merchandise), the Spanish legation in Washington had sought the blacks' return as murderers or assassins and *not* as property. Jay was wrong, Argaiz insisted. He had a poor understanding of the Spanish language. When Argaiz wrote in November 1839 that his government *"does not demand the delivery of slaves, but of assassins,"* this was not the essential demand as Jay thought. To prevent a second use of a substantive—the word *esclavos* (slaves)—Argaiz explained that he had not constructed the expression as it *should* have read: *"not only demands slaves, but slaves who are assassins."* In Spanish, Argaiz declared, "it is considered as understood, even though a conjunction or disjunction be omitted, in the expression in question, '*no pide esclavos sino asesinos,*' *(does not demand slaves but assassins)* the word *solo* (only) may be understood." Thus, Argaiz continued, the actual phrase should have been "no solo pide esclavos sino esclavos asesinos," or "not only demands slaves but slaves who are assassins." Spain, Argaiz asserted, consistently made its demand for the slaves as merchandise. The United States had to execute the treaty of 1795 as part of the supreme law of the land.[14]

Argaiz then referred to the second article in the Spanish paper, which claimed that according to the writings of Hugo Grotius, the famous Dutch theorist on international law, Spain also had the right to demand the blacks' surrender as murderers. Indeed, a former attorney general of the United States, William Wirt, cited Grotius in arguing in another case that "the usage, then, of demanding fugitives from a foreign Government, is confined . . . to crimes which affect the Government, and such as are of extreme atrocity." Wirt also quoted Emmerich de Vattel, the Swiss expert in international law: "If the sovereignty of the country in which crimes of this nature have been committed, demands the delivery of the persons who committed them, in order to punish them, they should be surrendered to him, as the person most interested in having them exemplarily punished." Argaiz declared that he "not only claimed the captured slaves as the property of Spanish subjects, but also . . . for their surrender as assassins, in order that they may be tried by competent courts." Spanish demands, he insisted, rested primarily on the treaty of 1795, but also on the law of nations and the *"good understanding and reciprocity"* of a "friendly nation."[15]

The Spanish minister had contributed to this confusion by writing a note that left his government open to the charge of shifting its stance in accord with believed necessity. Argaiz's argument is perhaps truthful, but on such an important point it seems careless for a seasoned European diplomat to have relied upon a State Department translator to *understand* the necessity of inserting the word *solo* (only) in the text. At the least, Argaiz was naively responsible for allowing his government's demands to mesh with the official position of the Van Buren administration.

It is perhaps understandable that Adams, a suspicious man anyway, could, on the basis of the published correspondence he had seen, believe that Argaiz had changed his predecessor's position in the controversy. In September 1839 Angel Calderón de la Barca initially asked for the blacks' return as criminals "to be tried by the proper tribunal, and by the violated laws of the country of which they are subjects." Five days later *Noticioso de Ambos Mundos* referred to the blacks as "mutineers & murderers." Whether they were slaves was a matter of opinion. Spain demanded their return as criminals who had broken Spanish law and had to stand trial. The following November, Argaiz himself declared that, on the basis of the treaty of 1795, he demanded the delivery of assassins. The technicalities regarding the literary construction of the Spanish language, even if accurate, did not matter: Argaiz was still demanding the blacks' return as assassins who were slaves. The Spanish had all along sought the blacks' surrender as criminals, and Forsyth, to serve the administration's purposes, had wrongly represented to the district attorney the Spanish demand. Now, in the January 1841 note to Forsyth, Argaiz combined the two demands into a single call for the slaves *as* assassins, appealing to both Pinckney's Treaty and reciprocity between the nations.[16]

It was no coincidence that in Argaiz's attempt to show that he was emphasizing the return of slaves as assassins, he was at the same time trying to leave the impression that no violation of Anglo-Spanish treaties against the African slave trade had occurred. Spain had grown increasingly concerned that England might intervene in Cuba as part of an effort to establish control over the Caribbean. The government in London could not justify intervention on the ground that slaves had committed murder, but if Argaiz were to demand the blacks as assassins without drawing attention to their status as slaves, he would not only have substantiated the abolitionists' claims in court but also have implicitly admitted that Ruiz and Montes had broken treaty agreements with England and that the Spanish government had merely looked the other way. Above all, Argaiz had to establish that the *Amistad* captives were slaves who had committed murder in the course of the mutiny.

The informal trilateral relationship among the United States, Spain, and England over the *Amistad* affair and Cuba had become more evident by mid-January 1841. America's chargé in Madrid, Aaron Vail, had had a "long and desultory conversation" with the Spanish minister of foreign affairs, Don Joaquín María de Ferrer, on the subject of America's political and commercial relations with Cuba and other Spanish possessions. Ferrer expressed concern over "supposed designs" by England to establish control over the West Indies. After abolishing slavery in its colonies, England began to put pressure on Spain to do the same. With "extreme dissatisfaction," as Vail termed Ferrer's feeling, Ferrer referred to the "official interposition" of the British minister in Washington, Henry S. Fox, in the *Amistad* case. Dispatches from the Spanish minister in Washington had claimed British interference on behalf of the blacks. Vail expressed doubt that Ferrer's information was correct. As far as Vail could determine, instructions had gone out for such an interposition; but at the time when he left Washington, they had not been carried out.[17]

Vail assured Ferrer that the American government, too, was concerned about British designs on Cuba. The island, he explained, had attractions—geographical location, good soil, high population, wealth, and agriculture—that fitted England's aim of global domination. Thus the administration in Washington had been watching any English move that might lead to intervention. To prevent such an occurrence, the United States was prepared to use military and naval forces. Ferrer seemed surprised, for he had not had time since coming to office to determine the American government's views on the matter. Without expressing an opinion, he inquired about the strength of the American navy.[18]

Vail was correct in believing that the British had not officially intervened in the *Amistad* case; but they had moved alarmingly close to that point, and nothing would have delighted the abolitionists more. Amos Townsend, Jr., had asked Tappan about the chances for British intervention if the Supreme Court awarded the blacks to the Spanish. Perhaps it would be a good idea to warn the British agent in Havana to be "on the lookout" for the arrival of the blacks. In Washington, Fox shared the same anxieties. He visited Adams in mid-January 1841, expressing concern that the Supreme Court would return the blacks to the Spanish claimants. His government in London would not like this, he emphasized. Three days later Fox again met with Adams. Palmerston had asked Fox to use his good offices on behalf of the blacks without interfering in the judicial proceedings. Fox therefore needed Adams's advice on what to do in the event of an unfavorable decision by the Supreme Court. Fox claimed to have had no discussion with the Van Buren administration about the matter, and Adams advised him to send a note to the secretary of state, asking the president to intervene on the blacks' behalf if the Court opted for their return to Cuba. Perhaps Adams hoped that Van Buren could lay political considerations aside, now that he would soon be leaving office. Fox wrote the note and brought it to Adams for his perusal the following evening.[19]

On January 20, Fox delivered the note to the State Department, informing Forsyth that the attention of the British government had been "seriously directed" to the *Amistad* case. He noted that his government had signed a treaty with Spain in 1817 that prohibited the African slave trade. England thus had "special and peculiar reasons" for being interested in these "unfortunate Africans" who were "illegally and feloniously reduced to slavery by subjects of Spain." Fox also reminded Forsyth that the United States and England had agreed to Article 10 of the Treaty of Ghent, which had established mutual efforts to halt the African slave trade. The United States now had to decide whether the blacks should "recover the freedom to which they [were] entitled" or be "reduced to slavery," in violation of laws against Spanish participation in the traffic. The British position, Fox insisted, was that the blacks could only be "free persons." The British government hoped that the president would secure the blacks' lawful right to liberty.[20]

But the Van Buren administration, either out of pique at British connections with the abolitionists or out of genuine concern that the government in London was searching for a pretext to intervene in Cuba, made it clear to Fox that the *Amistad* case was not a proper subject for Anglo-American diplomacy. In February, Forsyth informed Fox that he would accept his letter as an expression of "benevolence." The president insisted that only America's courts could determine the outcome; he had neither the power nor the disposition to interfere with legal tribunals acting within their proper jurisdiction. Forsyth also pointed out that Spanish facts about the case did not coincide with those cited by Fox. The evidence had not established that the blacks were recent imports from Africa and hence illegal. If the courts awarded the blacks to the Spanish minister, Forsyth allowed, that would raise the issue of whether there had been violations of Spanish laws and Spanish treaties with England. Only at that point could England appeal to treaty stipulations—and then, merely with Spain. The United States, Forsyth emphasized, could not act as a tribunal between the nations.[21]

Strictly speaking, the Van Buren administration was correct in declaring that the *Amistad* affair was not a legitimate subject for Anglo-American diplomacy. But that position was undoubtedly one of convenience. Forsyth's refusal to accept Fox's note on an official basis illustrates the problem facing the abolitionists in trying to prove the charge of executive interference: any action the administration took was subject to an interpretation falling within the bounds of legality. Enough problems between the Atlantic nations existed already by early 1841—specifically, a crisis over the Alexander McLeod affair—and Forsyth was not interested in creating another one.[22] To accept Fox's note, Forsyth knew, would invite British involvement in Cuba, which would have been injurious to American interests.

III

As the time for the trial approached, the abolitionists deluded themselves into believing they could obtain a writ of habeas corpus if the administration won its case and attempted to remove the blacks to Cuba. Simeon Jocelyn from the *Amistad* Committee had asked about a writ. Townsend declared, "If anything can be done legally to pluck the prey from the jaws of human tigers I hope it will be done." Tappan asserted that the committee wanted to guard against "any unconstitutional measure" adopted by the executive office or by other officials. It seemed wise to have a writ of habeas corpus ready. He instructed Townsend and another abolitionist, John F. Norton of Farmington, to make such preparations. Tappan was convinced that it would be easy to secure a writ and get the blacks before a judge, but the question was whether they would be remanded or sent back to jail for a further investigation of charges.[23]

In reality, the abolitionists had no chance of securing a writ of habeas corpus in the event of an adverse decision by the Supreme

Court. Indeed, the mere proposal suggests the abolitionists' naïveté regarding the law. Such a writ was tantamount to appealing a verdict by the highest court in the land. There was no remedy beyond the Supreme Court.

In the final moments before the trial, some of the abolitionists, nearly desperate about the probable outcome, were themselves willing to violate the law by considering a scheme to liberate the blacks from jail. Townsend wrote Tappan that he had received a letter from Tappan's friend A. F. Williams of Farmington, who argued that the blacks had to "be put into a place of safety" and that he wanted to help. Townsend wrote, however, "I am not prepared for such a movement." The "friends of human rights" had already "suffered so much" from "illegal violence" and had "so loudly & constantly" called for the supremacy of law over necessity that such a step would encourage more violence. The resort to "necessity against legality," Townsend warned, would put the "liberty of private responsibility" in the "place of legal decisions." He was reluctant to enter "any such arrangement," although he admitted that he was open to persuasion by Tappan and the committee. If they tried to free the blacks, Townsend allowed, the action would have to take place before suspicions arose and the officers holding them in custody placed a closer watch over them. Townsend hoped for a response by return mail if Tappan thought Williams's suggestion worth consideration.[24] Apparently Tappan held off, pending the outcome of the trial.

Another abolitionist concern was that someone else might abduct the blacks during the night and turn them over to the Spanish. Townsend wrote Tappan that he had asked Cinqué not to accompany anyone after dark. They should keep the blacks together "and make all the resistance in their power & not suffer themselves to be carried off by stealth." Cinqué said, "[I]f they come we all hulloo loud, & make plenty noise." Townsend later warned Tappan that if the Court decided to return the blacks to the Spaniards, there would probably be an attempt to get them out before the decision became publicly known.[25]

In the meantime the abolitionists were coming under pressure to sidestep an administration move to return the blacks to Cuba by raising money either to send them to Africa or to buy their freedom from the Spaniards. But Tappan and the others rigidly opposed both of these moves as admissions to the captives' status as slaves. In the Supreme Court room just before the judges arrived to open proceedings in mid-January, Francis Scott Key, author of "The

Star-Spangled Banner" and now a district attorney and member of the American Colonization Society, asked Adams about the *Amistad* case and then lamented that the *Antelope* decision left little hope for the blacks. Key himself had argued that case of 1825 for the blacks' freedom from bondage but had lost on the ground that international law upheld the right of nations to institute the slave trade. He now insisted that the best approach would be to raise money for the *Amistad* blacks' return to Africa. Key later wrote Tappan about the possibility of purchasing the captives from the Spaniards. But Tappan would not consider the proposal. To Baldwin he explained that it was not wise to let "such men as Mr. Key" think that the abolitionists doubted a favorable outcome. Moreover, the abolitionists could not permit "such a concession to slavery."[26] They had to place their hopes in the Supreme Court.

The abolitionists had to counter what appeared to be yet another White House effort to influence the outcome. In early January the Washington *Globe* argued that the district court decree was wrong and that the president had to surrender the blacks to Spain. Two weeks later, "Veto" (Theodore Sedgwick) wrote a long article in the *National Anti-Slavery Standard* of New York that criticized the *Globe* for interfering in the judicial process. Though the editorial preceding the *Globe* article declared that it came from "one of the first intellects of the south," Veto noted that the article appeared on the eve of the Supreme Court trial and in the "leading organ" of the government. Though not "cool and dispassionate," as it claimed to be, Veto held that the article was an extreme defense of slavery.[27]

The *Amistad* question, Veto argued, could not turn either on sympathy for the blacks or on the alleged merits of slavery; the only issue could be whether the district court decree was in accord with the law. The main problem was that the captives were black, Veto claimed. Had they been white, they would have had no problem proving themselves free men. But their blackness made everything different: "All justice, all ordinary rules are to be set aside for fear, forsooth, lest the abolitionists should have a triumph—lest some slaveholder on the shores of the Mobile or the Mississippi should tremble for the safety of his property." Fanatics in both the North and the South, but particularly in the latter, because they seemed to make up that region's entire population, were pushing for a settlement of "that great question," which "involved the destinies of the American republic." Many Northerners could not understand how the surrender of the blacks would promote slav-

ery, as the abolitionists declared. Yet these same Northerners realized that most of the Supreme Court justices were from the South
and that "the whole Southern voice [was] raised in one united
appeal to the passions, the prejudices, the fears, the interests of
these magistrates as slaveholders." Every question allegedly
involved the "interests of the South." "In the name of Heaven,"
Veto lamented, "can no decision ever be made in the cause of liberty without periling Southern interests? Can no slave ever be dis-
charged, no master ever defeated, no imprisoned free men ever liberated, without awakening the whole fury of the South?"[28]

Indeed, one of the South's major spokesmen, Senator John C.
Calhoun, had drawn the abolitionists' ire for publicly insisting that
the Court had to return the blacks to Cuba. Tappan had moved
quickly, writing rebuttals in the press that drew praise from Joshua
Leavitt. The articles, Leavitt declared, would "make Calhoun's
stuff appear exceedingly flimsy." But Townsend complained to
Tappan that Calhoun's demands would lead to the blacks' "slaughter" or to their being forced to "wear out their wretched existence
on the plantations of Cuba." Should the Supreme Court in "our
boasted land of freedom," Townsend wrote, "so truckle to the
Spirit of Slavery as to deliver these men into the hands of slave
drivers then is our liberty but a name & the Union of the States a
union of thieves & robbers."[29]

The abolitionists were becoming increasingly worried about the
options before the Supreme Court. Judge William Jay could not
believe that the Court would order the blacks' return; it would be
a "judicial massacre." The justices would probably attempt to send
them to Africa. "To *liberate* them would be a triumph to the abolitionists, & a sore & bitter mortification to most of the slaveholders." To send them to Africa would be a victory for colonizationists and "far more acceptable" to slaveholders. Many Northerners
neither abolitionists nor colonizationists, would be appalled if the
Court ordered their return to Cuba for murder. And yet it appeared
illegal to send them to Africa. The Court seemed inclined to surrender them but "*may* be induced to transport them." Was it better to entrust them to Africans than to "Cuban Savages"? If others
wanted to send them to Africa, Jay "would not acquiesce, but
would *not oppose.* Our lawyers should simply urge the court to
grant them liberty."[30]

For obvious reasons, Tappan believed that the best decision
would be to declare the blacks free. He wrote Adams that some of
them wanted to stay in the United States, and he warned that if

they returned to Africa it was likely that most of them would not make it back to Mende. In any case, they ought to have the option "to remain here or go where they choose." He later informed Adams that the *Amistad* Committee had instructed Baldwin to oppose any attempt by court or president to send the blacks to Africa. "They are entitled to their freedom *here,*" Tappan wrote. Though this point had not yet come up, Tappan declared that the attorneys intended to pursue it in court because of its "great importance to the cause of human rights." Some of the Africans, in particular the three girls, had expressed a desire to remain in the United States: "Just in proportion as these Africans have been enlightened has been their desire to remain here to be better instructed." The abolitionists had to fight the idea that the American government had the right to "force them away." The case involved the rights of the blacks, "the cause of human freedom," and the nation's honor.[31]

Tappan had again advocated the broad view of constitutional liberties. If the president won court sanction to dictate what should happen to the blacks, the executive office would have assumed a great hold over free blacks and perhaps over slavery itself. As Tappan earlier explained to his brother, real democracy meant "universal liberty." "I am," Tappan declared, "for the largest liberty for the poor man—for the oppressed."[32]

As the court date neared, Tappan wrote Baldwin that many people had "strong apprehensions" about the trial and that community feeling was "deepening." Leavitt urged Tappan to trust in God to "bring light out of darkness." Whatever the result, Leavitt believed, God would "use it or overrule it for great & good results in favor of justice and mercy & liberty."[33] Yet the abolitionists recognized that, for their cause to succeed, more Americans had to become concerned about individual liberties. So far little evidence of such concern had appeared.

10

"The Eternal Principles of Justice"

I

The Supreme Court under Chief Justice Roger B. Taney of Maryland had gained a reputation for protecting national supremacy while also safeguarding the rights of states, individuals, and property.[1] These stances were not always compatible and necessitated compromise decisions. But a compromise in the *Amistad* case could only leave the captives as casualties and the abolitionists' objectives unfulfilled. The abolitionists feared that the justices would opt to protect national supremacy and decide against the blacks. The easiest way out of the morass, a way that would affirm the administration's position without challenging the states' rights position, would be to award the blacks to the Spanish minister. If unity depended upon keeping arguments over slavery to a minimum, the Court would surely prefer that course.[2]

The makeup of the Court added substance to the rumors that the captives would soon be en route to Cuba. A congressional act of March 1837 had increased the number of associate justices from six to eight, and to one of the new positions Jackson had appointed John Catron of Tennessee; soon afterward Van Buren had filled the other with John McKinley of Alabama. Catron had been chief justice of his state's supreme court, a strong Union supporter during the nullification crisis, and a staunch advocate of federal supremacy. McKinley was a Southern Democrat and former United States senator.[3] The two newcomers joined Taney, Joseph Story of Massachusetts, Smith Thompson of New York (who had already been involved in the *Amistad* case on the circuit level), John McLean of Ohio, Henry Baldwin of Pennsylvania, James M. Wayne of Georgia, and Philip P. Barbour of Virginia. Thus five of the nine Court members were Southern, including the chief justice.

There would be countervailing factors. Two of the Southerners would be absent when the verdict was rendered—McKinley was in poor health and unable to attend any of the proceedings, and Barbour died in his sleep from a heart attack midway through the hearings. Furthermore, two other justices, Thompson and Story, had made plain their feelings against slavery. During the early stages of the *Amistad* case, Thompson had expressed his repugnance for slavery while conceding that American law upheld its existence; Story had voiced the same sentiments in the *Eugénie* circuit court case. In developing the importance of comity among nations, which was part of Story's conflict-of-laws theory, he drew heavily from the English *Somerset* decision of 1772, which had decreed that the law of slavery in one country had no binding effect on another country. By that doctrine of comity a nation condoning slavery possessed the right to ask for the return of fugitive slaves; but by that same doctrine the nation holding the alleged fugitives was not required to surrender them, unless by specific treaty obligations. Thus both slavery and freedom existed only by positive law. Story, it soon became clear, would receive the responsibility of writing the Court's opinion in the *Amistad* case.[4]

Before the small but packed courtroom, Attorney General Henry D. Gilpin opened the trial on February 22 with a two-hour presentation. He stood before the Supreme Court justices in a room shaped like a half circle and comparable to a cellar, for it lay beneath the Senate chamber and was often insufferably hot and damp. The room's only windows, three of them, were behind the raised bench, which meant that the attorneys and spectators had to strain to see the justices' faces because of the light beaming in behind them. Thus, in a room taking on the atmosphere of a catacomb, Gilpin began his case, walking back and forth, passing in and out of sight because of the huge pillars that held up the ceiling.[5]

Gilpin's introductory remarks repeated the arguments given in Hartford and New Haven, the stance outlined to Van Buren in autumn 1839 by the former attorney general Felix Grundy. On appeal from the circuit court, Gilpin declared, two points were under consideration: whether there was, according to the treaty of 1795, "due and sufficient proof concerning the property thereof"; and, if so, whether the United States had the right to intervene in securing the property of the Spanish claimants. Comity among nations demanded that the United States accept a ship's papers as prima facie evidence. The issue in the *Amistad* case was not "right" or "wrong" but whether the granting of the papers fell within the official's authority. The blacks' attorneys had failed to prove fraud concerning the captain general's certificate. Madden's deposition was "chiefly hearsay" and was contradicted by other witnesses. The treaties of 1817 and 1835 related only to the slave trade; they had no bearing on whether the blacks were slaves. The captives were therefore returnable to Spain as property.[6]

Gilpin insisted that the executive had acted legally in attempting to secure a court decree to return the property. According to precedents, the delivery of foreign property went through public officials of those foreigners' government. In the *Eugénie* case the French consul and owners had proved their legal claim to the vessel, and Justice Story ordered its surrender to the public official. In the *Antelope* case of 1825, there was more than one claim: by the captain as captor; by the Spanish and Portuguese vice-consuls for their citizens; by the United States. Again, Gilpin noted, the court accepted the claims as documented and directed delivery partly to the Spanish consul and partly to the United States. In the case of the *Amistad,* Gilpin declared, the Spanish minister requested a return of property in accord with the treaty of 1795. The documentation of ownership was in order, and the lower courts should have directed the return of the vessel, the blacks, and every item aboard.[7]

Baldwin consumed the remainder of the first day and all of the next in delivering what Adams termed a "sound and eloquent but exceedingly mild and moderate argument." Baldwin proclaimed that the case affected not only the Africans but also America's "national character in the eyes of the whole civilized world." It presents, he said, "for the first time, the question whether that government, which was established for the promotion of JUSTICE, which was founded on the great principles of the Revolution, as proclaimed in the Declaration of Independence, can, consistently with the genius of our institutions, become a party to proceedings for the enslavement of human beings cast upon our shores, and found in the condition of free men within the territorial limits of a FREE AND SOVEREIGN STATE." Baldwin insisted that the law of nations guaranteed justice to the African as well as to the Spaniard. In a foreign court all parties bringing suit on questions of freedom or slavery were on equal ground. The Africans were never domiciled in Cuba and therefore owed no allegiance to its laws. The only law applying to the Africans was "universal obligation"—that of nature.[8]

Baldwin proceeded to his major purpose: to seek dismissal of the case. He argued that the federal government had no right to participate in an admiralty court on behalf of foreigners claiming property and that it therefore had no power to help foreigners recover fugitive slaves. Furthermore, the United States could not appear in a case involving victims of the African slave trade who had found asylum in a free state. The Africans of the *Amistad* were never slaves; they were certainly free upon entering New York. The captives fell under the protection of the state, which, as the Supreme Court had in 1837 said in *New York* v. *Miln,* "has the same undeniable and unlimited jurisdiction over all persons and things within its territorial limits, as any foreign nation, when that jurisdiction is not surrendered or restrained by the Constitution of the United States."[9]

The United States government had no power to establish slavery, Baldwin argued, and no right to restore the blacks to claimants. The Constitution did not authorize the government to "establish or legalize" slavery; its existence depended on the laws of states. In a statement doubtless reflecting his reading of James Madison's recently published notes on the Constitutional Convention, Baldwin pointed out that the Founding Fathers had made no references to "property in men," although they recognized slavery within states that allowed it. Madison had declared at the convention that it was "wrong to admit in the Constitution" that "there could be property in men." The Constitution, Baldwin emphasized, did not refer to human beings as "merchandise or legitimate subjects of commerce." Similarly in the *Miln* case, Justice Barbour had declared that persons were not "the subjects of commerce." If Congress had the power to authorize the importation of slaves as commerce, Baldwin insisted, it could force slavery into every state, regardless of state laws. The Constitution was a compact among the states requiring them to respect the laws of others; the federal government had no duty or power to act on this matter. The *Amistad* blacks were free men, and once the courts had declared them free, the president could not intervene. America's courts must not become "actors in reducing them to slavery."[10]

The American people, Baldwin asserted, had never considered it the duty of their government to force free people into bondage by giving "extra-territorial force to a foreign slave law." The president of the United States had no business seeking recovery of slaves for their owners, whether the slaves were foreign or domestic. Ruiz and Montes, as Spanish subjects, had no right to call on the government in Washington to use the legal process for reenslavement. "Did the people of the United States," he asked, "whose government is based on the great principles of the Revolution, proclaimed in the Declaration of Independence, confer upon the federal, executive, or judicial tribunals, the power of making our nation accessories to such atrocious violations of human right?" If the United States upheld a foreign nation's slave laws inside this country, Baldwin declared, it would be violating man's natural rights. Another country's laws could not apply in the United States where it violated America's own laws, the law of nature, or the "law of God."[11]

Baldwin argued that the *Amistad's* blacks were not pirates or robbers subject to seizure and punishment. Cinqué sought only to free himself and his companions from unlawful bondage. They owed no allegiance to Spain and were on the schooner only by "constraint." Impressed American seamen, Baldwin pointed out, had the right to use any means in winning their freedom. In a similar fashion, the actions taken by the *Amistad's* blacks constituted no crime.[12]

Baldwin insisted that, according to comity, the United States government could not interfere with either a state's right to recover fugitive slaves or its duty to return them, whether foreign or domestic. To support this stand, he referred to the experience of John Quincy Adams, who as secretary of state had in 1818 dealt with a proposal to cooperate with England in suppressing the African slave trade. Adams declared that the United States government could have nothing to do with the idea, because blacks in America fell under state laws. The federal government, Baldwin declared, had to respect the laws of a state when they did not conflict with the supreme law. American courts had to do the same in matters affecting the "personal rights of men found within the jurisdiction of a free state." There could be no return of fugitive slaves without a treaty provision.[13]

In his concluding statements, Baldwin pressed the argument that Ruiz and Montes were guilty of fraud. His clients had not filed charges against the Cuban captain general, because he had never tried to assume jurisdiction over the blacks as slaves or to settle any question concerning their status. The captain general simply took the applications of Ruiz and Montes and issued passports for *ladino* slaves. Under those papers, Ruiz and Montes fraudulently put *bozales* on the *Amistad.* Reshipment under passports erroneously calling them *ladinos* and "passengers for the government" was an "artifice" used for the "double purpose" of evading British cruisers and legalizing the shipment of captives. Baldwin noted that it was remarkable that over a year had passed since the district court decision declaring the blacks free, and the Spaniards had still not produced evidence for their claims. "And yet," Baldwin said, "strange as it may seem, during all this time, not only the sympathies of the Spanish minister, but the powerful aid of our own government have been enlisted in their behalf!"[14]

Baldwin's performance drew favorable reaction. According to the New York *American,* it carried "research and force." He had talked for four hours in an effort to persuade the Court to dismiss the right of the United States to appear as a party in the case. It was not a national matter, he insisted; it belonged to the states. Furthermore, the blacks had a right of self-emancipation on the basis of the law of nature. Yet, when making the latter claim, Adams observed, Baldwin did so in "cautious terms, to avoid exciting Southern passions and prejudices, which it [was] our policy as much as possible to assuage and pacify." Adams considered it a "powerful and perhaps conclusive" speech, but he worried that "executive influence" would affect the Supreme Court's decision.[15]

Baldwin had raised the inflammatory issue of whether the states rather than the federal government through Congress should determine the status of blacks in America. This question had profound implications for later controversies over fugitive slaves. The irony was that here the abolitionists were seeking to protect blacks from the federal government by appealing to states' rights. By the 1850s Southerners had adopted the same argument turned inside out, appealing to states' rights to protect slavery (though not in the case of fugitive-slave-law enforcement) from the federal government.

II

At long last, after an absence from the courtroom of over three decades, John Quincy Adams prepared to stand before the Supreme Court to do what he never would have believed conceivable: to defend helpless blacks from what he considered to be the machinations of the White House in veritable collusion with a foreign government. Adams was a troubled man, and not only because of the coming trial. On February 19, the day proceedings were originally scheduled to have begun, a close friend of Adams's had died; Taney had agreed to postpone the argument until Monday, the twenty-fourth. As Adams rose to present his case, he felt "deeply distressed and agitated," but once under way his "spirit did not sink." In his diary he wrote that he had a "grateful heart for aid from above" and felt "humiliation for the weakness incident to the limits of my powers." But he had risen to the occasion because the case depended on the "steady and undeviating pursuit of one fundamental principle"—the "ministration of *justice.*" The Court had to protect the blacks against the "immense array of power" exerted by the executive and the Spanish minister "on the side of *injustice.*"[16]

Adams repeated many of the arguments presented by Baldwin, but his central thrust was the charge of executive interference. The guiding principle in the case, he insisted, had to be the Declaration of Independence. Pointing to a copy of the document mounted on a courtroom pillar, he declared, "I know of no other law that reaches the case of my clients, but the law of Nature and of Nature's God on which our fathers placed our national existence." The court was a protector of "JUSTICE," which meant the "constant and perpetual will to secure to every one his own right." And yet the executive had combined with the government of Spain to deny human rights to the blacks of the *Amistad.* From the beginning of the case, Adams argued, the White House had shown sympathy for the whites and antipathy toward the blacks. To Argaiz on December 13, 1839, Forsyth had written that "all proceedings in the matter, on the part of both the executive and judicial branches of the government have had their foundation in the assumption that those persons alone were the parties aggrieved; and that their claim to the surrender of the property was founded in fact and in justice." By what right, Adams indignantly asked, had the administration extended sympathy to the two Spanish perpetrators of the violence and not to their victims?[17]

Adams repeated his earlier charge that there was a pattern of executive behavior opposed to the blacks. On September 5, 1839, District Attorney Holabird of Connecticut had written to Forsyth that the blacks were under indictment for murder and that the next term of the circuit court would begin on September 17—at which time, Holabird wrote, "I *suppose* it will be my duty to bring them to trial, unless they are in some other way disposed of." Adams remarked that it was "easy to understand in what 'other way' he wished them disposed of." Holabird had closed the note by declaring, "Should you have any instructions to give on the subject, I should like to receive them as soon as may be." Four days later, on September 9, the district attorney wrote that, after examining the law, he had found no basis for American court jurisdiction over the case, because the alleged offenses had occurred on a ship belonging to a foreign nation. Thus, according to Adams, the district attorney had recommended that the United States search for treaty provisions that would allow it to surrender the vessel and blacks to Spain—and preferably "before our court sits." These events, Adams argued, demonstrated the administration's sympathy with the whites—a feeling that Forsyth had wrongfully insisted was national.[18]

The actions of the secretary of state, Adams believed, left the impression of unwarranted executive interference. At one point Forsyth had told Argaiz that the delay in resolving the case arose from reasons which "*it would serve no useful purpose to discuss at this time* [emphasis added], farther, than to say that they are beyond the control of this department, and that it is not apprehended that they will affect the course which the Government of the United States may think it fit ultimately to adopt." Thus, Adams insisted, Forsyth had led Argaiz to believe that "care had been taken to prevent the Africans from being placed beyond the control of the Executive, and therefore he need be under no apprehension that the decision of the courts, whatever it may be, 'will affect the course which the Government of the United States may think it fit ultimately to adopt.'" What other meaning could there be? Adams asked.[19]

According to a British abolitionist and observer at court, Joseph Sturge, Adams accused Forsyth and the Spanish ministers of *"conspiracies"* against the blacks that were characterized by incredible ineptitude by the administration in Washington. Despite the certainty of death upon the captives' return to Cuba, the "American Government deliberately adopted the design of delivering them up, either as *property* or as assassins." The White House found "willing agents" in Holabird and the United States marshal. Adams's major evidence was twofold: Forsyth's note of January 7, 1840, to the secretary of the navy, acknowledging that the USS *Grampus* was under orders to take the blacks to Cuba as soon as the court rendered the expected decision; and Forsyth's note of January 12, 1840, instructing the district attorney to have the blacks put onto the ship without waiting for a defense appeal— "You are not to take it for granted that it will be interposed." Adams demanded, "Was this JUSTICE?"[20]

The *Grampus* affair, Adams declared, was evidence. At the suggestion of the State Department and at the request of the Spanish minister, the ship "in the dead of winter" moved into New Haven carrying secret orders from President Van Buren that instructed the marshal to deliver to Lieutenant John S. Paine all the blacks "under process" before the court. This "memorable order," Adams asserted, was in conformity with the written opinion given earlier by Attorney General Grundy. It was not "*conditional* to be executed only in the event of a decision by the Court against the Africans, but positive and unqualified to deliver up *all* the Africans in his custody under process *now* pending." Nothing in the order, Adams pointed out, prevented Paine from fulfilling his mission while the trial was pending. More important, the order was "sufficient to supersede the whole protective authority of the judiciary." Thus, the executive expected the marshal to obey the president rather than the judge. Did not the president recognize that "the right of personal liberty is individual?" No order could speak in general terms; as the *Antelope* case showed, an order must state a specific number and designate the individuals involved. The presence of the *Grampus,* Adams stated, demonstrated the president's intentions to comply with the Spanish minister's demand. It was also a "signal equally intelligible to the political sympathies of a judge, presumed to be congenial to those of a Northern President with Southern principles."[21]

The White House committed a "singular blunder," Adams declared, for the president's directive to the marshal contained three major flaws: Van Buren had not signed it; it was not a warrant but "a mere order" enclosed in a letter to the marshal; and it made the same mistake as Forsyth's January 7 letter in that it contained a reference to the *circuit* court rather than to the district court. The district attorney had immediately tried to rectify the situation by sending Lieutenant Meade to Washington for corrections. Holabird feared that these mistakes would furnish legal grounds for dismissing the blacks on a writ of habeas corpus. On January 12, Adams explained, Forsyth wrote Holabird that the order had been corrected—although he did not say by whom. The files did not contain the final warrant, Adams asserted, and when the House later called for documents on the case, the original order of January 7 was in the package sent by the president, but not the corrected one. Adams lamented the State Department's carelessness in a case involving lives.[22]

Adams also denounced the president's supposed effort at fairness in agreeing to send Gedney and Meade to Cuba to testify in a trial affecting the blacks' lives. This was not sympathy, he declared. This was not "the abundance of his kindness." What could Gedney and Meade know of the captives' status? "They could testify to nothing but the circumstances of the capture." How could the blacks prove their freedom in Cuba, if in the "capacity of slaves" they could not present evidence? The president's offer was a "mere pretense, to blind the public mind with the idea that the Africans were merely sent to Cuba to prove they were not slaves."[23]

If the president complied with the Spanish demand, Adams declared, he would desecrate the American judicial system. The demand violated the Constitution by calling for interference with the court's jurisdiction. It also infringed upon "the rights of the negroes, of the citizens, and of the States." Adams asserted that Forsyth should have immediately refused Spain's demands as "most extraordinary, inadmissible, and insolent." By not doing so, he led observers to believe that the president was "earnestly desirous" to comply. This in turn encouraged the Spanish minister to repeat his demands. Adams asserted that the president had no power to halt judicial proceedings in Connecticut and to restore the blacks to the government in Madrid.[24]

Spanish demands, Adams explained, were also inconsistent and confusing. On the one hand, they denied American court jurisdiction over the case and sought the return of persons to stand trial for a crime as subjects of Spain; on the other, they wanted the blacks as property, with indemnity to the owners for any injuries. Article 9 of the treaty of 1795 relating to ships and merchandise did not apply to human beings. Even the Spanish recognized a difference between "merchandise" and "persons." In a dispatch of September 6, 1839, Minister Calderón wrote Forsyth that the *Amistad* had left Havana "laden with sundry merchandise, and with fifty-three negro slaves on board." Calderón had distinguished between "merchandise *and* negroes," Adams insisted. The wording in the treaty article made it absurd to argue that merchandise included persons. It required the return of merchandise to port officials, "in order to be *taken care of* and restored *entire* to the true proprietor." Did "entire" apply to human beings? "A stipulation to restore human beings *entire* might suit two nations of cannibals," he sarcastically remarked, "but would be absurd, and worse than absurd, between civilized and Christian nations." Asserting that he spoke from personal experience, he noted that when the nations renewed the treaty in 1819, he as secretary of state had conducted the American side of the negotiations and that no one had considered merchandise to include human beings.[25]

Furthermore, Adams asked, if the court had no right to institute proceedings, how could it determine the merchandise? How could it decide whether the blacks were Spanish subjects? Or pirates and robbers? The Spanish had based their first claim on the treaty of 1795 in declaring that the blacks were "merchandise, rescued from pirates and robbers." Yet, as Adams discerned, the Spanish minister had combined "merchandise" and "robbers" into one and the same. The situation had become ridiculous. "The merchandise was rescued out of its own hands, and the robbers were rescued out of the hands of the robbers." Surely this was not the treaty's meaning. Vattel had said that "no construction shall be allowed to a treaty which makes it absurd." Adams asked, is "any thing more absurd than to say these forty Africans are robbers, out of whose hands they have themselves been rescued? Can a greater absurdity be imagined in construction than this, which applies the double character of robbers and of merchandise to human beings?"[26]

Spanish demands, Adams declared, also violated decency. The ministers had not asked the president for the blacks as property, nor had they sought delivery under Spanish law. Instead, they expected the president to "turn himself into a jailer, to keep these people safely, and then into a tipstaff to take them away for trial among the slave-traders of the barracoons." These demands would negate the writ of habeas corpus, Adams insisted. "Has the 4th of July, '76," he wondered, "become a day of ignominy and reproach?" In answer to Argaiz's claim that the "public vengeance has not been satisfied," Adams exclaimed, "The 'public vengeance'! What public vengeance? The vengeance of African slave-traders, despoiled of their prey and thirsting for blood! The vengeance of the barracoons!" The Spanish wanted the president to act as "man-robber" and *"rescue"* the blacks from the court so as to deliver them to satisfy the public vengeance of African slave traders. "Where in the law of nations is there a warrant for such a demand?" Adams asked. Despite the attorney general's claim that a ship's papers were not subject to scrutiny, Adams believed that such documents were open to examination when the outcome could mean that the president might send the blacks to Cuba, "to be sold as slaves, to be put to death, to be burnt at the stake."[27]

Adams also complained that Forsyth had rebuffed British efforts to intervene. When Fox had expressed the hope that the president would act on behalf of the blacks, Forsyth accepted the note only as "evidence of the *benevolence* of Her Majesty's Government, under *which aspect alone* it could be entertained by the Government of the United States." Yet Fox's letter had a tone different from that of the Spanish note. His was "courteously worded," casting "no imputations" upon the United States and seeking "no unconstitutional and despotic interference" of the executive with the judiciary. Fox had only expressed his government's *"anxious hope"* that the president would secure the liberty to which the blacks were entitled by law. But when Fox called for presidential action, Forsyth made his government's opposition clear: "You must be aware, sir, that the Executive has neither the power nor the disposition to control the proceedings of the legal tribunals when acting within their own appropriate jurisdiction." Adams derisively exclaimed, "How sensitive the Secretary is now! ... How alive to the honor of the country." Yet when the Spanish minister demanded the "most inadmissible, the most unexampled, the most offensive," Forsyth made no effort to vindicate his nation's honor in the face of humiliating demands that reeked of vengeance.[28]

At 3:30 P.M. the Court adjourned and Adams closed the first four and a half hours of his defense. He was not satisfied. He had reviewed the correspondence between Forsyth and the Spanish ministers, but, as he lamented in his memoirs that evening, his lack of access to the communications had not allowed him "half the acuteness" and a "tenth part of the vigor" he wanted. In addition, he had ended his presentation "somewhat abruptly," unable to give a detailed review of the *Antelope* decision. Indeed, he had left it "almost entirely untouched." Francis Scott Key, who had argued and lost the *Antelope* case, had recently warned him of its potential impact on the *Amistad* blacks. Somehow, Adams had to counter its influence by emphasizing the importance of natural law and simple morality. He did not despair. "I did not," he wrote, "I could not, answer public expectation; but I have not yet utterly failed. God speed me to the end!"[29]

Assessments of Adams's first day in court varied. Romantics discerned the symbolism of a descendant of the Revolutionary generation recalling the principles of the Declaration of Independence; others noted that he had rambled. One observer praised Adams's "masterly vindication" of "those great & eternal principles of right, of liberty, & of law that lie at the foundation of all genuine democratic and righteous government." The New York *Commercial*

Advertiser remarked that his performance was "eloquent and affecting," but the New York *American* asserted that his argument related more to the politics of the case than to its merits and was "certainly not so much to the point as could have been desired." The New York *Evening Post* called his defense a "harangue" and a "violent political declamation," and it urged abolitionists to keep the justice of their claim to freedom separate from extraneous matters. Though William Lloyd Garrison praised Adams for his powerful defense, another abolitionist, John F. Norton, told Tappan that they would further the cause more through legal means than by emotional appeals and invectives. Norton was probably correct. Justice Barbour remarked to Story that evening as they were returning to the boardinghouse that he was "somewhat surprised" at the line of Adams's argument. But perhaps the most telling comment came from Story himself. In a letter to his wife, he called Adams's defense an "extraordinary argument . . . extraordinary . . . for its power, for its bitter sarcasm, and its dealing with topics far beyond the record and points of discussion."[30]

Adams, however, was optimistic about his second day. He awakened with "much encouraged and cheerful feelings" after an "uneasy restless night," ready to continue his defense. But at 11:00 A.M., the justices entered the courtroom to announce that Barbour had died and that proceedings would not resume until the following Monday, March 1. By that time Washington was rippling with excitement over several events. Americans had flocked into the city for William Henry Harrison's inauguration as president, and the House of Representatives reverberated with speeches by congressmen before their newly arrived constituents. Great feeling had also arisen over the ongoing Alexander McLeod controversy with England, which had resulted from the sinking of the *Caroline* and the longstanding border tensions with Canada. But, according to the New York *American*, the major attraction was the Supreme Court, which was filled early that day, mainly by ladies who had gathered to hear the remainder of Adams's remarks. After appropriate respects to Justice Barbour, Adams spoke for nearly three hours, repeating his condemnation of the Van Buren administration and calling again for justice.[31]

III

After Baldwin and Adams completed their case for the defense, Gilpin returned to the floor on March 2 to conclude his argument for the United States. In a three-hour presentation, he reviewed Baldwin's argument with, according to Adams, "great moderation of manner" while "very slightly noticing mine." Gilpin emphasized two points: that satisfactory evidence of property required the return of the *Amistad,* its cargo, and the blacks to Spanish subjects on the basis of the treaty of 1795; and that the United States had the right to intervene in securing the return of property demanded by the Spanish minister. On the first point, Gilpin at last took notice of the Spanish government's demand for criminals when he argued that the call for extradition of the blacks as fugitives did not interfere with a demand for them as property. On the second, he maintained that even though private parties were seeking the return of private property, the United States government still had an obligation to act when the Spanish minister asked for assistance in representing the parties. Private claims, Gilpin declared, had merged with those of the United States.[32]

Adams's charges against the Van Buren administration had had an effect, for Gilpin now vehemently denied executive interference in the case. At the Spanish minister's urging, Gilpin declared, the president fulfilled treaty obligations by filing the case before the judiciary, which had the property within its custody. His "suggestion" on file stated the Spanish minister's argument that the blacks were property, to be restored under treaty terms, and sought the court's inquiry into how America could meet its obligations. Yet the defense inexplicably called this "executive interference" and "executive dictation." Since a treaty was the supreme law of the land, the executive's duty was to enforce its provisions, and the White House had taken "proper steps" toward this end. It was a "daily occurrence" for the executive to implement judicial decrees; no special laws were necessary.[33]

Gilpin was correct in asserting that the executive had the power to intervene as the first step toward bringing in the courts. The execution of a treaty *was* the responsibility of the executive. If the judiciary believed the case satisfactory, the executive's interposition constituted what Gilpin called a proper part of judicial proceedings. But the problem was that Gilpin had described an action that was legal and had then attempted to square that action with the president's behavior. The two actions were not synonymous. As the abolitionists suspected but were unable to prove without documentation from State Department files, the executive had intervened not in order to bring in the courts but to *avert* their involvement. The executive acted *before* and *without* the judiciary.

Only when the White House failed to circumvent the judicial process did it retreat into the position that it had taken proper action
toward the courts' participation. Perhaps Gilpin, who was not in
office at the time the case originated, did not realize this; but an
examination of pertinent documents would have established this
chronology.

Gilpin now also allowed that the Spanish had made a "double
demand" for the return of the blacks as both property and criminals. From the first, however, the Spanish ministers had consistently appealed to the treaty of 1795. Calderón's letter of September 6, 1839, called for a recognition of the law of nations and of
treaties between the United States and Spain. Both Calderón and
Argaiz, Gilpin insisted, repeatedly referred to the "double character" of the demand for the slaves. Argaiz on November 25, 1839,
sought the "same double demand"—that the United States should
surrender the blacks as property and as criminals. He based his
demand for property on John C. Calhoun's Senate resolutions of
April 15, 1840: that a ship on the high seas in peacetime and on a
legal voyage was, by international law, under sole jurisdiction of
the country signified by the flag overhead; that if such a ship was
forced into the port of a friendly power, its cargo, all persons on
board, their property and their rights, fell under the protection of
international law. These resolutions, Gilpin argued, referred to
slaves as property and were passed in relation to slaves recently
taken into Bermuda and freed. On the basis of these resolutions,
as well as the treaty of 1795, Argaiz called for the return of the
Amistad blacks as property.[34]

Gilpin's reference to Spain's double demand is perhaps explain-
able. Adams's focus on the issue had forced the attorney general to
acknowledge the Spanish government's view of the blacks as both
criminals *and* slaves. But it is noteworthy that Gilpin made no references to potentially inflammatory terms used by Argaiz—"assassins" and satisfying the "public vengeance." Instead, Gilpin
referred to "pirates" and "robbers"—arousing fewer emotions and
fitting the wording in the treaty of 1795. He did not admit to either
an error or a deception (as Adams charged) in Forsyth's handling
of the case. Gilpin ignored that allegation by focusing on America's
interest in complying with the treaty terms. Whether the Van
Buren administration returned the captives as property or as criminals, the move would be above reproach: it would not alter the
White House's insistence that the blacks were legally slaves, and

their delivery would be in accord with treaty obligations with Spain.

Executive intervention in the case was proper, Gilpin asserted; the appellees had no justification for attempting to censure the president. On several grounds—treaty agreement, constitutional requirements, international relations, legal precedents—the interposition of the executive was attributable to "duty and propriety." Gilpin argued that no principle was "better settled" in the country's political affairs than that the judiciary deferred to the executive on diplomatic issues. When America's executive sought redress for a foreign court's decision, it dealt with that country's executive. If Spain disagreed with a court decision, that conflict had no effect on rights under a treaty or procedure by the American executive. In the *Amistad* case, the president was awaiting the court's findings, which would provide the "just and only basis of ultimate decision by the executive."[35]

Gilpin insisted that the United States had to adhere to a "golden rule" in international relations: "let us do to them as we wish them to do to us." If the United States was someday in the same situation as the Spanish were, the American minister in Madrid would interpose on behalf of fellow citizens. If that foreign government did not facilitate such interposition, the United States would have grounds for complaint. This was the procedure adopted by the Spanish minister on behalf of Ruiz and Montes. The United States had to allow a procedure that it claimed for itself.[36]

Gilpin argued that slaves were property within the United States. Citizens owned them as property; they bought and sold them as property; Congress passed legislation on them as property. States were admitted into the Union with congressional approval only after their constitutions recognized slaves as merchandise capable of being owned, transported, and bought and sold. The Constitution of the United States allowed states to regulate their internal property—and at the time of its formation, slaves were one type of property. The Constitution also protected the rights of states to enlarge upon this property by importing slaves until 1808. If slaves were not property, the United States government had no right to demand indemnity from England for slaves freed in Bermuda. Calhoun's resolutions of 1840 won the Senate's unanimous support in declaring that slaves, though freed as persons and so affirmed by a foreign court, were by international law still property, if the institution of slavery was condoned by the country in which the owner resided.[37]

Despite Gilpin's earlier reference to Spain's double demand, he returned to the administration's original position by concluding that the *Amistad* blacks were slaves and that slaves as well as other species of property were returnable under the treaty of 1795. The terms of the treaty were so general that neither party could exclude slaves as property without the other's approval. Article 16 referred to all kinds of merchandise except that of contraband. The Adams-Onís Treaty of 1819, ratified in 1821, renewed this article. Both nations' executive officials believed that the treaty terms included slaves as property. Regardless of the court's decision, this was evidence of each party's intentions, Gilpin argued, and should receive the highest consideration in interpreting the treaty.[38]

Adams had admonished that when doubt existed over a treaty issue, the safest principle was to choose the interpretation that made greater common sense. But that admonition worked against his case. To reduce confusion, Gilpin had advanced the simplest construction that slaves were property under the terms of the treaty. The overwhelming weight of judicial decisions and legislative enactments leaned toward Gilpin's argument. To have excluded slaves as property under the treaty of 1795 would have required a special provision. Theodore Sedgwick, one of the blacks' defense attorneys, had warned Tappan in the initial stages of the battle that the abolitionists could not win the *Amistad* case if they argued that slaves were not property in the United States. Therefore, common sense dictated that if American diplomats used the term *merchandise* in treaties, they meant it to include slaves as well as inanimate objects. The only way to defeat the government's case, as Sedgwick emphasized, was to undermine the Spaniards' claim to having property rights to the blacks.[39]

And yet common sense argued against Gilpin's allegation that the blacks had committed piracy and robbery. He claimed, "If they are property, they are property rescued from pirates, and are to be restored."[40] Gilpin's argument meant that slaves as persons had acted as pirates in seizing *themselves* as property, requiring the wresting of themselves as slave property from themselves as slave pirates. This argument approached the absurd, which, according to Adams's earlier citation of Vattel, could not apply to treaty interpretations.

Gilpin argued that the blacks were prima facie slaves. In line with the 1795 treaty provision calling for due and sufficient proof, he declared that there could be no doubt that the blacks were slaves owned by Spanish subjects. They were blacks in a country allowing slavery, transported from one Spanish port to another in a licensed coasting vessel, and, at the time of its departure from Havana, in the owners' possession. The "first evidence of property," Gilpin declared, was "their actual existence in a state of slavery, and in the possession of their alleged owners, in a place where slavery is recognized, and exists by law." In addition, Ruiz and Montes had documents required by Spanish law to prove ownership. Their certificates carried the signature of the captain general and the countersignature of the port captain, affirming that the blacks belonged to the Spanish citizens holding them. The court of another country had no right to question such prima facie evidence. These rules were vital to international relations. If the United States disregarded the above proofs of property, it would violate its own proofs of property.[41]

In answer to the claim that the certificate was a "mere passport" and not evidence of property, Gilpin asserted that testimony indicated that it was the "necessary and usual evidence of property." Though it was Ruiz's "personal passport," it was not a "mere personal passport," because it allowed him to take property with him, and it "ascertained and described that property." Despite the defense attorneys' assertion that the blacks were imported into Cuba from Africa after the Anglo-Spanish treaty of 1817, their evidence was not legally sufficient to permit the American court to rule the importation a violation of law. Only a Spanish court could establish violations of Spanish law. Since only municipal law could deal with the question, it would serve no purpose to prove that the importation was illegal. If fraud was clear, Gilpin insisted, the remedy would have to come from Spanish courts, not from the United States. In the *Antelope* case, Chief Justice John Marshall had declared, "The Courts of no country execute the penal laws of another." In the *Eugénie* case, Justice Story relied upon documentation of ownership in directing the return of a French ship operating in violation of French laws against the slave trade. Story explained that this enabled "the foreign sovereign to exercise complete jurisdiction," and promoted the "great interests of universal justice." These principles governed relations among nations.[42]

Gilpin concluded that the blacks' actions had not put them "in the actual condition of freedom." If slaves by Spanish law, they remained so on Spanish ships. A similar act of revolution in Cuba would not have made them legally free: "No nation recognizing slavery, admits the sufficiency of forcible emancipation." American courts could not rule that such an act constituted a "release from slavery." Not only would the ruling be applying America's municipal regulations in Spanish territory, but it would be contrary to America's own laws. If the blacks were free, it could only be because they were not slaves when they first boarded the *Amistad,* not because of some subsequent action. Without evidence proving their freedom, the captives were of necessity slaves.[43]

Gilpin's closing statements were long and elaborate but, to Adams's relief, contained no new ideas. Though mentioning Spain's double demand, the attorney general argued on the principles set out first by his predecessor during the autumn of 1839.

IV

On March 9, after the Court dispensed with a brief order of business, Justice Story prepared to give the decision. A native of Massachusetts, Story was conservative, strongly nationalistic, an eminent scholar and jurist, as sensitive to an individual's rights as to a strict adherence to the law. He had served on the Supreme Court since 1811, distinguishing himself by legal treatises and learned decisions. Though opposed to slavery, Story had no use for abolitionists, whom he regarded as a threat to ordered society. Story was a staunch supporter of property rights who agreed with a colleague on the bench, Smith Thompson, that as long as American law protected property in slaves, his duty as judge was to uphold the law.[44] If politics created strange bedfellows, so did the law. It seemed likely that those members of the Court who detested slavery would ally with the Southern justices to return a verdict favorable to the administration in Washington and that of Spain. The lack of confidence on the part of Adams and the abolitionists seemed justified.[45]

Story read the decision; only Justice Baldwin dissented, and without submitting a written opinion. Story explained that the justices found an error in the circuit court's affirmation of the district court decree ordering the blacks' delivery to the president of the United States for transportation to Africa in accord with the congressional act of March 3, 1819. According to Story, the blacks did not fall under its provisions, for their captors had not taken them from Africa and into the United States in violation of America's laws prohibiting the slave trade. The captives had not been imported or sold as slaves. In the initial claim by the United States government, Story observed, it had expressed a willingness to accept one of two options: either return the blacks to their Spanish owners as property or, if the Court ruled that they were not slaves, define them as blacks illegally brought into the country, returnable to Africa under the congressional act of 1819. Story assumed that the United States had dropped the second claim, since Gilpin had not mentioned it. Although the district court had decreed the captives' delivery to the executive for transportation to Africa under the act, the United States was correct in not insisting on this now. That act did not apply to the *Amistad.* When the schooner entered American waters, the blacks were in possession of themselves and claiming freedom. They had had no intention "to import themselves here as slaves, or for sale as slaves."[46]

The main issue in the case, Story declared, was whether the blacks were the property of Ruiz and Montes and returnable under Article 9 of the treaty of 1795, which dealt with ships and merchandise. Story ruled that the prosecution had not proved its claim to property and that the blacks were free. Since they had never been slaves, they could not have been pirates or robbers, and the treaty of 1795 did not authorize their restoration to Spain. Indeed, Story insisted that the treaty was not applicable to the case. Article 6, still in force because of the Adams-Onís Treaty, had no bearing, because it referred to instances in wartime where property of subjects of either signatory nation had by force come under the territorial jurisdiction of the other. Article 8 related to incidents involving some uncontrollable factor—weather, pirates, enemies— forcing the ship of one country to seek refuge in a port of the other. Article 9 stipulated that ships and cargo saved from pirates or robbers at sea and brought into the port of either signatory nation should be taken to port officials and "restored entirely to the proprietary, as soon as due and sufficient proof shall be made concerning the property thereof." For the *Amistad* to fit either Article 8 or 9, Story explained, certain conditions had to be plain: that the blacks fit the meaning of merchandise stipulated in the treaty; that American officials rescued them from pirates or robbers on the high seas; that the blacks were pirates or robbers, unlawfully seeking escape from slavery; that Ruiz and Montes could document their claim to ownership. The *Amistad,* Story declared, did not fit either article, because weather and enemies had not determined the vessel's landing in American waters and because the blacks were not pirates.[47]

But the most important point making the treaty inapplicable, Story declared, was that the *Amistad* blacks were not slaves. If slaves under Spanish law, they would fall into the category of merchandise referred to in the treaty. In wording that followed closely that found in Baldwin's original arguments in the lower courts, Story ruled that the blacks had never been lawful slaves of Ruiz and Montes. They were "natives of Africa," "kidnapped" and "unlawfully transported to Cuba, in violation of the laws and treaties of Spain, and of the most solemn edicts and declarations of that government." Evidence was "cogent and irresistible" that Ruiz and Montes had made a "pretended purchase" with "full knowledge of all the circumstances." The United States district attorney had admitted in the courts that the blacks were native Africans recently taken into Cuba. Spanish laws, treaties, and decrees had abolished the African slave trade and made participation in it a "heinous crime." Africans brought into Spanish territories were free. The *Amistad* captives were free blacks, and the treaty of 1795 did not apply.[48]

Story affirmed the right of self-defense by persons held illegally. In his own writings, he had admitted that a situation could arise in which the checks-and-balances principle ceased to work and the various branches of government concurred in "a gross usurpation." There would be no usual remedy by changing the law or passing an amendment to the Constitution, should the oppressed people be a minority. Story concluded, "If there be any remedy at all . . . it is a remedy never provided for by human institutions." That was the "ultimate right of all human beings in extreme cases to resist oppression, and to apply force against ruinous injustice." Mutiny was a right of persons illegally enslaved. They might commit "dreadful acts" to win freedom, Story allowed, but they could not "be deemed pirates or robbers in the sense of the law of nations."[49]

The real issue in the *Amistad* case, Story explained, was a conflict of rights between parties. Since neither Spanish law nor treaty was applicable, "conflict of rights between the parties under such circumstances [became] positive and inevitable, and [had to] be decided upon the eternal principles of justice and international law." If the case centered on the ship's goods and American citizens claimed a title against Spanish protestations, those Americans could take their claims before an American court, regardless of the treaty with Spain. All the more, Story declared, a conflict of rights had to be the "very essence of the controversy" when "human life and human liberty [were] in issue." Signatories of the treaty of 1795 never intended to deny equal rights to foreigners who claimed equal justice before American courts. They never sought to deny foreigners the protection afforded them by other treaties or by general laws of nations. The *Amistad* captives, Story insisted, had equal rights to equal justice before American courts. Without positive law, the "eternal principles of justice" had to prevail.[50]

Story admitted that government documents accompanying property on board private vessels of foreign nations were prima facie evidence of the disposition of the cargo; but he did not accept the argument that the mere presence of such documents precluded an examination of their legitimacy. The Court was not attempting to "meddle" with the question of "connivance" in the illegal slave trade by Cuban officials. But it recognized that documents were "always open to be impugned for fraud." Story insisted that nothing was "more clear in the law of nations" than the doctrine that if a vessel's papers were "shown to be fraudulent," they were "not to be held proof of any valid title." A ship's papers were "to be construed as intended to be applied to bona fide transactions." And yet they were subject to fraud, whether in the original acquisition or in their later use. In either case, Story asserted, the existence of fraud undermined the "most solemn transactions" and made a title "utterly void." The treaty of 1795 required the owner to provide "due and sufficient proof" of his property. There could be no proof when there was a "stained tissue of fraud."[51]

Finally, Story upheld Gedney's seizure of the *Amistad* as a "highly meritorious" and "useful service" to the owners of the ship and the cargo. Maritime law always considered such a service to be a just reason for salvage. The one-third rate seemed "sound discretion" because of the "very peculiar and embarrassing circumstances of the case."[52]

The Court's decision showed remarkable restraint in view of the issues involved in the case. Eighteen months of controversy had come to a quiet and undramatic end in the Washington courtroom as Story read a decision that could not have surprised anyone who had examined the matter on strictly legal grounds. The evidence was conclusive. It is impossible to determine the impact of other considerations: popular opinion favored the blacks; their counsel, especially Baldwin, had prepared the case well; Adams had repeatedly reminded the court of its duty to human rights and to the American Republic. In the decision, however, Story had emphasized the law.

Particularly noteworthy was the Court's decision not to examine Adams's charges of executive interference in the case. Story had explained to his wife that Adams had stressed too many extraneous

matters in his defense, and to an extent this was true. His long per-
orations on justice and liberty were somewhat airy. This was
unfortunate, for while they satisfied the abolitionists by becoming
part of the public record, they tended to shift the focus from
Adams's central argument concerning executive misbehavior. And
yet his charges that the president had obstructed the judicial process were serious—so serious that they constituted grounds for a
congressional investigation. Story, however, did not deal with the
question, and since Adams was slow in delivering the manuscript
of his speech to the court reporter, his argument did not appear in
the published *Reports.*[53] Contemporaries who wanted to read
Adams's comments either had to piece them together from newspaper accounts or had to await their publication as an abolitionist
tract. And those who were not abolitionists were probably never
aware of Adams's accusations. Story kept the focus on legal issues
and declared that since the blacks were free, the Court found it
unnecessary to render an opinion on whether the United States
government had a right to intervene in the case. Inasmuch as by
March 1841 Van Buren was no longer president, the Court perhaps
saw no sense in fueling allegations raised by the abolitionists. Harrison from the Whig party was now in the White House, and,
almost as important to the abolitionists, Daniel Webster had taken
Forsyth's place in the administration. Chances for executive interference had diminished markedly, and though Webster was no
abolitionist, he certainly was no Georgia slaveholder.[54] Whether or
not the Court considered these matters in making its decision, it
had fulfilled its constitutional function: to hand down a decision
grounded in the law, relatively free of emotion, and seemingly
devoid of political considerations.

A major point in the Supreme Court's decision was that slaves
were property. When Story declared that in the absence of positive
law the eternal principles of justice had to prevail, he had implicitly legitimized that principle's corollary—namely, that with the
existence of positive law, the same eternal principles became secondary. No matter how immoral the slave trade and slavery itself,
international law required that one nation's decision to legalize
either or both deserved recognition by others. Had the Spanish
government proved that the *Amistad* blacks were legally slaves,
Story would doubtless have accepted the White House argument
and ordered their surrender to Spain. Whether the abolitionists
recognized the ramifications of Story's argument is not clear; if so,
they were wise in saying nothing about them.

The decision also sanctioned the right of revolution when captives were illegally enslaved and no positive law applied. The law was the decisive consideration: if the slavery was legal, there could be no right of revolution; if illegal, any means of escape was acceptable. The *Amistad* decision was a warning to those dealing in the outlawed slave trade that, according to international law, their captives had a right to kill them. It also implied that the law could require society to accept an act contrary to morality and eternal justice. To the disdain of antislavery groups, the decision underlined the supremacy of positive law over natural law and revealed how wide the gap between them had grown. Furthermore, it extended that supremacy into international affairs. Natural law had virtually become residual, although revolution could stem from an appeal to natural law. The abolitionists had not wanted municipal law to apply to territorial waters, and, in a technical sense, they had achieved only a limited victory despite the Court's ruling that the *Amistad* blacks were free.[55]

The abolitionists failed to take advantage of Story's decision to ignore differences in color in affirming the blacks' right to a fair trial in America's courts. He had ruled that the Africans were free blacks, though of foreign nationality, and had recognized their status as persons having the right to participate in the nation's legal process. Instead of highlighting the fuzzy impact that the Court decision allegedly had on the antislavery movement, the abolitionists might have been wiser to focus on the Court's recognition of the individual rights of free blacks. Cinqué and some of the others had personally testified in the lower courts, and their depositions had been accepted as testimony; they had instituted civil suits in the New York courts at a time when their status as either free blacks or slaves was still undefined. Now the highest court in the land ruled that the *Amistad* captives were free and entitled to legal rights usually granted only to white persons. That part of the decision was clear: black people had made a plea for freedom in the American legal system and had won their case.

In the *Amistad* case, the Court had decided along purely legal lines. Story had affirmed that slaves were property and that if the Spanish claimants had proved ownership, he would have ordered their return under the treaty; but the only impression the public received—and the one the abolitionists repeatedly exalted—was that the Court had set the blacks unequivocally free. To heighten the impact, the abolitionists had numerous copies of Adams's defense printed as a propaganda tract advertising that black per-

sons had secured freedom through the American courts. Many sub-
tleties not supportive of the cause disappeared in the excitement
over the victory—that Story had reiterated the slaves' status as
property; that slaves had no rights as human beings; that Story had
by implication affirmed that slave property taken from one jurisdiction to another was subject to return upon appeal; that President Van Buren, if guilty of either illegalities or improprieties,
would go unscathed. At the least, Leavitt bitterly remarked, the
president's executive order attempting to return the blacks to the
Spanish government should be "engraved on his tomb, to rot only
with his memory."[56] No matter how immoral or unethical the
actions of slaveholders and supporters of the White House, the
abolitionists had been unable to furnish proof of a broken law; and
in that absence of evidence the Court rendered its decision.

Adams expressed it best in letters to Tappan and Baldwin: "The
captives are free!" The elderly statesman believed Tappan most
responsible for the outcome. "Thanks," he wrote, "Thanks! in the
name of humanity and of Justice, to *you*."[57] Despite the legal limitations of the abolitionists' victory, they could proclaim to the
American public that the Supreme Court had decreed the freedom
of these black people. Morally speaking, of course, the outcome
appeared at best a Pyrrhic victory in that more than a third of the
captives were dead and the survivors had suffered all manner of
indignities. Denied bail, the thirty-six male captives had undergone eighteen months of incarceration in a dingy and unsanitary
room that measured a bare twenty by thirty feet and contained
cribs arranged in rows as beds. Furthermore, they had been
treated like caged animals on display before fascinated Connecticut citizens who, in the carnival spirit of the age of P. T.
Barnum, paid a few cents to gaze on the so-called savages as cannibals and tattooed pagans rather than human beings held captive
thousands of miles from home. If Tappan and friends could hang
their hopes on nothing else in the Court decision, they could high-
light Story's comments upon the eternal principles of justice in
celebrating a victory for freedom.

11

In Perspective

The reaction to the Supreme Court decision was predictable. Southerners were not pleased, Northerners praised the verdict without discerning any implications for slavery, and the abolitionists pronounced it a milestone for their cause. Expressions of dissatisfaction in the South were mild, which perhaps suggested that the *Emancipator* was correct when it had earlier observed that the Southern press wished to keep the *Amistad* affair quiet for fear of its setting a dangerous precedent for American slaves. The Mobile *Commercial Register & Patriot* considered the court decree an "insult" to Spain and "no small triumph" for the abolitionists, whereas the Charleston *Courier* and the New Orleans *Times Picayune* merely reported the outcome. The *Courier* remarked, however, that Story's ruling had not "come up to the expectation of many in its arguments." The New York *Commercial Advertiser* meanwhile called it a victory for "life and liberty," a "great and glorious triumph for humanity," vindication of the "universal law of the Creator," a "great moral spectacle." Indeed, the decision seemed providential since it coincided with the recent breakup of two of the largest slave-trading establishments in Africa—including Pedro Blanco's, the one the *Amistad* blacks had come through. Baldwin rejoiced in the "Glorious result of our cause" and praised Adams for saving the "national character from reproach and dishonor." To the *Amistad* Committee of Tappan, Leavitt, and Jocelyn, Baldwin noted its "constant & assiduous exertions in the cause of justice." According to another observer, the committee had managed to "awaken a sympathy in the public mind" on behalf of the blacks. Leavitt hailed the "glorious triumph of *justice*—of liberty, of law, over *sympathy,*—& slavery & executive power." The decision marked "a revival of the Common Law doctrines of the Revolution." Gerrit Smith exclaimed to Theodore Dwight Weld, "What an occasion of thankfulness to God!"[1]

Despite the exultation, the emergence of two major problems soon showed that the *Amistad* affair was still not over: what to do with the captives until the abolitionists could arrange their transportation home, and how to close the *Amistad* issue once it became entangled with domestic politics and America's growing interest in Cuba. After the court decision, the federal government made clear that it would no longer provide their upkeep. Furthermore, some of the abolitionists grew concerned that the captives could become a burden on society and an embarrassment to the cause. In addition, there was the danger of someone's exploiting the blacks as household servants or common laborers, or perhaps attempting to sell them as slaves in the South. Finally, the *Amistad* affair continued to irritate both domestic and foreign affairs as politicians tried to capitalize on Spain's claims for damages in such a way as to encourage that nation to sell Cuba to the United States. Not until the Civil War ended slavery was the *Amistad* case closed.

I

In Westville, Connecticut, Cinqué and his people had anxiously awaited news of the court decision. They had been disappointed before. And what made their repeated disappointments more bitter was that their hopes had risen with the steady encouragement of the abolitionists and then with the district court decision, only to have the seemingly interminable delays of the legal process bring them a sense of both helplessness and hopelessness. But the Supreme Court was the highest tribunal in the land, and there could be no more appeals—and, most of all, no more delays. They knew that the end of the ordeal had come—for better or worse.[2]

When Willcox and Pendleton learned the results, while in New Haven, they rode the two miles to Westville to inform the captives. As they prepared to tell the blacks, Cinqué signaled his countrymen to sit. With worried looks, they heard the marshal declare, "The big Court has come to a decision—they say that you—one and all—are free, and no slaves." Cinqué immediately replied, "Me glad—me thank the American men—me glad." He turned to his people to tell them the news in their own language. They laughed and began talking in Mende. The marshal then called to Cinqué, "You want to go home to Africa?" Expecting a hearty yes, the marshal was surprised to hear Cinqué say, "I don't know. I think one or two days—then say—we all talk—think of it—then me say." Sensing the blacks' distrust, the marshal showed them a newspaper. "There it is in this paper," he said; "read it." Cinqué beckoned to the young boy, Kale, to read it aloud. But Kale was skeptical: "Paper lie sometimes."[3]

At this point, two of the blacks' trusted friends arrived—Townsend and the Reverend Henry G. Ludlow, who assured them that the news was accurate: they were free. Townsend noted that although the blacks showed great joy, they did not exude a "tumultuous outbreak of feeling" similar to that after the district court decision. This was "a more christianlike & dignified gladness, chastened & modified no doubt by the remembrance of their former disappointed hopes." Ludlow agreed to speak to the blacks: "Cinqué, I want you, and all of you, to know that Christ has watched over you—raised up friends for you—and inclined the Court to decide favorably." They replied, "We very glad—love God—love Jesus Christ—He over all—we thank Him." The entire group knelt in prayer while Ludlow thanked God. Banna soon afterward wrote Tappan, thanking him, Adams, and God for deliverance from the "wicked men from Havanas." Kinna repeatedly wrote Tappan, his "Dear friend."[4]

The abolitionists used the Supreme Court decision to promote their cause. They continued to educate the blacks, managed to convert some to Christianity, and raised money for their transportation home by asking for donations and by putting the blacks on public exhibition. All the while they publicized the outcome of the case in books, pamphlets, sermons, and newspapers. The *Amistad* Committee soon arranged to publish two thousand copies of Baldwin's argument. As Leavitt told Adams, they had to "make the most of it" in establishing "great principles."[5]

As part of this publicity effort, Tappan emphasized that the *Amistad* Committee hoped the case would appear as a philanthropic effort and that Baldwin would not expect full compensation for his services. Tappan wrote him confidentially, "You will take into consideration the interesting nature of the case—the essential aid it will give you in your profession—that the funds are derived from men, women & children out of their charity fund." "In view of all," Tappan added, "please let me know what you think would be reasonable. If it appears too much I will take the liberty to tell you so. As we shall publish all our disbursements we wish to do what will be considered proper." The committee assured Baldwin that the pay was the "smallest part" of his reward. Perhaps one day the "Savior and Judge of the World" would say at the Judgment Day, "I was sick and ye visited me, I was in *prison* and ye came unto me." Inside Tappan's personal copy of *The Amistad Case,* there is his penciled notation that Baldwin received only about $700 for at least seventy days of work on the case.[6]

Since the abolitionists regarded the *Amistad* decision not as an end but as a means toward the greater objective of abolishing slavery, the *Amistad* Committee wrote Adams that it was vital to carry the case into all of its ramifications "as fast and as far as prudence and justice would admit." As Tappan emphasized to Baldwin, the committee members were "determined to push the matter as far as they legally *could.*" They thought that Gedney, Willcox, Pendleton, Holabird, and Forsyth were all liable for false imprisonment. Also, they believed that the government of England should be fully apprised of the "shameless prostitution of legal forms and functions" by Spaniards like Ruiz and Montes. Madden's affidavit about the open flaunting of the anti-slave-trade treaties in Cuba had to be brought to the attention of the British government. The committee wanted the "utter nullification" of the Spanish treaty with England and the repudiation of Vega's decree on the right to enslave recently imported Africans into Cuba. In pursuit of these aims, Leavitt wrote George W. Alexander, a leader of the British and Foreign Anti-Slavery Society in London, that the *Amistad* Committee wanted to bring these points before the ministry. The committee asked Adams to send a note to Palmerston, relating a history of the subject and enclosing Vega's statement, the passport, the clearance, and Madden's affidavit. Adams, however, refused to open a correspondence on the matter with any British officials; such a procedure would be improper and illegal because he was not a diplomatic representative of the United States. Undaunted by Adams's reaction, Leavitt notified the British and Foreign Anti-Slavery Society that the *Amistad* Committee had sent Palmerston a note containing documents on the case.[7]

More than once, Baldwin and Adams had to remind the abolitionists that there was no legal recourse beyond the Supreme Court. In response to an inquiry from the *Amistad* Committee about whether the abolitionists might secure the schooner and cargo for the blacks as their property, Baldwin insisted that it was too late. The courts had decided that the schooner belonged to Spanish subjects and that the blacks had been "parties to the proceedings from the first, without interposing any claim to the property." He had been aware of this issue from the first, Baldwin explained, but had not pursued it out of fear that it would prejudice the question of whether the courts might construe the blacks as pirates under the terms of the treaty of 1795. The committee then asked whether Baldwin might seek redress from the federal government for the "unlawful, unreasonable and oppressive" incarceration of the blacks. Baldwin replied that the "regular" judicial process had detained the captives and that liability for false imprisonment could turn only on whether the officials' acts were *"malicious* and without probable *cause."* Adams agreed that the *Amistad* matter was closed. In answer to another suggestion from the committee, he called it futile to prosecute Ruiz and Montes. British authorities had numerous volumes of diplomatic correspondence on the slave trade that showed colonial officials in Cuba openly defying the law. Culpability lay with them rather than with those who exploited the system. Adams put it well when he wrote to Tappan that although the eighteen months of imprisonment grated upon his spirit "harsh discord," there was no way to win compensation.[8]

The *Amistad* Committee remained unhappy with the part of the Court's decision that awarded Antonio to his owners in Cuba. It feared an immediate attempt to remove him from the country and wanted Baldwin to seek Antonio's discharge by securing a writ of habeas corpus. Baldwin immediately replied that Antonio had said in court that he *wanted* to return to Havana—that he did not want freedom. "Unless *he desires* it no Court would issue a habeas corpus for his liberation," Baldwin wrote. "He is not in fact kept as a prisoner but goes about the streets without restraint." The committee persisted. Within two weeks it wrote Baldwin that if Judson refused to order Antonio's release, and if Antonio said he was held against his will, it wanted a writ of habeas corpus. The committee did not believe that there should be any delay or warning, because it had "no favors to expect."[9]

The abolitionists were pushing too far. Story's decision had affirmed that slaves were property and that the *Amistad*'s blacks were free solely on the ground that neither the Spaniards nor the United States government had proved that the captives were slaves. On that same ground, the Court had ordered the return of Antonio, who was unquestionably a slave. But the abolitionists insisted upon a higher principle—that all blacks on the schooner should go free because of the natural right of freedom. Tappan and the others refused to recognize that appeals to morality had not

generated sufficient public pressure to change the law or Story's
defense of it. Under no circumstances could they have established
legal justification for Antonio's freedom.

But, failing legal sanction, there was another way—which again
suggested that the abolitionists did not believe themselves bound
by what they considered an immoral law: the underground railroad. By late March, Antonio had disappeared. Marshal Willcox
saw Tappan immediately, asking assistance in finding the slave.
But Tappan refused. When Willcox insisted that, as a "conscien-
tious and christian man," Tappan had to help him, Tappan replied
that the marshal's "rhetoric & moral philosophy" were "utterly
ineffectual." Tappan confided to Baldwin that Antonio had told
him in New Haven that he did not want to return to Havana.
Tappan added, "I advised him to leave & go where he pleased."
Indeed, Tappan offered assistance, and Antonio soon arrived at
Tappan's house. Tappan had already contacted the "Committee of
Vigilance," whose duty was to help fugitive slaves. By late April,
Antonio was living and working in Montreal.[10]

II

Meanwhile, stories circulated that the *Amistad* blacks were suffering ill treatment in Westville. In mid-March, Kinna wrote Baldwin
that the jailer, Colonel Stanton Pendleton, was "not good man."
Men working for Pendleton had challenged Cinqué to a fight, but
he refused. The New Haven *Herald* reported that arrangements
had been made for the blacks' protection by moving them to an
interior town. An order for their release had gone to the marshal.

But problems developed over custody of the three girls, for even
though Townsend went before the probate court of the district of
New Haven and secured the right of guardianship over them,
Pendleton refused to comply. The were living with him and his
wife, and, according to Pendleton, preferred to remain. The abolitionists had expected this type of trouble, for at the opening of
court in New Haven on March 16, Baldwin, who appeared on
behalf of Townsend, applied to Judge Samuel Hitchcock for a writ
of habeas corpus to win custody of the girls. As plaintiff, Townsend
contended that the probate court had appointed him their guardian. But Pendleton had denied the right of custody, which meant
that the girls were illegally detained. Pendleton's attorneys, Ralph
and Charles A. Ingersoll, intended to establish that the girls were

old enough to make their own decision and that they stayed with Pendleton by choice.[12]

The next morning, Baldwin asked the court to allow "friends of the girls" to meet with them privately. But Judge Hitchcock agreed only to grant an argument on a writ of habeas corpus, which permitted the three girls to appear in court that same afternoon. The defendant denied that Townsend was a legally appointed guardian of the girls and claimed that the "pretended appointment" by the probate judge was "extra-judicial, invalid, and void." The girls, each at least twelve years old, were of "competent age" to choose guardians. Since the appointment was without their knowledge and consent, they should go free with whomever they pleased. Baldwin applied again to talk with the girls in private with the aid of Cinqué, Covey, and others. He wanted to counteract what he believed to be the intimidation by Pendleton and his family, who were present at the trial.[13]

The defense objected to a private meeting. It would be unfair to allow Cinqué to talk with them privately; everyone knew he had absolute control over the blacks. The girls had to decide for themselves. Tappan noted that the Ingersolls' argument was a "long harangue" and "very abusive." It contained a "perversion of facts" and "false charges" and accused Tappan of holding Pendleton's family "up to odium" in the newspapers. Tappan, according to the defense, had interrupted Pendleton's household affairs by sending Covey to see the African girls. In court, Tappan declared, Ralph Ingersoll "abused" two of the abolitionists who came to testify, "imitating their mode of conversing with the Africans & raising loud laughter at their expense & at the expense of the friends of the Africans."[14]

But then the opposing attorneys arranged a compromise that caused the case to take on the air of a circus. Cinqué received permission to explain to the girls in open court, according to Tappan, what Tappan and his friends intended for them. Standing before the girls, Cinqué began talking in his native language, according to the New York *Commercial Advertiser,* "with great power of expression and gesture" and in a "style said to be one of the finest specimens of Mende eloquence." He drummed on until defense counsel suddenly realized that Cinqué was warning the girls that if they stayed with Pendleton, he would transport them to the South and sell them as slaves. After a bitter objection, the court ruled that Cinqué was to speak in English.[15]

But still the spectacle went on. The girls were asked which person they preferred as protector. Frightened by the proceedings, they could barely reply. Were they afraid of Cinqué? No. Of Townsend? No. Of Pendleton? No. Tappan? No. They were "afraid of men." Some "white man" at Pendleton's house told them that Tappan wanted them whipped and sold as slaves. When order returned, the hearings continued that afternoon and into the late evening, many witnesses testifying as to the condition of the girls and to the propriety of their staying with Pendleton. Several of the blacks appeared, including Kinna, who spoke in English, along with Tappan and the Reverend Leonard Bacon of New Haven. Pendleton's family and others pointed to the three girls' "attainments" in religion and other matters, as Tappan wrote, to leave the impression that they had been well taught and that they loved the Pendletons. The investigation was still not completed at the noon adjournment of March 18. Tappan wrote Jocelyn that the marshal "behaved very well" but that Pendleton had been like a "wild beast."[16]

As expected, on March 19 the court placed the girls under Townsend's custody, but not without incident. After the judge's decree, the girls cried and held on to Mrs. Pendleton as Townsend approached. Pulled loose and taken outside, the girls boarded a carriage surrounded by Yale law students, who hissed and criticized Tappan and others for forcibly taking the youths from a family that wanted only to help them.[17] Such an atmosphere further suggested that the central concern of Americans lay with the captives as *individuals* rather than as a race of people and that the abolitionists' call for universal principles of liberty was still drawing little public attention. To Americans, it seems, the *Amistad* blacks, and in particular the youths, were helpless victims who posed no threat to the community, and who *should not* become tools in promoting the aims of the abolitionists.

The girls soon joined the other captives whom Tappan and friends had relocated from Westville to Farmington, a quiet town of two thousand people, accessible by road from Hartford and by canal from New Haven. It had few proslavery residents; over a hundred of its people, including some of the town's leaders, were members of two antislavery societies. Moreover, the underground railroad had a network there. After hearing Pendleton's threats, Tappan thought it advisable to move the blacks into New Haven by railroad cars. That night he received a note from a contact in Farmington that they had arrived safely and would take lodging on a farm belonging to the abolitionist A. F. Williams. The "Mende Indians," as they became known, were housed in barracks, while the three girls moved in with private families. In a school established above a store, the blacks resumed studies with Professor George E. Day, doctor of divinity of Yale. Cinqué was called the Black Prince, who performed native dances and somersaults on the lawn.[18]

For all this apparent exultation, signs of impatience had appeared among the blacks. Kale sent a deeply moving letter to Adams, which the *Emancipator* published. "We want you to ask the Court what we have done wrong," Kale wrote. "What for Americans keep us in prison. Some people say Mendi people crazy; Mendi people dolt, because we no talk American language. Merica people no talk Mendi language; Merica people dolt? . . . Some people say, Mendi people got no souls. Why we feel bad, we got no souls? We want to be free very much. . . . Dear friend, we want you to know how we feel. Mendi people *think, think, think.* Nobody know what he think; teacher he know, we tell him some. Mendi people have got souls. We think we *know* God punish us if we tell lie. We never tell lie; we speak truth. What for Mendi people afraid? Because they got souls. . . . Cook say he kill, he eat Mendi people—we afraid—we kill cook; then captain kill one man with knife, and cut Mendi people plenty. We never kill captain, he no kill us. . . . All we want is make us free."[19]

As the blacks became increasingly restless about additional delays in returning home, tragedy struck again. In August 1841 Foone, a good swimmer, drowned in the canal under circumstances leading some to believe that he had committed suicide out of despondency caused by absence from home and family. Perhaps more than any event, this sorrowful news convinced Tappan and the other abolitionists that they could not wait through the winter to send the Africans home.[20]

"What shall be done with them now that they are free?" was the poignant question Baldwin had asked of Adams shortly after the Court decision. The blacks' freedom "was a barren gift," he lamented, adding, "They were here, separated from their homes by the distance of half the globe and in a state where they might be pitied but were not wanted." Baldwin warned Leavitt that the blacks had to return to Africa before they became a burden on society. Tappan had earlier expressed his belief that if the abolitionists did not facilitate the blacks' return, they would become "worthless vagabonds." Baldwin believed that there was no reason for delay.

The Court decision was correct, and the Reverend Ludlow affirmed that the captives wanted to go home. If they could be taken to Sierra Leone, Baldwin asserted, they "might, *perhaps,* reach their own country."[21]

Adams indignantly wrote Baldwin that the government of the United States was bound by "honor and justice" to help the blacks return to Africa. Since the district, circuit, and supreme courts agreed upon a verdict of freedom, the blacks had to have been free when Gedney found them. The Van Buren administration had used *"military, executive and judicial* authorities" to deprive the blacks of liberty and property by confiscating the *Amistad* and its cargo and putting the blacks in prison for eighteen months. Now they were "adrift in a strange land" and in need of assistance. In "conscience," the federal government should provide their way home and give them indemnification for false imprisonment. Adams recommended that "Friends" of the *Amistad* send a memorial to the president, asking for a vessel to take the blacks to Sierra Leone. If the president felt that he lacked authority, they should send a memorial to Congress. Approval of aid would be "suitable and proper atonement."[22]

Adams asked Secretary of State Webster if John Tyler, the new president following Harrison's sudden death, could arrange passage for the Africans. The courts had declared them free, and yet the government had taken the vessel from them—the one "found in their possession"—along with its cargo, which was "their lawful prize of war." Adams argued for the equity in returning them home, and he noted that the act would be in harmony with congressional enactments on the slave trade. But Webster, according to Adams, seemed "startled" at the argument that the *Amistad* and its cargo were the Africans' property. He nonetheless raised no objection to passage in a public ship and agreed to discuss the matter with the secretary of the navy.[23]

Considerable time passed without a reply, however, and in late August 1841 the *Amistad* Committee directly asked the president for help in returning the blacks to Africa. But when Adams talked with Webster and Tyler in September, he got the impression that the president would do nothing until Congress passed an act allowing assistance. Instead, Tyler proposed that the American Colonization Society assume the burden. This suggestion, of course, aroused no interest among the abolitionists. Later the president told Tappan that he would like to furnish transportation but that there was no law authorizing a public vessel for that purpose. Tyler was not going to act without congressional approval, and Leavitt had learned that most members of Congress opposed the move. The abolitionists were fearful of returning the blacks in a merchant ship because of the risk of recapture by the Spanish. As Tappan noted to Sturge, "What a triumph they would have if they could re-enslave Cinqué & his companions."[24]

The abolitionists were more successful in soliciting British assistance in returning the blacks to Africa. The foreign secretary, Lord Aberdeen, met with members of the British and Foreign Anti-Slavery Society and, according to John Scoble, was "exceedingly well disposed to the blacks of the *Amistad.*" Aberdeen thought it probable that a British ship of war could assist their return to Africa.[25]

With winter coming, the abolitionists decided that they could not wait for a British decision. On November 27, 1841, the thirty-five black survivors (two others had died) of the initial fifty-three on the *Amistad,* including the three girls, along with James Covey, departed New York on the barque *Gentleman.* Money to support the voyage had come from private donations, public exhibitions, and from the Union Missionary Society, which blacks had formed in Hartford to oversee the five white missionaries and teachers who were sent with the *Amistad* captives to found the first Christian mission in Africa, the American Missionary Association.[26] With assurances from the British minister Fox of the "good offices and protection" of British naval commanders along the African coast as well as the British governor of Sierra Leone, the vessel reached its destination in January 1842, after a fifty-day voyage—nearly three years after the blacks had left their homeland.[27]

III

The controversy over the *Amistad* did not end with the blacks' departure. It repeatedly affected the issues of slavery and race relations at home and diplomatic concerns with England and Spain regarding Cuba. Indeed, foreign and domestic arguments inside the United States soon became entangled in the debate over slavery. Charges lingered of executive interference in the judicial process, dramatically revived in 1848 when Martin Van Buren made another run for the presidency. In the meantime John Quincy Adams led a public attack on a House committee report containing a mysterious change in date on documents relating to the *Amistad* case—a change that, like earlier ones, worked solely in the administration's favor. All the while, America's interest in Cuba grew, providing the Spanish government with leverage for demanding indemnification for the *Amistad* and its cargo. Southern influence in Washington became evident when that region's supporters in Congress disregarded the Supreme Court decision and expressed a willingness to award compensation to the government in Madrid, implying, not surprisingly, that the blacks of the *Amistad* had been legitimate slaves belonging to Ruiz and Montes.

Spanish reaction to the Supreme Court decision had been predictable. Argaiz complained to his home government that the "abolitionist spirit" had taken over the Court and that the decision had come at the "sacrifice of justice, treaties, and reciprocity." He again cited Pinckney's Treaty in lodging a formal protest with Secretary of State Webster and in demanding indemnification for the *Amistad* and its cargo, including the "negroes found on board," and for the injuries and losses sustained by Ruiz and Montes during their imprisonment. On December 12, 1839, Argaiz asserted, Forsyth had promised that the final decision would come "from no other source, than the Government of the United States." With considerable sarcasm, Argaiz suggested that perhaps the courts should conclude treaties—especially since they apparently had the right of "interpreting, considering and deciding" them. In a short time he learned that the "self-styled friends" of the blacks had persuaded Antonio to board a steamboat for New York. The Spanish consul in that city followed Antonio but learned from Tappan that the slave would not be returned to Spanish authorities. Antonio, according to the consul, was "beyond . . . reach." Spain had lost every argument in the *Amistad* case.[28]

It was evident that Argaiz had misinterpreted the role of the government in Washington or that Forsyth had led him to believe that the president alone would dispense with the matter. Whether or not intentional, the secretary's unfortunate use of the phrase *Government of the United States* left his words open to the interpretation that he was referring to the executive, not to the courts. And yet if one takes into account the Van Buren administration's unmistakable efforts to control the case, Forsyth's dispatch of December 1839 perhaps has added meaning. It seems likely that the secretary used the term *government* interchangeably with *executive office,* and that he was confident the president would be the final arbiter. The central issue was a treaty obligation, as the White House saw it, and that matter fell into the domain of nations or governments. The only role of the Supreme Court was to facilitate the implementation of treaty terms.

The Van Buren administration's efforts to steer those events left problems for succeeding presidents. Not only did the *Amistad* difficulty irritate relations with Spain, but that government's repeated protests over the Court decision made the issue susceptible to political exploitation in the United States. As American interest in Cuba grew during the next few years, the *Amistad* claims became subject to political manipulation. To Northern congressmen who feared that acquisition of the island would be a boon for slaveholders, it became expedient to oppose reparations payments as part of a strategy designed to keep relations with Spain unsettled and thereby obstruct negotiations over Cuba. To Southerners who wanted the island, the Spanish argument regarding the *Amistad* was valid. In the context of the turbulent 1850s, the *Amistad* argument was another critical issue dividing the nation.

For the time being, however, President Tyler faced more-pressing matters and his only objective was to close the *Amistad* case. To him, the Supreme Court's decision was final. After assuring Argaiz that American authorities would search for Antonio, he assumed that there would be no further correspondence on the issue. As Webster explained to the Spanish minister in September 1841, the executive could not "review or alter" the Court judgment. If Ruiz and Montes wanted reparations, they had to go through the American courts. Webster informed Argaiz in June 1842 that Forsyth's use of the term *government* had included the Court as well as the executive and that the Spanish minister would have a legitimate complaint only if he showed that the American courts had acted "corruptly" or been legally wrong. If the courts were "respectable, impartial, and independent," their decisions were final.[29]

For several reasons the Spanish minister would not let the *Amistad* matter rest. Argaiz's persistence was partly attributable to national pride, although on a personal level he doubtless suspected that a failure to win reparations could cost him his ministry. But the government in Madrid had a more important consideration: freedom for the *Amistad* blacks could become a license for slave rebellions in Cuba and the surrounding islands. British abolitionists also kept the situation in an uproar. The Spanish government feared that the British intended to extend the powers of the mixed commission to seek freedom of slaves imported after 1820. Such a policy would "shake the Island of Cuba to her foundations" and constitute "the first alarm bell" of Spain's overthrow. The Spanish now were apprehensive that the British might regard the Supreme Court's decision as an excuse for some form of intervention in Cuba to enforce the Anglo-Spanish treaties against the slave trade. Indeed, Spanish officials feared that England sought the immediate emancipation of all slaves in the West Indies, and the "universal supremacy" of England—at any costs.[30]

Both in Madrid and in Washington, the Spanish government continued to make demands for reparations. The American chargé in Madrid, Aaron Vail, reported on his long conversations with the Spanish minister of foreign affairs, Don Antonio González, who repeatedly called for a settlement that would resolve the controversy and help thwart British designs on Cuba. At one point Vail inquired about the rumor, ultimately unsubstantiated, that the captain general on the island intended to compensate owners of the *Amistad*'s blacks from funds set aside for indemnities to the United States under a treaty of 1834. González denied the story, insisting that he could not assume compensation payments until the American government had recognized the claim. In late 1842 the Spanish first minister of state, Count Almodóvar, told the American minister in Madrid, Washington Irving, that his government had made no effort to link the *Amistad* claims with those of the treaty of 1834. In the meantime Argaiz warned of "horrible consequences" if slaves could murder their owners and flee to the United States.[31]

By early 1843 there was evidence that some members of the Tyler administration were beginning to question Webster's stance and to yield to Southern pressures to meet Spain's demands. To the House of Representatives, the president remarked that although strict legality required that the American naval officers receive salvage rights, it might seem "wise" to refund the payments as evidence of the "entire good faith" of the United States in meeting treaty requirements. Attorney General Hugh Legaré of South Carolina had already told Webster that the secretary of state's arguments on the recent *Creole* slave revolt made Spain's position in the *Amistad* matter "quite irresistible." In November 1841, slaves on the American coastal slaver *Creole* had mutinied and entered the Bahamas, where British officials set them free on the basis of their home government's emancipation act. Webster had called for indemnification on the grounds of comity. At first glance the *Amistad* and *Creole* mutinies were remarkably similar—except that, as Legaré failed to note and as Webster fully realized, there was no question that the *Creole*'s blacks were legally slaves. When Argaiz

likewise claimed that the *Creole* and *Amistad* cases were analo-
gous, Webster remained firm in resisting the demands for
compensation.[32]

In early 1844 Washington became concerned that the recent
recall of Argaiz signaled a change in policy that might hurt American interests in Cuba. The secretary of state at that time, Abel
Upshur of Virginia, regarded the move with "uneasiness and suspicion" and warned Irving in Madrid that relations with Spain
were of a "delicate nature," particularly because of "supposed
designs of another Power" upon Cuba. Irving had to convince the
government in Madrid that a crisis over Cuba would cause the
United States to act. Upshur instructed him to gather information
on any British action suggesting imminent intervention. Some
time later Irving reported that Argaiz's recall was due to several
factors—among them his "mismanagement" of the *Amistad*
affair.[33]

IV

During the spring of 1844, events in the House of Representatives
indicated that America's interest in Cuba was going to lead to
greater pressure on the government to give in to Spain's demands
on the *Amistad.* The Committee on Foreign Affairs agreed with
President Tyler's recommendation to pay the *Amistad* claims as a
sign of good faith and in accord with admiralty and international
law. The Southerners and their sympathizers on the committee,
including its Democratic chairman, Charles J. Ingersoll of Pennsylvania, adopted the argument presented by Spain and the Van
Buren administration in advocating a maneuver that ignored the
ruling of the Supreme Court. The committee report declared that
"piratical negroes" had committed murder and that the papers of
the ship were "perfectly authenticated and regular." Under maritime law the president of the United States should have returned
the vessel, cargo, and blacks to the Spanish minister. Understand-
ings of comity bound governments to surrender "pirates, murderers, robbers, and other criminals."[34]

The House committee had taken the Southern position on the
Amistad affair and blamed the abolitionists for America's failure
to honor treaty obligations with Spain. It declared that a "lawless
combination" had argued on behalf of the blacks, erroneously
claiming that the captives had exercised their "natural right of self-
defense" and were "justified by law for the murder, robbery, and

piracy they had committed." The committee insisted that abolitionist claims were a "perversion of law" by "zealots" encouraged
by the press. Their "fanatical denunciation" of slavery had made
these blacks into "heroes and martyrs."[35]

According to the House committee report, the Supreme Court
based its decision on questionable evidence. The justices had relied
on the claim of a "half-civilized, totally ignorant African [James
Covey], found in some English vessel, who could hardly be conscious of the obligation of an oath, and who swore to no knowledge
of such circumstances as should decide any question." That testimony was "seconded" by the testimony of another (Charles Pratt),
a second African from an English ship, "who scarcely pretended to
know anything, but was permitted to swear that he believed the
other." This "tissue of fabrication" was completed by the opinion
of a professor (George E. Day of Yale College) who in a few weeks
claimed to have learned the African language and thought the
blacks to be *bozales* and not *ladinos.* The professor's teacher of the
African language was one of the African sailors, who claimed to
have been taken from his country and brought to America by a
British man-of-war. The other African, a cook on a British sloop
of war, affirmed that the first African's deposition was credible.
Then two of the slaves, Cinqué and Grabeau, who had led the
mutiny, testified to events. On this "proof"—by Madden, "who
knew nothing," by "an extremely ignorant negro," by "another
very ignorant negro," and by a "professor's opinion"—the district
attorney admitted in court that the blacks were native Africans
brought into Cuba recently.[36]

The committee based most of its argument on a factual error
that remains a mystery. The report alleged that Lieutenant Gedney
had seized the *Amistad* on August 26, 1840 (the year was actually
1839), and that since the blacks had been in Cuba for "at least four-
teen months" (after their arrival from Africa, in June 1839), they
had been domiciled. There was no evidence that Ruiz and Montes
believed that the blacks had come from Africa recently. If the
Amistad was engaged in the illegal African slave trade, the committee noted, the captain, crew, and owners aboard took strangely
little precaution. The vessel left Havana during the day with over
fifty blacks, none in irons or "any slavish restraint," and with only
the captain, his slave, two seamen, and the cook, who was also a
slave. It was "extremely improbable" that Ruiz and Montes, the
captain general, and other officials in Cuba all "conspired in the
perilous guilt" of certifying the blacks with fraudulent papers and

transporting them to plantations without adequate force to put down a mutiny.[37]

The House committee report emphasized that its concern was not only with the effect of the case on foreign relations but also with its impact on America's "own institutions and harmony." The Constitution and congressional legislation condoned slavery, and yet for years the nation had been unsettled by "new and extreme—your committee believed unnecessary, and unwarrantable, and unconstitutional interference with vested rights." The committee discerned a "menacing attitude of part of a community," which had "overpowered the law of nations, of treaties, and of the United States." The report concluded, "The law must be supreme, if liberty is to be preserved; and it must be everywhere the same, north and south."[38]

The committee made two recommendations. First, proper indemnity to Spain should be $70,000 for all the property involved. Second, to publicize the correction, Ingersoll presented a motion to print ten thousand copies of the report.[39]

It is difficult to believe that Ingersoll, as chairman of the committee, did not know one of the most basic facts in the *Amistad* case—that Gedney seized the vessel in 1839, not in 1840. The year of the seizure was important because it affected the question of domicile, which helped to determine slave status. Since Ingersoll's private papers provide no answer as to motive, it is impossible to be certain; and yet it does seem fair to assume that he saw the obvious political advantage in showing the year of the seizure to be 1840.[40] Ingersoll's party affiliation was Democratic, his political allegiance Southern, his committee Southern dominated. Furthermore, the report appeared within the context of the South's growing desire for Cuba, which necessitated better relations with Spain; and it became public on the eve of the presidential election of 1844. The Democratic party still rested on a tenuous alliance of North and South that would have been threatened by a debate over slavery.

Ingersoll's report underwent bitter attack by the Whig representative from Ohio, Joshua Giddings, a staunch opponent of slavery. He angrily pointed out that while the House "gag rule" blocked antislavery petitions, the Committee on Foreign Affairs was attempting to "send out this vindication of the slave trade to the people at the public expense." Whereas Ingersoll had voted for the gag rule to prevent agitation in Congress of the slavery question, he was willing to pay claims that would condone the slave trade and involve the people of the North in the "guilt of this commerce." The gag resolutions, he said, "present the majority of this House in the attitude of holding a gag in the mouths of their constituents with one hand, while the other is employed in taking from their pockets the funds to be paid over to these slave dealers, as a compensation for their intended victims, who possessed the heroism to escape from their grasp." Giddings insisted that the mutiny was justified by the blacks' "natural and inalienable right of life and liberty"—by "natural law." It was self-defense, "the first law of nature."[41]

Perhaps in part because of Giddings's attack, the House on April 19 voted to table Ingersoll's motion to print extra copies of the committee report. Giddings had proclaimed that a vote for compensation to Spain was a vote for the African slave trade. Chances are that he influenced Northern congressmen concerned about standing accused of contributing to the traffic. Adams must have thought so. That night he recorded in his memoirs that Giddings's hour-long speech of the preceding day had "sickened the Democracy of Ingersoll's report."[42]

The controversy over the report did not end, however, for in the spring of 1845 Adams publicly charged that someone had tampered with the record in an attempt to prove that the blacks were legally slaves. His case rested upon the claim that Gedney had seized the *Amistad* in 1840 rather than in 1839. This "gross and glaring forgery" was central to the claim for indemnity because it helped determine whether the blacks were *bozales* or *ladinos.* It thus affected the blacks' disposition as either "piratical murderers" or free men resorting to "justifiable homicide" in escaping the illegal slave trade. The change in date also had an impact on the issue of whether the passport was a fraud. Previous hearings before the courts had established that the blacks were *bozales,* Adams noted; the United States district attorney had made this admission. If the seizure of the *Amistad* had taken place in 1840, that fact alone would have invalidated the entire testimony by suggesting that the blacks could *not* have been recent imports. Though Adams was unable to prove his allegation, he continued to believe that the "error" was so blatant that it had to have been intentional.[43]

V

Sensing that the timing was propitious, the Spanish minister to Washington, once again Angel Calderón de la Barca, renewed his government's demands for reparations. He had additional reason for optimism: the secretary of state was now the outspoken Southerner, John C. Calhoun. Calderón warned in December 1844 that a further delay in honoring the *Amistad* claims would cause the Spanish king shortly to adopt those measures that he judged "most conducive toward the reparation of the wrongs suffered by the owners of the *Amistad.*" Failing to win satisfaction, Calderón waited before trying again—this time in January 1846, when the United States was embroiled in controversies with England over the Oregon question, and with Mexico over the Texas issue and other matters that led to war in the spring of that year.[44]

To President James K. Polk's secretary of state, James Buchanan of Pennsylvania, Calderón renewed the *Amistad* claims. The secretary was a Democrat with known Southern sympathies, and he was from the same state as Ingersoll. Furthermore, the possibility of wars with both England and Mexico made good relations with Spain imperative in order that either potential antagonist might be prevented from securing a foothold in the Caribbean. Buchanan informed Ingersoll, still chairman of the House Committee on Foreign Affairs, that the *Amistad* was a "source of irritation and discord" with Spain and "highly prejudicial" to American interests, and that there were "strong reasons" for accepting Spain's interpretation of the treaty of 1795. After the Mexican War began, Calderón was so confident that the United States would pay the claims that he informed Buchanan that the government in Madrid had instructed its people to observe strict neutrality during the war.[45]

Ingersoll was likewise certain that the committee report would pass and agreed to resubmit it to the House of Representatives—where it again encountered Adams's opposition. Amid additional appeals from Calderón during the latter part of 1846, Senator Ambrose Sevier, a Democrat from Arkansas, made a motion to insert in the House civil and diplomatic bill an amendment calling for the reduced amount of $50,000 to the *Amistad* claimants in exchange for Spain's agreement to relinquish claims against the United States. It passed without a count in February 1847. In March, however, Adams launched another assault on those who sought to reverse his triumphs in the case. Afterward the House voted down the Senate amendment by a wide margin. The sectional alignment of voters suggests that questions of morality had less to do with the outcome than did political viewpoints on slavery.[46]

The *Amistad* issue did not lie dormant for long. Polk and Buchanan made known their wishes that the next session of Congress
would make the appropriation, and this news doubtless encouraged the Spanish government to search for some means of exert-
ing pressure on the United States to settle the claims. If there was
no truth in the earlier allegations that the government in Madrid
had tried to link these reparation demands with an unrelated debt,
evidence now suggested that Spain was ready in the summer of
1847 to withhold these payments in lieu of an *Amistad* settlement.
The United States was still at war with Mexico, and again it
seemed an auspicious time to force a settlement of the claims controversy. But the Polk administration refused to give in to these
tactics. Such a move, Buchanan warned the Spanish minister for
foreign affairs, might jeopardize relations with Spain.[47]

The Polk administration adopted its position in the claims controversy more out of expediency than on the basis of the facts. In
late 1847 Andrew T. Judson, the district judge who had rendered
the decision of January 1840, wrote the blacks' attorney, Roger S.
Baldwin, that he was sorry the president favored the claims payment and that he wished Polk "had taken the trouble to have
investigated the fact" before recommending that Congress honor
Spanish demands. "The *false names,* and the fictitious *permit* or
pass could not strengthen a title wholly groundless before."[48] But
the president agreed with Buchanan, who in turn agreed with
Ingersoll, and the result was a Southern position on the *Amistad*
claims controversy that hurt relations with Spain when no settlement was forthcoming and sharpened the sectional division over
slavery at home.

In January 1848 the *Amistad* issue flared once more in Congress,
when Giddings revived the claim that Ingersoll had falsified the
record of the Supreme Court and on that basis had called for
indemnification to Spain. Giddings wanted the issue brought
before a select committee that would have Adams and others on it
and that might settle the issue before someone altered more government records.[49]

These were inflammatory charges, but they soon gave way to
more-pressing concerns. By early 1848 the war with Mexico was
winding down, and Adams's death in February 1848 temporarily
ended the accusations of executive interference and impropriety.
Despite his efforts of nearly a decade, Adams had been unable to
establish culpability. Questions of guilt remain, even though the

best evidence still rests only on a pattern of events that promoted the administration's political interests.

The *Amistad* claims issue refused to die, however, for in the presidential election of 1848 the candidate on the Free-Soil ticket was Martin Van Buren. Representative John Rockwell of Connecticut, a Whig, revived the charges against the former president in bitterly denouncing the efforts to pay the Spanish indemnity. In the *Amistad* decision of 1841, Rockwell declared, Southerners on the Supreme Court "rose above their prejudices, if they had any; neither sectional nor party feelings prevented their deciding the case upon its merits—of finding the facts according to the evidence, and of administering justice according to law." Rockwell echoed Adams's charges in accusing the Van Buren administration of wrongdoing. Though no one would ever know all details of this "conspiracy," Rockwell admitted, the suggestive evidence was plentiful. To achieve its objective, Rockwell exclaimed, the White House had been prepared to violate the "laws of God and man."[50]

Rockwell's charges led Van Buren's supporters to attempt to exonerate their candidate. Salmon P. Chase of Ohio urged Van Buren to write a letter explaining the views that had governed administration policy during the *Amistad* affair. Though there is no reply in the Chase papers, Benjamin F. Butler, the New York attorney involved in the Ruiz episode of 1839–40, saw the letter and lamented to Van Buren that it was not "very satisfactory." In mid-October 1848 another supporter, apparently doubting the wisdom of voting for Van Buren, asked the former president how he had justified White House policies. Within a week, Van Buren deftly explained that he had been moved by the injustices committed against the *Amistad* blacks and that he had promoted the "most humane policy" possible at the time. Van Buren added that he had "endeavoured to make the terms of it as just & liberal as the nature of the cases would admit of."[51]

Van Buren's explanation could not have been satisfactory to those who questioned his behavior in the *Amistad* case. In accord with political demands of 1839–40, he had perhaps adopted the "most humane" and "liberal" stand conceivable; but by any other standard he had failed to present a convincing case for his administration's willingness to send the captives to near certain death in Cuba. Nor was that all. Van Buren had not responded to the charges of misconduct in office. There can be no doubt that much of Rockwell's speech was politically inspired; and yet if one considers his charges against the Van Buren administration within the context of the persistent accusations made by Adams and the abolitionists, the suspicion of executive interference lingers.[52]

During the early 1850s Daniel Webster returned to the position of secretary of state, where he must have experienced a sense of déjà vu in confronting the *Amistad* issue.[53] This time, however, the focus shifted to the Senate. In February 1851, and again in 1852 and 1858, Senator James Mason of Virginia, chairman of the Committee on Foreign Relations, presented a committee report based entirely on Ingersoll's House committee report—including the erroneous date of 1840—and calling again for payment of the *Amistad* claims.

Like the House during the early 1840s, the Senate split along sectional lines in arguing the question of whether to accept the Mason committee report and pay the *Amistad* claims. In February 1851 Chase of Ohio denounced the proposal and declared that the *Amistad* blacks were "absolutely free," and John P. Hale of New Hampshire, a prominent Democrat with Free-Soil convictions, exclaimed that the payment would make Americans participants in the illegal and immoral slave trade. Henry Clay of Kentucky, a Whig renowned for his ability to resolve bitter political arguments by compromise, tried to calm the angry senators by calling for an inquiry into the matter. Emphasizing that he did not lean toward making the payment, he declared that his central concern was to draw attention to those in the North who seized hold of everything they could "to reagitate the country" on the issue of slavery. After an acrimonious debate, the Senate overwhelmingly voted in favor of Clay's proposal. The *Amistad* claims question had become a live issue in the Senate.[54]

Sectional divisions repeatedly blocked the *Amistad* compensation effort. According to the Mason committee report first submitted to the Senate on February 19, 1851, only the executive had responsibility for assuring fulfillment of treaty terms. A decision to surrender the vessel and its cargo did not rest in the courts. The executive and legislative departments had never been subordinate to judicial decisions in foreign affairs. The committee concluded that the attorney general was correct in autumn 1839 when he stated that the United States had no right to question the *Amistad*'s papers; they were conclusive evidence that the blacks were slaves. The committee recommended payment in excess of $50,000, which was based on the value of property when shipped out of Havana, and reasonable compensation for Ruiz and Montes for their detention inside the United States. The Senate, however, took no action. Despite appeals from the executive office, Mason's later attempts likewise failed to convince the Senate to honor the claims. In each instance the issue led to heated exchanges along sectional lines.[55]

Meanwhile, in the House, the *Amistad* issue kept resurfacing. In late 1853 Giddings reviewed the legal issues involved in the case and revived the charges of date falsification. Five years later, during a House debate over the *Amistad* claims, Representative DeWitt Leach of Michigan accused Buchanan, now president, of bringing up the matter "at the behest and for the interests of slavery." The president, Leach declared, had supported the Dred Scott decision of 1857—that slaves taken into American territories were the property of their masters—and now denounced the *Amistad* decision for one reason: the Scott decision was "proslavery" and the *Amistad* "antislavery." Buchanan had succumbed to "the power behind the throne"—the "slave power."[56]

During a Senate debate of February 1859 over the acquisition of Cuba, Mason called for the removal of what he tried to dismiss as "one little obstruction" to the negotiations—the *Amistad* bill. Senator William H. Seward, a strong antislavery advocate from New York, immediately remarked that if resolution of the *Amistad* case facilitated passage of the Cuba bill, that was yet another reason for his opposition to paying the *Amistad* claims. Senator William Fessenden of Maine agreed with Seward that if that "trifling matter" of the *Amistad* stood in the way of Cuba's acquisition, he, too, opposed the claims bill.[57]

As the *Amistad* claims remained unpaid by Congress despite presidential appeals, the Spanish continued their protests and repeatedly related the issue to others that arose between the nations. In February 1854, relations between Spain and the United States seriously deteriorated over the *Black Warrior* affair. Spanish officials in Cuba were bitter over American filibustering expeditions on the island, and they seized the *Black Warrior,* an American steamer en route from New York to Mobile. The charge was that it did not have proper papers. Angry Americans throughout the country demanded punishment of the Spaniards. Calderón, however, declared that his government refused to pass sentence without hearing the accused officers' defense. The affair blew over, but not without Calderón's remarking that even though the United States had not made indemnity for the *Amistad,* his government had never accused Washington of an "unfavorable disposition."[58]

Over three years later the *Amistad* matter arose again when the United States minister to Spain, Augustus Dodge, was having little success in adjusting a series of unrelated American claims—the so-called Cuban claims, originating in 1844. He finally complained to Secretary of State Lewis Cass that America's failure to pay the *Amistad* claims had caused him "mortification" because the Spanish brought up that issue every time he pressed them for "just and long delayed claims" owed the government in Washington.[59]

By the time of the American Civil War, the *Amistad* claim was becoming a dead issue. On March 5, 1860, the two nations signed a convention in Madrid designed to settle all claims between them. Spain agreed to pay most of the Cuban claims that the United States held against the government in Madrid, while leaving the remainder unpaid until the *Amistad* matter was settled by arbitration. These two major issues, along with a host of minor claims, were sent to a joint board of commissioners for arbitration. But the Senate in June divided along proslavery and antislavery lines in twice refusing to approve the treaty because of the deduction of the *Amistad* claims. That December, on the eve of the secession crisis in South Carolina, President Buchanan told Congress that the Senate's refusal to approve the treaty had placed America's relations with Spain in an "awkward and embarrassing position."[60]

Since the *Amistad* issue had become entangled with arguments involving slavery, it was predictable that the Civil War would resolve the controversy. Domestically, once the war resolved the debate over slavery, the *Amistad* ceased to have political appeal and was no longer subject to exploitation. In foreign affairs, the Spanish government realized that its hope for compensation had collapsed with the defeat of America's slaveholding interests. The death of slavery in the United States closed the *Amistad* case.

American law had won freedom for the *Amistad* captives; and yet many of the abolitionists considered this victory as incomplete because the verdict had not rested on the law of nature. The Christian abolitionists continued to insist that slavery was a moral evil that lay beyond man-made law. They realized that in the *Amistad* decision, positive law had triumphed over natural law—so they soon resumed their demands based on a higher law. A careful reader of the great English legal scholar Sir William Blackstone might have recalled his warning that "the liberty of considering all cases in an equitable light must not be indulged too far, lest thereby we destroy all law, and leave the decision of every question entirely in the breast of the judge." Blackstone asserted that "law, without equity, though hard and disagreeable, is much more desirable for the public good, than equity without law." Otherwise, the result will be "infinite confusion" as every judge becomes a legislator.[61] But because the abolitionists' purpose was high and noble, their enemies were necessarily immoral and sinful. Many of those who occupied extreme positions against slavery felt that the laws of the land were immoral and thus not binding on them.

Among the abolitionists, Baldwin and Sedgwick early recognized that lasting justice could come only within the system. Others would soon join them in searching for remedies inside the legal and constitutional framework of the nation. Slavery, some declared, might be undercut by focusing on congressional control over interstate commerce and over territories. Shortly after the circuit court decision of September 1839, Lewis Tappan realized that only by arousing public opinion against unjust laws could the abolitionists succeed in changing those laws and making the nation adhere more closely to Christian virtue. Perhaps he, too, had grasped the real lesson of the *Amistad* affair—that the captives were free because America's legal system had performed its function of securing justice.

The *Amistad* decision constitutes an historic milestone in the long struggle against slavery and for the establishment of basic civil rights for everyone, regardless of color. In a monumental decision, Justice Story ignored all contemporary restrictions based on color or race in declaring the captives free as "kidnapped Africans"—that under what he called "the eternal principles of justice," they had the inherent right of self-defense and could kill their captors to win freedom. Baldwin and his defense team had made this argument from the beginning of the court battle and had emerged triumphant. Adams likewise advocated these ideas before the U.S. Supreme Court; but he went one important step further in attempting to strike a mortal blow at slavery itself by appealing to the natural law principles underlying the Declaration of Independence. Story privately expressed amazement at the irrelevance of such a far-reaching argument. And yet, he too must have recognized the value of a strategy that stood natural law next to man-made law, thereby exposing the huge chasm between them and making it clear that justice prevailed only when the two forms of law existed in harmony. Story surely grasped the lack of cohesion between the Declaration of Independence and the Constitution itself. Adams's moving words, however, had challenged Americans to examine their racial attitudes.

The importance of the *Amistad* case lies not so much in the reasoning behind the Supreme Court's decision but in the fact that the blacks, in collaboration with white abolitionists, had won freedom. Legal technicalities did not matter. Adams emerged as the great champion of freedom based on what the *Amistad* supporters could exalt as "the eternal principles of justice." Although Story had focused on self-defense in his decision, the victorious abolitionists could expand his words to include a condemnation of the immorality of slavery. Thus the popular impression of blacks liberated from slavery spoke much more loudly than did the legal limitations of the decision. Positive law had come into conflict with natural law, resulting in the captives going free. In that sense the *Amistad* case made a significant contribution to the fight against slavery.

Appeals to morality had also fostered a climate of opinion among Americans that encouraged questions about the wisdom of continuing such glaring incongruities between positive law and natural law. How could the Constitution, in protecting slavery, exist in harmony with the Declaration of Independence, which did not? For positive or man-made law to change for the better, some sort of awakening experience must expose the shortcomings of that law. The *Amistad* incident provided that experience. The black captives did not go free on the basis of universal principles of moral right; but the fervent arguments raised by the abolitionists ultimately forced the truth onto Americans—that slavery did not exist on the basis of natural law but out of man-made laws attributable to a selfish mixture of economic, political, social, and racial motivations. Such passionate issues led to a bitter conflict between human and property rights that helped bring on the Civil War.

In the long perspective of history, the *Amistad* case dealt a serious blow to slavery that, seemingly minor at the time, constituted one more debilitating injury to the peculiar institution. After sustaining an increasingly steady succession of attacks by antislavery advocates, slavery would finally collapse and die in the Civil War.

A final note: No conclusive evidence has appeared to determine whether or not Cinqué was reunited with his wife and three children, and, for that same reason, there is no justification for the oft-made assertion that he himself engaged in the slave trade on his return home. The period following his arrival in Africa in early 1842, like many other parts of this Shakespearean-like drama, remains a matter of speculation.

Notes

Abbreviations

African Captives	*The African Captives: Trial of the Prisoners of the "Amistad" on the Writ of Habeas Corpus before the Circuit Court of the United States for the District of Connecticut, at Hartford; Judges Thompson and Judson, September Term, 1839* (N.Y.: American Antislavery Society, 1839)
African Repository	*The African Repository and Colonial Journal* (Wash., D.C.: American Colonization Society, monthly)
AHN	Estados Unidos, Expedientes, Sección de Estado, Archivo Histórico Nacional, Madrid, Spain
AMA	American Missionary Association
ARC	Amistad Research Center, New Orleans, La.
DS	Department of State
FARC	Federal Archives and Records Center, Waltham, Mass.
GPO	Government Printing Office
H. Exec. Doc. 185	U.S. Congress, *House Executive Documents,* no. 185, 26th Cong., 1st sess. (1840)
JQA	John Quincy Adams
LC	Library of Congress, Washington, D.C.
Memoirs of JQA	Charles Francis Adams, ed., *Memoirs of John Quincy Adams, Comprising Portions of His Diary from 1795 to 1848,* 12 vols. (Philadelphia: Lippincott, 1874–77)
MHS	Massachusetts Historical Society, Boston, Mass.
NA	National Archives, Washington, D.C.
Side-light	Annie Heloise Abel and Frank J. Klingberg, eds., *A Side-light on Anglo-American Relations, 1839–1858; Furnished by the Correspondence of Lewis Tappan and Others with the British and Foreign Anti-Slavery Society* (N.Y.: Augustus M. Kelley, 1979; originally published in 1927)
Yale	Sterling Memorial Library, Yale University, New Haven, Conn.

Introduction

1. This account is based on the following sources: Testimony of Lt. Richard W. Meade, Nov. 19, 1839, 7–9, U.S. District Court, Records for Conn., FARC; Deposition of Dr. [?] Sharp, Nov. 19, 1839, 10, ibid.; Deposition of James Ray (crew member of *Washington*), Dec. 3, 1839, 147–48, ibid.; Deposition of George W. Pierce (crew member of *Washington*), Dec. 3, 1839, 149, ibid.; 15 Peters 518, 521–22 (1841); John W. Barber, *A History of the Amistad Captives* (New Haven, Conn.: E. L. & J. W. Barber, 1840), 3–6; Joseph Sturge, *A Visit to the United States in 1841* (London: Hamilton, Adams, 1842), app. E, xxxii, xxxiv; Augustus F. Beard, *The Story of the "Amistad,"* pamphlet published by AMA (n.d.), in ARC; N.Y. *Commercial Advertiser,* Aug. 27, 1839, 2; N.Y. *Evening Star,* Aug. 30, 1839, 2; N.Y. *Morning Herald,* Sept. 2, 1839, 2; Albany (N.Y.) *Argus,* Sept. 7, 1839, 3; Boston *Liberator,* Sept. 6, 1839, 143.

2. As reported by an observer in the Albany (N.Y.) *Argus,* Sept. 7, 1839, 3.

3. R. Kent Newmyer, *Supreme Court Justice Joseph Story: Statesman of the Old Republic* (Chapel Hill: U. of North Carolina Press, 1985), 368.

4. Russel B. Nye, *William Lloyd Garrison and the Humanitarian Reformers* (Boston: Little, Brown, 1955), 41–43.

5. Garrison privately admitted that for practical reasons abolition would have to be gradual. Louis Filler, *The Crusade against Slavery, 1830–1860* (N.Y.: Harper & Row, 1960), 61 n. 28.

6. Elbert B. Smith, *The Death of Slavery: The United States, 1837–65* (Chicago: U. of Chicago Press, 1967), 34.

7. Ibid., 36. Lawrence J. Friedman shows how abolitionists often moved from one position to another, depending on circumstances. See his *Gregarious Saints: Self and Community in American Abolitionism, 1830–1870* (Cambridge, Eng.: Cambridge U. Press, 1982). On the concept of a government of God, see ibid., 48, 64; Lewis Perry, *Radical Abolitionism: Anarchy and the Government of God in Antislavery Thought* (Ithaca, N.Y.: Cornell U. Press, 1973), esp. 45, 47, 48, 50, 51, 57; James B. Stewart, *Holy Warriors: The Abolitionists and American Slavery* (N.Y.: Hill and Wang, 1976), 53.

8. See George M. Fredrickson, *The Black Image in the White Mind: The Debate on Afro-American Character and Destiny, 1817–1914* (N.Y.: Harper & Row, 1971), chap. 2. On mob violence of the 1830s, see Leonard L. Richards, *"Gentlemen of Property and Standing": Anti-Abolition Mobs in Jacksonian America* (N.Y.: Oxford U. Press, 1970); Leon F. Litwack, *North of Slavery: The Negro in the Free States, 1790–1860* (Chicago: U. of Chicago Press, 1961), 100–102; Stewart, *Holy Warriors,* chap. 3.

9. Richard K. Crallé, ed., *The Works of John C. Calhoun,* 6 vols. (N.Y.: D. Appleton, 1853–57), 2:631.

10. On the shift to political abolitionism during the late 1830s, see Merton L. Dillon, *The Abolitionists: The Growth of a Dissenting Minority* (De Kalb: Northern Ill. U. Press, 1974), 121. See also Richard H. Sewell, *Ballots for Freedom: Antislavery Politics in the United States, 1837–1860* (N.Y.: Oxford U. Press, 1976).

11. Lewis Tappan to Benjamin Tappan, March 9, 13, 1840, Benjamin Tappan Papers, MS Div., LC; Stewart, *Holy Warriors,* 50, 53, 142–43; Perry, *Radical Abolitionism,* 45, 47, 48, 50, 51, 57; Friedman, *Gregarious Saints,* 48, 64, 75, 93, 104–

5; Staples quote from *African Captives,* 36–37. Staples's position probably came from Locke's argument that every man had a right to his life, liberty, and estate, the three of which he designated as "property."

Chapter 1. The Mutiny

1. Testimony of Grabeau (black captive on *Amistad*), Nov. 19, 1839, 20, U.S. Dist. Ct. Records for Conn., FARC. Testimony of David F. Bacon (observer in Africa), Nov. 19, 1839, 25, ibid.; Curius Dentatus to JQA, Dec. 19, 1840, John Adams Family Papers, MHS; N.Y. *Advertiser & Express,* Oct. 12, 1839, 1; N.Y. *Commercial Advertiser,* Nov. 5, 1839, 2; Joshua Leavitt to George W. Alexander, March 25, 1841, AMA Papers, Box 197, "Sierra Leone" folder, ARC; Basil Davidson, *The African Slave Trade: Precolonial History, 1450–1850* (Boston: Little, Brown, 1961), 84 (originally published as *Black Mother*); Daniel P. Mannix and Malcolm Cowley, *Black Cargoes: A History of the Atlantic Slave Trade, 1518–1865* (N.Y.: Viking, 1962), 107–8; William H. Smith, *A Political History of Slavery,* 2 vols. (N.Y.: Putnam's, 1903), 1:53–60; Christopher Fyfe, *A History of Sierra Leone* (London: Oxford U. Press, 1962), 184, 220, 229; Edwin P. Hoyt, *The "Amistad" Affair* (N.Y.: Abelard-Schuman, 1970), 24–25, 29–30.

2. Bacon testimony on Africa before U.S. Dist. Ct., Jan. 9, 1840, in newspaper clipping in Baldwin Family Papers, Box 186, Yale.

3. Ibid.; Lewis Tappan to *Amistad* Committee, Sept. 10, 1839, printed in N.Y. *Advertiser & Express,* Sept. 14, 1839, 1; N.Y. *Evening Star,* Aug. 30, 1839, 2; Grabeau's account in George E. Day to eds. of N.Y. *Journal of Commerce,* Oct. 8, 1839, printed in "Narrative of the Africans," in *African Captives,* v. Published by the abolitionists, this account of the trial is the fullest available and contains useful background information. Affidavit by Bahoo (African from Bandaboo), Sept. 29, 1839, U.S. Dist. Ct. Records for Conn., FARC; Mannix and Cowley, *Black Cargoes,* 47–48; Hoyt, *"Amistad" Affair,* 26–27.

4. N.Y. *Evening Star,* Aug. 30, 1839, 2; Testimony of Fuliwa (black captive on *Amistad*), Nov. 19, 1839, 21, U.S. Dist. Ct. Records for Conn., FARC; Bacon testimony, Jan. 9, 1840, Baldwin Family Papers, Box 186, Yale; Cross-examination of Cinqué at district court trial of Jan. 1840, cited in N.Y. *Advertiser & Express,* Jan. 11, 1840, 2; Cinqué's explanation to jailer in New Haven, Conn., cited ibid., Jan. 15, 1840, 1.

5. Tappan to *Amistad* Committee, Sept. 10, 1839; Grabeau's account, *African Captives,* v; Testimony of Fuliwa, 21, U.S. Dist. Ct. Records for Conn., FARC.

6. Grabeau's account, *African Captives,* v; Tappan to N.Y. *American,* Sept. 16, 1839, 2; Charles Butler to JQA, Dec. 25, 1840, Adams Family Papers, MHS; U.S. Dist. Ct. Records for Conn., 68-insert, FARC.

7. Tappan to N.Y. *American,* Sept. 16, 1839, 2; Butler to JQA, Dec. 25, 1840, Adams Family Papers, MHS.

8. Public letter from Tappan to Leavitt, Nov. 15, 1841, cited in Joseph Sturge, *A Visit to the United States in 1841* (London: Hamilton, Adams, 1842), app. E, xliv; Arthur F. Corwin, *Spain and the Abolition of Slavery in Cuba, 1817–1886* (Austin: U. of Texas Press, 1967), 39.

9. David Turnbull, *Travels in the West: Cuba, with Notices of Porto Rico and the Slave Trade* (London: Longman, Orme, Brown, Green, and Longmans, 1840),

57, 59–61. See also Butler to JQA, Dec. 25, 1840, Adams Family Papers, MHS. A few months after his withdrawal, Turnbull, accompanied by free British blacks, returned to Cuba as superintendent of liberated Africans. The Cuban governor, Gerónimo Valdés, accused him of organizing a rebellion, had his companions shot, and had Turnbull imprisoned and then deported. See Corwin, *Spain and the Abolition of Slavery in Cuba,* 75–77.

10. Turnbull, *Travels,* 61–62.

11. U.S. Dist. Ct. Records for Conn., 68-insert, FARC; Corwin, *Spain and the Abolition of Slavery in Cuba,* 28. For a good account of the situation in Cuba, see David R. Murray, *Odious Commerce: Britain, Spain and the Abolition of the Cuban Slave Trade* (Cambridge, Eng.: Cambridge U. Press, 1980).

12. Philip S. Foner, *A History of Cuba and Its Relations with the United States,* 2 vols. (N.Y.: International Publishers, 1962), 1:189–90; Corwin, *Spain and the Abolition of Slavery in Cuba,* 40–43; Murray, *Odious Commerce,* chap. 13.

13. Foner, *History of Cuba,* 1:190–91; Corwin, *Spain and the Abolition of Slavery in Cuba,* 42; Murray, *Odious Commerce,* 272, 274, 276.

14. Foner, *History of Cuba,* 1:172–74; Corwin, *Spain and the Abolition of Slavery in Cuba,* 46, 51; Murray, *Odious Commerce,* 82, 114–16.

15. Murray, *Odious Commerce,* ix, 51, 71, 77, 78; Foner, *History of Cuba,* 1:174; reformer quoted ibid., 179–80.

16. Corwin, *Spain and the Abolition of Slavery in Cuba,* 39, 47, 50, 54–55, 62; Murray, *Odious Commerce,* 100, 103, 106.

17. Corwin, *Spain and the Abolition of Slavery in Cuba,* 61–63; Murray, *Odious Commerce,* 101, 103; Hubert H. S. Aimes, *A History of Slavery in Cuba, 1511–1868* (N.Y.: Putnam's, 1907), 125–28, 133–35; Royal Decree from Ministry of Marine, Commerce, and Colonies in Madrid to governor-general (captain general) of Cuba, Nov. 2, 1838, U.S. Dist. Ct. Records for Conn., FARC; Thomas F. Buxton, *The African Slave Trade, and Its Remedy* (London: John Murray Albemarle, 1840), 26.

18. Turnbull, *Travels,* 343–44, 348–49. See also Murray, *Odious Commerce,* 120.

19. Trist to J. Kennedy & [?] Campbell & [?] Dalrymple, July 2, 1839, U.S. DS, Dispatches from U.S. Consuls in Havana, 1783–1906, NA. Trist, consul in Havana from 1833 to 1841, came under heavy attack for allegedly collaborating in the slave trade for personal gain, but a congressional and State Department investigation in 1840 turned up insufficient evidence to sustain the charge. See Corwin, *Spain and the Abolition of Slavery in Cuba,* 63; Warren S. Howard, *American Slavers and the Federal Law, 1837–1862* (Berkeley: U. of Calif. Press, 1963), esp. chap. 2.

20. Turnbull, *Travels,* 155–57.

21. Ibid., 62–63, 344; Charles Butler to JQA, Dec. 25, 1840, Adams Family Papers, MHS.

22. Butler to JQA, Dec. 25, 1840, Adams Family Papers, MHS.

23. For the Spanish foreign minister's suspicion of British interests in Cuba, see Aaron Vail, American minister to Spain, to sec. of state, Jan. 15, 1841, U.S. DS, Dispatches from U.S. Ministers to Spain, 1792–1906, NA. On Spanish fears of British intervention in Cuba, see Murray, *Odious Commerce,* esp. chap. 7, but also 113, 286. For Spain's internal problems, see James M. Callahan, *Cuba and*

International Relations: A Historical Study in American Diplomacy (Baltimore: Johns Hopkins U. Press, 1899), 16, 171–72, 365–66, 414–16; Corwin, *Spain and the Abolition of Slavery in Cuba,* 64, 66; Raymond Carr, *Spain, 1808–1975* (Oxford, Eng.: Clarendon Press, 1982), chap. 5; Eric Christiansen, *The Origins of Military Power in Spain, 1800–1854* (London: Oxford U. Press, 1967), chap. 3.

24. Grabeau's account, *African Captives,* v; Ruiz and Montes version of mutiny, translated from the Spanish paper *Noticioso de Ambos Mundos* of New York, and printed in N.Y. *Advertiser & Express,* Oct. 5, 1839, 2; Testimony of Fuliwa, U.S. Dist. Ct. Records for Conn., FARC; Testimony of Antonio (cabin boy slave belonging to Captain Ferrer of *Amistad*), Nov. 19, 1839, 21–23, ibid.; Passports enclosed ibid., 68-insert; Public letter from Tappan to Leavitt, Nov. 15, 1841. Among the popularized versions of the *Amistad* affair, two of the best are Fred J. Cook, "The Slave Ship Rebellion," *American Heritage* 8 (Feb. 1957): 60–64, 104–6; William A. Owens, *Black Mutiny: The Revolt on the Schooner "Amistad"* (Philadelphia: Pilgrim Press, 1968), originally published in 1953 as *Slave Mutiny.*

25. Ruiz and Montes translated version of mutiny; Tappan to *Amistad* Committee, Sept. 10, 1839; Grabeau's account, *African Captives,* v; Testimony of Antonio, Nov. 19, 1839, 21, U.S. Dist. Ct. Records for Conn., FARC; 15 Peters 522 (1841); Hoyt, *"Amistad" Affair,* 33–34. Cinqué's Mende name was Sengbeh Pieh.

26. Public letter from Tappan to Leavitt, Nov. 15, 1841; Ruiz and Montes translated version of mutiny; Testimony of Antonio, Nov. 19, 1839, 21, U.S. Dist. Ct. Records for Conn., FARC; Hoyt, *"Amistad" Affair,* 36–37.

27. Public letter from Tappan to Leavitt, Nov. 15, 1841; Testimony of Antonio, Nov. 19, 1839, 22–23, U.S. Dist. Ct. Records for Conn., FARC; Cinqué testimony before district court in Conn., Jan. 8, 1840, cited in N.Y. *Commercial Advertiser,* Jan. 10, 1840, 2; Sturge, *Visit,* app. xliv–xlv.

28. Testimony of Antonio, Nov. 19, 1839, 21–23, U.S. Dist. Ct. Records for Conn., FARC; Simeon E. Baldwin, "The Captives of the *Amistad,*" *Papers of the New Haven Colony Historical Society,* vol. 4 (New Haven, 1888), 333.

29. Testimony of Fuliwa, Nov. 19, 1839, 21, U.S. Dist. Ct. Records for Conn., FARC; Testimony of Antonio, Nov. 19, 1839, 21–23, ibid.; Ruiz and Montes translated version of mutiny; Judicial investigation of Aug. 29, 1839, Montes account of mutiny, printed in Albany (N.Y.) *Argus,* Sept. 7, 1839, 3; Judicial investigation of Aug. 29, 1839, Montes, Ruiz, and Antonio accounts of mutiny, printed in N.Y. *Evening Star,* Aug. 31, 1839, 4; Sturge, *Visit,* app., xlv–xlvi.

30. Ibid.

31. Testimony of Antonio, Nov. 19, 1839, 22–23, U.S. Dist. Ct. Records for Conn., FARC. The fate of the two sailors remains in question. At least one writer believes that they lowered the stern boat and made it to shore. See Hoyt, *"Amistad" Affair,* 38–39. But this seems unlikely. Hoyt himself admits that the *Amistad* was nearly twenty miles offshore. Besides, one wonders whether the two men could have fought off the blacks while lowering a boat. Furthermore, if they survived either a swim or a rowing to shore, word of their exploits would surely have reached the newspapers. Probably the *Amistad* blacks were correct when they later declared that the two sailors drowned. Sturge, *Visit,* app. xlv.

32. Testimony of Antonio, Nov. 19, 1839, 22–23, U.S. Dist. Ct. Records for Conn., FARC; Ruiz and Montes translated version of mutiny.

33. Testimony of Antonio, Nov. 19, 1839, 23, U.S. Dist. Ct. Records for Conn., FARC; Ruiz and Montes translated version of mutiny; "Introductory Narrative," *African Captives,* iii; Sturge, *Visit,* app., xlv.

34. Ruiz and Montes translated version of mutiny.

35. Ibid.; "Introductory Narrative," *African Captives,* iii; N.Y. *Evening Star,* Aug. 31, 1839, 4.

36. N.Y. *Commercial Advertiser,* Aug. 26, 1839, 2; Ruiz and Montes translated version of mutiny; "Introductory Narrative," *African Captives,* iii; Sturge, *Visit,* app., xlv. The merchant vessel was the *Eveline.*

37. N.Y. *Commercial Advertiser,* Aug. 26, 1839, 2; N.Y. *Whig,* Aug. 28, 1839, 2; N.Y. *Advertiser & Express,* Oct. 5, 1839, 2.

38. From among many newspaper stories highlighting the mysterious black schooner, see the following: N.Y. *Whig,* Aug. 26, 1839, 2; N.Y. *Commercial Advertiser,* Aug. 26, 1839, 2; Aug. 30, 1839, 2; Sept. 4, 1839, 2; N.Y. *Advertiser & Express,* Aug. 28, 1839, 2; Aug. 31, 1839, 2; N.Y. *Sun,* Aug. 29, 1839, 3; *Morning Courier & N.Y. Enquirer,* Aug. 30, 1839, 2; N.Y. *Evening Star,* Aug. 31, 1839, 4; Wash. *National Intelligencer,* Aug. 28, 1839, 3; Boston *Liberator,* Sept. 6, 1839, 143.

39. N.Y. *Commercial Advertiser,* Aug. 26, 1839, 2.

40. Testimony of Antonio, Nov. 19, 1839, 22, U.S. Dist. Ct. Records for Conn., FARC.

41. Ruiz and Montes translated version of mutiny; Cross-examination of Schyler Conklin (one of the five men encountered by blacks on beach), Nov. 19, 1839, 12–13, U.S. Dist. Ct. Records for Conn., FARC; N.Y. *Advertiser & Express,* Oct. 5, 1839, 2.

42. Testimony of Cinqué, Nov. 19, 1839, 19, U.S. Dist. Ct. Records for Conn., FARC; Testimony of Grabeau, Nov. 19, 1839, 20, ibid.; Testimony of Henry Green, Nov. 19, 1839, 1–4, ibid.; Cross-examination of Green, Nov. 19, 1839, 5–6, ibid.; Testimony of Peletiah Fordham (one of the five men encountered by blacks on beach), Nov. 19, 1839, 13–14, ibid.; N.Y. *Evening Star,* Aug. 31, 1839, 4; N.Y. *Commercial Advertiser,* Aug. 30, 1839, 2. The four men with Green were Fordham, Conklin, Aaron Fithing, and Seymor Sherman. Green et al. suit, Sept. 19, 1839, 2, U.S. Dist. Ct. Records for Conn., FARC.

43. Testimony of Green, Nov. 19, 1839, 2–4, U.S. Dist. Ct. Records for Conn., FARC; Cross-examination of Green, Nov. 19, 1839, 5–6, ibid.; Testimony of Fordham, Nov. 19, 1839, 14–15, ibid.; N.Y. *Commercial Advertiser,* Aug. 30, 1839, 2.

44. See the Introduction for details of Gedney's capture of the *Amistad.*

45. *Morning Courier & N.Y. Enquirer,* Aug. 30, 1839, 2.

46. N.Y. *Commercial Advertiser,* Aug. 26, 1839, 2; Wash. *National Intelligencer,* Aug. 28, 1839, 3.

47. N.Y. *Commercial Advertiser,* Sept. 4, 1839, 2; N.Y. *Evening Star,* Aug. 31, 1839, 4.

48. "Introductory Narrative," *African Captives,* iii.

49. Ibid.; N.Y. *Evening Star,* Aug. 31, 1839, 4; Boston *Liberator,* Sept. 6, 1839, 143; Warrant from president of U.S. to Marshal Norris Willcox, Aug. 29, 1839, U.S. Circuit Ct. Records for Conn., Sept. Term, FARC; Andrew T. Judson to Willcox, Aug. 29, 1839, ibid.

50. Willcox to Judson, Sept. 19, 1839, U.S. Circ. Ct. Records for Conn., FARC.

51. Gedney's libel claim, Sept. 19, 1839, U.S. Dist. Ct. Records for Conn., FARC. In admiralty law, a libel is the written claim filed by the plaintiff.

Chapter 2. Abolitionists and "This Matter of Color"

1. Larry Gara, "Who Was an Abolitionist?" in Martin Duberman, ed., *The Antislavery Vanguard: New Essays on the Abolitionists* (Princeton, N.J.: Princeton U. Press, 1965), 33, 40, 51.

2. Gerald Sorin, *Abolitionism: A New Perspective* (N.Y.: Praeger, 1972), 17; Lawrence J. Friedman, *Gregarious Saints: Self and Community in American Abolitionism, 1830–1870* (Cambridge, Eng.: Cambridge U. Press, 1982), 18.

3. Louis Filler, *The Crusade against Slavery, 1830–1860* (N.Y.: Harper & Row, 1960), 61 n. 28; Russel B. Nye, *Fettered Freedom: Civil Liberties and the Slavery Controversy, 1830–1860* (East Lansing: Michigan State U. Press, 1949), 5–6; idem, *William Lloyd Garrison and the Humanitarian Reformers* (Boston: Little, Brown, 1955), 94–96; Betty Fladeland, *Men and Brothers: Anglo-American Cooperation* (Urbana: U. of Ill. Press, 1972), 223; Merton L. Dillon, *The Abolitionists: The Growth of a Dissenting Minority* (DeKalb: Northern Ill. U. Press, 1974), 37; Ronald G. Walters, *The Antislavery Appeal: American Abolitionism after 1830* (Baltimore: Johns Hopkins U. Press, 1978), introd. and n. 1; Aileen S. Kraditor, *Means and Ends in American Abolitionism: Garrison and His Critics on Strategy and Tactics, 1834–1850* (N.Y.: Random House, 1967), 29, 207, 264-65 n. 22, 270-71 n. 55.

4. Bertram Wyatt-Brown, *Lewis Tappan and the Evangelical War against Slavery* (Cleveland: Case Western Reserve U. Press, 1969), ix–x.

5. Quoted in *Emancipator*, Sept. 26, 1839, 87.

6. Sorin, *Abolitionism*, 41, 59–60; Dillon, *Abolitionists*, 67.

7. Dillon, *Abolitionists*, 106.

8. Ibid., 106–7.

9. Ibid., 60; Sorin, *Abolitionism*, 41; Friedman, *Gregarious Saints*, 15, 21, 26.

10. Wyatt-Brown, *Lewis Tappan*, xi; Sorin, *Abolitionism*, 47; Dillon, *Abolitionists*, 57; Friedman, *Gregarious Saints*, 18.

11. Dillon, *Abolitionists*, 29.

12. Sorin, *Abolitionism*, 18, 19, 55; Wyatt-Brown, *Lewis Tappan*, 45–46, 55.

13. Dillon, *Abolitionists*, 58, 59.

14. See Wyatt-Brown, *Lewis Tappan*, 230; Friedman, *Gregarious Saints*, 16-21.

15. Sorin, *Abolitionism*, 47, 57.

16. David Brion Davis, "Slavery and Sin: The Cultural Background," in Duberman, ed., *Antislavery Vanguard*, 31.

17. Fladeland, *Men and Brothers*, 225.

18. Wyatt-Brown, *Lewis Tappan*, 81-83.

19. Sorin, *Abolitionism*, 17; *National Anti-Slavery Standard* (N.Y.), Oct. 22, 1840, 78.

20. Sorin, *Abolitionism*, 55; Dillon, *Abolitionists*, 40.

21. Leonard L. Richards, *"Gentlemen of Property and Standing": Anti-Abolition Mobs in Jacksonian America* (N.Y.: Oxford U. Press, 1970), 42ff., 114, 115, 122, 155, 166.

22. See ibid. for an excellent study showing that the anti-abolitionists were primarily "gentlemen of property and standing" concerned about their social positions as well as about miscegenation.

23. Ibid., 36; Nye, *Garrison,* 94.

24. Wyatt-Brown, *Lewis Tappan,* 84.

25. Ibid., 83.

26. Davis, "Slavery and Sin," 3.

27. Janes to Rev. Joshua Leavitt, Aug. 30, 1839, AMA Papers, Box 197, "Sierra Leone" folder, ARC. Janes to Roger S. Baldwin, Aug. 30, 1839, ibid.; Lewis Tappan to Baldwin, Nov. 11, 1839, Baldwin Family Papers, Box 35, Yale; Testimony of Sullivan Haley, Nov. 19, 1839, 17, U.S. Dist. Court Records for Conn., FARC. Testimony of Janes, Nov. 19, 1839, 17, ibid.; N.Y. *Commercial Advertiser,* Jan. 10, 1840, 2; N.Y. *Advertiser & Express,* Jan. 11, 1840, 4. An attempt to identify Janes's official position yielded no results. Neither the Sterling Memorial Library of Yale University nor the New Haven Colony Historical Society has information on him. Janes probably worked in the customs office.

28. Janes to Leavitt, Aug. 30, Sept. 2, 1839, AMA Papers, Box 197, "Sierra Leone" folder, ARC; Janes to Baldwin, Aug. 30, 31, 1839, ibid.

29. Janes to Leavitt, Aug. 30, 1839, ibid.; Janes to Baldwin, Aug. 30, Sept. 2, 1839, ibid.

30. Janes to Baldwin, Aug. 31, Sept. 2, 1839, ibid.

31. Janes to Baldwin, Sept. 2, 1839, ibid.

32. Wyatt-Brown, *Lewis Tappan,* 87, 89; Gilbert H. Barnes, *The Antislavery Impulse, 1830-1844* (N.Y.: American Historical Association, 1933), 25–27; Dwight L. Dumond, *Antislavery: The Crusade for Freedom in America* (Ann Arbor: U. of Mich. Press, 1961), 171; Horatio T. Strother, *The Underground Railroad in Connecticut* (Middletown, Conn.: Wesleyan U. Press, 1962), 111; Samuel W. S. Dutton, *An Address at the Funeral of Roger Sherman Baldwin, February 23, 1863* (New Haven, Conn.: Thomas J. Stafford, 1863), 4–18, in ARC. A writ of habeas corpus is a court order instructing officials to release a prisoner from unlawful imprisonment unless they file formal charges.

33. Simeon Jocelyn's brother, Nathaniel, who later painted the famous portrait of Cinqué, also worked for the underground railroad by opening his house as a refuge for runaways. He was prepared to use force to free the *Amistad*'s blacks. Strother, *Underground Railroad in Connecticut,* 110–11; Townsend to Baldwin, Aug. 30, 1839, Baldwin Family Papers, Box 35, Yale; Seth Staples to Baldwin, Sept. 4, 1839, ibid.; Staples to Tappan, Sept. 4, 1839, Lewis Tappan Papers, Correspondence, 1809–72, MS Div., LC; Townsend to Tappan (erroneously listed as to Simeon Jocelyn or Joshua Leavitt), Sept. 6, 1839, AMA Papers, Box 197, "Sierra Leone" folder, ARC.

34. Clarence W. Bowen, "Arthur and Lewis Tappan" (Paper read at the fiftieth anniversary of the N.Y. City Anti-Slavery Society, at the Broadway Tabernacle, Oct. 2, 1883), 1–2, 10–13, in ARC; Joseph Sturge, *A Visit to the United States in 1841* (London: Hamilton, Adams, 1842), 4–5; Sorin, *Abolitionism,* 50; Dumond, *Antislavery,* 218.

35. Wyatt-Brown, *Lewis Tappan,* 176.

36. Ibid., xiv, 177; Tappan Papers, Journals and Notebooks, 1814–69, May 2, 1841, 26, MS Div., LC.

37. Dillon, *Abolitionists*, 129–30; Tappan Papers, Journals and Notebooks, 1814–69, Nov. 14, 1839, 105-07, MS Div., LC; Tappan to Benjamin Tappan, Nov. 14, 1839, Papers of Benjamin Tappan, MS Div., LC.

38. Wyatt-Brown, *Lewis Tappan*, 180–81.

39. R. Earl McClendon, "The *Amistad* Claims: Inconsistencies of Policy," *Political Science Quarterly* 48 (Sept. 1933): 388; Strother, *Underground Railroad in Connecticut*, 69; Lewis Tappan, *History of the American Missionary Association: Its Constitution and Principles* (N.Y.: AMA, 1855), in ARC; Augustus Field Beard, *The Story of the "Amistad,"* pamphlet published by AMA (n.d.), in ARC.

40. Barnes, *Antislavery Impulse*, 35; Nye, *Garrison*, 59–61.

41. Barnes, *Antislavery Impulse*, 164; Wyatt-Brown, *Lewis Tappan*, 206.

42. *Emancipator*, Sept. 5, 1839, 74; N.Y. *Commercial Advertiser*, Sept. 6, 1839, 2; Sept. 11, 1839, 2; N.Y. *American*, Sept. 12, 1839, 3. Many letters containing small contributions are in the AMA Papers, Box 197, "Sierra Leone" folder, ARC.

43. Choate wrote a letter to the *Emancipator* in which he argued that if the blacks' counsel could show that the purpose of the mutiny was to win liberty rather than to commit robbery or piracy, no American court would convict the accused. See Jean V. Matthews, *Rufus Choate: The Law and Civic Virtue* (Philadelphia: Temple U. Press, 1980), 195–96, 241; Choate to Lewis Tappan, Sept. 7, 1839, ARC; Lewis Tappan to Baldwin, Sept. 12, 1839, Baldwin Family Papers, Box 35, Yale; *Emancipator*, Sept. 19, 1839, 82. Governor William W. Ellsworth of Connecticut had offered his assistance. Though in 1833 he had served as defense counsel in the Prudence Crandall case, involving an abortive attempt to establish a black girls' school in the state, the abolitionists apparently showed no interest. Dumond, *Antislavery*, 212; Filler, *Crusade against Slavery*, 168.

44. Townsend to Tappan, Sept. 6, 1839, AMA Papers, Box 197, "Sierra Leone" folder, ARC. For newspaper reaction favorable to blacks, see N.Y. *Sunday Morning News*, Sept. 1, 1839, quoted in *Emancipator*, Sept. 12, 1839, 77; N.Y. *Commercial Advertiser*, Sept. 2, 1839, 3; Buffalo *Commercial Advertiser and Journal*, Sept. 4, 1839, quoted in *Emancipator*, Sept. 26, 1839, 85; N.Y. *American*, Sept. 4, 1839, 2; *The Albion* (N.Y.), Sept. 7, 1839, 287; N.Y. *Advertiser & Express*, Sept. 7, 1839, 1; N.Y. *Whig*, Sept. 10, 1839, 2.

45. "Introductory Narrative," Oct. 15, 1839, *African Captives*, iv. Ferry deposition, Sept. 7, 1839, in U.S. Circuit Court Records for Conn., FARC; Tappan to *Amistad* Committee, Sept. 9, 1839, printed in N.Y. *Advertiser & Express*, Sept. 14, 1839, 1; Wyatt-Brown, *Lewis Tappan*, 206.

46. Visitors to the jail paid a small charge to the keeper, who perhaps for publicity reasons told greatly inflated stories of the mutiny. He claimed that he gave the proceeds to charity after first meeting the prisoners' needs. Leavitt to *Amistad* Committee, Sept. 6, 1839, printed in N.Y. *Advertiser & Express*, Sept. 7, 1839, 2; Tappan to *Amistad* Committee, Sept. 9, 1839, printed in N.Y. *Advertiser & Express*, Sept. 14, 1839, 1; Tappan to *Amistad* Committee, Sept. 10, 1839, printed in N.Y. *Advertiser & Express*, Sept. 14, 1839, 1; Tappan to N.Y. *American*, Sept. 16, 1839, 2; Wyatt-Brown, *Lewis Tappan*, 207.

47. Ibid.

48. Ibid.

49. Ibid.

50. L. N. Fowler, "Phrenological Developments of Joseph Cinques, Alias Ginqua," *American Phrenological Journal and Miscellany* 2 (1840): title page, 136–38, in ARC.

51. Strother, *Underground Railroad in Connecticut,* 69; Beard, "Story of the *Amistad,*" ARC; "Introductory Narrative," *African Captives,* iv–v; Roland H. Bainton, *Yale and the Ministry: A History of Education for the Christian Ministry at Yale from the Founding in 1701* (N.Y.: Harper, 1957), 87, 153–54; Rollin G. Osterweis, *Three Centuries of New Haven, 1638–1938* (New Haven, Conn.: Yale U. Press, 1953), 299.

52. Tappan to *Amistad* Committee, Sept. 9, 1839, printed in N.Y. *Advertiser & Express,* Sept. 14, 1839, 1; Tappan to N.Y. *American,* Sept. 16, 1839, 2. As was shown earlier, Portuguese slave merchants, not Spanish, had bought Cinqué in Africa.

53. In autumn 1841 the captives learned that a recent book described their homeland of Mende as Kossa. They explained to Tappan and others that this was not the correct name—that Kossa was a derogatory name applied to the Mendes by the British, who disliked them. See article entitled "The Mendi People," from N.Y. *Evangelist* (founded by Tappan family and at one time edited by Joshua Leavitt), reprinted in *African Repository* 17 (1841): 318. See also K. L. Little, *The Mende of Sierra Leone: A West African People in Transition* (London: Routledge & Kegan Paul, 1951), 72. Sorin, *Abolitionism,* 50, 79. For Cinqué's later district court testimony in January 1840, see below, chap. 7.

54. Lewis Tappan to Baldwin, Sept. 12, 1839, Baldwin Family Papers, Box 35, Yale; Leavitt to Baldwin, Sept. 16, 1839, ibid.; Henry B. Stanton to Tappan, Sept. 12, 1839, AMA Papers, Box 197, "Sierra Leone" folder, ARC; Ellis Gray Loring to *Emancipator,* Sept. 3, 1839, printed in *Emancipator,* Sept. 19, 1839, 82; Wyatt-Brown, *Lewis Tappan,* 161, 171, 189, 227, 230; Sorin, *Abolitionism,* 51.

55. JQA to William Jay, Sept. 17, 1839, John Adams Family Papers, JQA Letterbook, MHS; Wyatt-Brown, *Lewis Tappan,* 103; Dillon, *Abolitionists,* 116.

56. Staples and Sedgwick to president of U.S., Sept. 13, 1839, in *H. Exec. Doc.* 185, pp. 63–64.

Chapter 3. The Politics of Justice

1. Charleston *Mercury* quoted in N.Y. *Advertiser & Express,* Sept. 7, 1839, 2; Richmond *Enquirer,* Sept. 10, 1839, 3. The *Emancipator* later observed that Southern papers were generally silent on the *Amistad* issue, "doubtless feeling that it is quite desirable to quiet the matter as soon as possible." See issue of Oct. 10, 1839, 94.

2. N.Y. *American,* Sept. 4, 1839, 2. The N.Y. *Advertiser & Express* agreed with the *American.* See issue of Sept. 7, 1839, 2.

3. N.Y. *Sunday Morning News,* Sept. 1, 1839, quoted in *Emancipator,* Sept. 12, 1839, 77; N.Y. *Evening Star,* Sept. 5, 1839, 2; N.Y. *Daily Express,* Sept. 5, 1839, 20.

4. N.Y. *Evening Star,* Sept. 4, 1839, 2.

5. Ibid., Sept. 12, 1839, 2; N.Y. *Commercial Advertiser,* Sept. 13, 1839, 2.

6. See the following issues of N.Y. *Morning Herald:* Sept. 9, 1839, 2; Sept. 10, 1839, 2; Sept. 14, 1839, 2; Sept. 17, 1839, 2.

7. Calderón to Forsyth, Sept. 6, 1839, U.S. DS, Notes from the Spanish Legation in the U.S. to the DS, 1790–1906, NA. See also Calderón to First Secretary of State, Sept. 6, 1839, Leg. 5584, Exp. 1, no. 104, AHN

8. Ibid.

9. Spanish paper quoted in N.Y. *Advertiser & Express,* Sept. 11, 1839, 1.

10. Ibid.

11. Ibid.

12. For a further exploration of the chances for British intervention in Cuba, see below, chaps. 8 and 9. American and Spanish concerns over this matter become clear in Aaron Vail, American minister to Spain, to Forsyth, Jan. 15, 1841, U.S. DS, Dispatches from U.S. Ministers to Spain, 1792–1906, NA. On Spain's fears of British abolitionist activity in Cuba, see David R. Murray, *Odious Commerce: Britain, Spain and the Abolition of the Cuban Slave Trade* (Cambridge, Eng.: Cambridge U. Press, 1980), esp. chap. 7. On Canadian border issues, see Howard Jones, *To the Webster-Ashburton Treaty: A Study in Anglo-American Relations, 1783–1843* (Chapel Hill: U. of North Carolina Press, 1977).

13. See Major L. Wilson, *The Presidency of Martin Van Buren* (Lawrence: U. Press of Kansas, 1984), 153–54; Francis F. Wayland, *Andrew Stevenson: Democrat and Diplomat, 1785–1857* (Philadelphia: U. of Pennsylvania Press, 1949), 115–18; John B. Moore, *History and Digest of the International Arbitrations to Which the United States Has Been a Party,* 6 vols. (Wash., D.C.: GPO, 1898), 1:408–19; Charles M. Wiltse, *John C. Calhoun,* 3 vols. (Indianapolis: Bobbs-Merrill, 1944–51), 3:63; Jones, *Webster-Ashburton Treaty,* 80–81.

14. See Joseph Story, *Commentaries on the Conflict of Laws* (Boston: Hilliard, Gray, 1834).

15. Missouri Senator Thomas Hart Benton believed that the reason for the administration's support for Calhoun's resolution was that it promoted sectional unity, which translated into Van Buren's reelection. "This was one of the occasions on which the mind loves to dwell," Benton declared, "when, on a question purely sectional and Southern, and wholly in the interest of slave property, there was no division of sentiment in the American Senate." Thomas Hart Benton, *Thirty Years' View; or, A History of the American Government for Thirty Years from 1820 to 1850,* 2 vols. (N.Y.: D. Appleton, 1856), 2:183.

16. My examination of Trist's dispatches to Washington covered the period April 1839 through March 13, 1842. U.S. DS, Dispatches from U.S. Consuls in Havana, 1783–1906, NA.

17. See Alvin L. Duckett, *John Forsyth: Political Tactician* (Athens: U. of Ga. Press, 1962), 184; *Memoirs of JQA,* 10:255; Warren S. Howard, *American Slavers and the Federal Law, 1837–1862* (Berkeley: U. of Calif. Press, 1963), 33–36.

18. Duckett, *Forsyth,* 182–83.

19. Ibid., 33–34.

20. See Louisville Committee to Van Buren, April 2, 1840, Martin Van Buren Papers, MS Div., LC; Van Buren to Louisville Committee (published), April 21, 1840, ibid.; Dixon Lewis to Van Buren, July 15, 1840, ibid. See also Glyndon G. Van Deusen, *The Jacksonian Era, 1828–1848* (N.Y.: Harper & Row, 1959), 131–33, 136; Robert V. Remini, *Martin Van Buren and the Making of the Democratic Party* (N.Y.: Columbia U. Press, 1959), 132; Donald B. Cole, *Martin Van Buren and the American Political System* (Princeton, N.J.: Princeton U. Press, 1984), 361–63; John Niven, *Martin Van Buren: The Romantic Age of American Politics*

(N.Y.: Oxford U. Press, 1983), 385, 388–89, 466–68. Calderón to First Sec. of DS, Sept. 6, 1839, Leg. 5584, Exp. 1, no. 104, AHN.

21. Holabird to Forsyth, Sept. 5, 1839, *H. Exec. Doc.* 185, p. 39; Holabird to Forsyth, Sept. 9, 1839, ibid.; Forsyth to Holabird, Sept. 11, 1839, ibid., 40.

22. Duckett, *Forsyth,* 185–86; Wilson, *Presidency of Martin Van Buren,* 155; Forsyth to Van Buren, Sept. 18, 23, 1839, Van Buren Papers, MS Div., LC; Woodbury to Van Buren, Sept. 22, 1839, ibid. A search of the Kendall and Woodbury Papers in the Library of Congress revealed nothing on the *Amistad.* Nor is there any reference to the case in either the *Autobiography of Amos Kendall,* ed. William Stickney (Boston: Lee and Shepard, 1872), or in Joseph H. Parks, *Felix Grundy: Champion of Democracy* (Baton Rouge: Louisiana State U. Press, 1940). As Parks indicates, there are no substantial collections of Grundy papers.

23. For Grundy's opinion, see *Official Opinions of the Attorneys General of the United States,* 3:485–92. See also John B. Moore, *A Digest of International Law,* 8 vols. (Wash., D.C.: GPO, 1906), 5:852. Story was a highly respected legal scholar, but his nationalist point of view did not have universal appeal. "Comity" referred to courteous acceptance by one nation of the laws and institutions of another. On this subject see Paul Finkelman, *An Imperfect Union: Slavery, Federalism, and Comity* (Chapel Hill: U. of North Carolina Press, 1981).

24. The American legal scholar was Henry Wheaton. For the *Smith* case see 27 Federal Cases 1167 (1820). For *Palmer* see 3 Wheaton 610 (1818).

25. For the *Antelope* case see 10 Wheaton 66 (1825). See also John T. Noonan, Jr., *The Antelope: The Ordeal of the Recaptured Africans in the Administrations of James Monroe and John Quincy Adams* (Berkeley: U. of Calif. Press, 1977).

26. Duckett, *Forsyth,* 185; Wilson, *Presidency of Martin Van Buren,* 155.

27. See Justice Story's reasoning on this point in *U.S.* v. *Amistad,* 15 Peters 592, 593–94 (1841).

28. The final argument concerning the continuity of the slave trade from Africa to Puerto Príncipe was consistent with the Supreme Court's ruling in *Brown* v. *Maryland.* This was the "original package" case, although the Court was divided over the question. For the case see 12 Wheaton 419 (1827).

29. *Emancipator,* Sept. 12, 1839, 77–78; *Side-light,* 185, 185 n. 140.

30. N.Y. *Evening Post,* Sept. 17, 1839, 2.

31. *Emancipator,* Sept. 12, 1839, 78.

Chapter 4. "The Inherent Property of Liberty"

1. William M. Wiecek, *The Sources of Antislavery Constitutionalism in America, 1760–1848* (Ithaca, N.Y.: Cornell U. Press, 1977), 157 n. 24.

2. Rev. Francis Wayland to Lewis Tappan, Oct. 2, 1839, ARC; Leavitt's address before the convention, June 15, 1843, in *Proceedings of the General Anti-Slavery Convention, June 13–20, 1843,* 122, located in ARC. Lewis Tappan believed that if counsel could establish that the *Amistad* blacks were persons, the Spaniards' case for return of property would collapse. On Tappan's views see William S. Holabird, U.S. district attorney, to Sec. of State John Forsyth, Sept. 21, 1839, in *H. Exec. Doc.* 185, p. 40.

3. Wiecek, *Sources of Antislavery Constitutionalism,* 134, 157 n. 24; Robert M. Cover, *Justice Accused: Antislavery and the Judicial Process* (New Haven, Conn.: Yale U. Press, 1975), 183–87.

4. Harold M. Hyman and William M. Wiecek, *Equal Justice under Law: Constitutional Development, 1835–1875* (N.Y.: Harper & Row, 1982), 240–41. Section 14 of the Judiciary Act of 1789 provided that "either of the justices of the supreme court, as well as judges of the district courts, shall have power to grant writs of *habeas corpus* for the purpose of an inquiry into the cause of commitment.—*Provided,* That writs of *habeas corpus* shall in no case extend to prisoners in gaol, unless where they are in custody, under or by colour of the authority of the United States, or are committed for trial before some court of the same, or are necessary to be brought into court to testify." *U.S. Statutes at Large,* 1:82. In *Ex Parte Tobias Watkins* of 1830, Chief Justice John Marshall indicated the problems ahead when he declared that the act of 1789 authorized the Supreme Court "and all the courts of the United States and the judges thereof, to issue the writ 'for the purpose of inquiring into the cause of commitment.'" He noted the law's "general reference to a power which we are required to exercise, without any precise definition of that power." 3 Peters 201 (1830). The only reference to a writ of habeas corpus in the Constitution is in Article I, Section 9, which concerns suspension of the writ during emergencies. Amendments V and VI of the Bill of Rights allude to the writ, when they refer to the process of indictment and trial and permit one to read into it the judicial power to enforce these provisions. During the nineteenth century, however, the Bill of Rights was a limitation not on state courts but on federal courts.

5. *African Captives,* 7. Holabird to Forsyth, Sept. 21, 1839, *H. Exec. Doc.* 185, p. 40; Deposition of Theodore Sedgwick, blacks' attorney, Sept. 18, 1839, U.S. Circuit Court Records for Conn., FARC. Sedgwick warned Tappan that the federal courts had established the principle that slaves were property and that the only way to win the *Amistad* captives' freedom was to cite Spanish laws and treaties in proving that they were never legally slaves. See Sedgwick to Tappan, Oct. 12, 1839, Lewis Tappan Papers, Correspondence, 1809–72, MS Div., LC.

6. Tappan to *Amistad* Committee, Sept. 18, 1839, in *Emancipator,* Sept. 26, 1839, 86; N.Y. *Commercial Advertiser,* Sept. 20, 1839, 2; *African Captives,* 7.

7. N.Y. *Commercial Advertiser,* Sept. 20, 1839, 2; Tappan to *Amistad* Committee, Sept. 18, 1839, in *Emancipator,* Sept. 26, 1839, 86.

8. *African Captives,* 7; Richmond *Enquirer,* Sept. 24, 1839, 2; Wash. *National Intelligencer,* Sept. 21, 1839, 3; N.Y. *Advertiser & Express,* Sept. 21, 1839, 1; Gerrit Smith to *Emancipator,* Sept. 19, 1839, 82; letter (n.d.) from lady to *Emancipator,* Sept. 19, 1839, 82; Bryant's poem, ibid.

9. *African Captives,* 7, 30–34.

10. Ibid., 7, 8.

11. Holabird in U.S. Circ. Ct. Records for Conn., FARC; Ellsworth in U.S. District Ct. Records for Conn., FARC. See also Holabird, ibid, 33–34.

12. N.Y. *Commercial Advertiser,* Sept. 20, 1839, 2.

13. *African Captives,* 7–8.

14. N.Y. *Advertiser & Express,* Sept. 21, 1839, 1; Deposition of Augustus Hanson, U.S. Circ. Ct. Records for Conn., FARC. The defense later presented an affidavit of another native African, Bahoo from Bandaboo, who also testified that the girls were Mandingoes. He claimed that he had known them in Bandaboo and that they had come from Africa with him on the same slaver. *African Captives,* 27. See also ibid., 7.

15. *African Captives,* 8–9. For the congressional act of March 3, 1819, see *U.S. Statutes at Large,* 3:532–34.

16. *African Captives,* 9–12.

17. Ibid., 12–13.

18. Ibid., 13, 15.

19. Ibid., 14–15.

20. Ibid., 16–17. For the *Antelope* case see 10 Wheaton 66 (1825).

21. *African Captives,* 15–18.

22. Ibid., 19–20.

23. Ibid., 20.

24. Ibid., 20–21.

25. Ibid., 21–22.

26. Ibid., 28.

27. Ibid., 29.

28. Ibid., 30.

29. Ibid. 34–35.

30. Ibid., 35–36. According to a vague statement found in the New York *Advertiser & Express,* Ruiz was partly educated in Connecticut. See issue of Sept. 21, 1839, 1.

31. *African Captives,* 36–37; N.Y. *Advertiser & Express,* Sept. 25, 1839, 1. For the *Eugénie* case, see 26 Federal Cases 832 (1822).

32. *African Captives,* 37.

33. Ibid., 38.

34. Ibid., 38–39.

35. Ibid., 39–40.

36. Ibid., 42.

37. Ibid., 43–44.

38. Ibid., 44, 47; N.Y. *Commercial Advertiser,* Sept. 24, 1839, 2.

39. *African Captives,* v, 47; Augustus F. Beard, *The Story of the "Amistad",* pamphlet published by AMA (n.d.), in ARC; N.Y. *Commercial Advertiser,* Oct. 8, 1839, 2; Rollin G. Osterweis, *Three Centuries of New Haven, 1638–1938* (New Haven, Conn.: Yale U. Press, 1953), 273; Horatio T. Strother, *The Underground Railroad in Connecticut* (Middletown, Conn.: Wesleyan U. Press, 1962), 70–71.

40. *African Captives,* 47; Charleston *Mercury,* Sept. 28, 1839, quoted in *Emancipator,* Oct. 31, 1839, 106; N.Y. *Commercial Advertiser,* Sept. 24, 1839, cited ibid., Sept. 26, 1839, 86; N.Y. *American,* Sept. 28, 1839, 2; N.Y. *Morning Herald,* Oct. 1, 1839, 2; *Emancipator,* Oct. 10, 1839, 94. Numerous papers called for the blacks' freedom on the bases of natural rights and self-defense. See *Emancipator,* Sept. 26, 1839, 85–86, for a list of these in New Hampshire, New York, Connecticut, Pennsylvania, Massachusetts, and New Jersey. See also N.Y. *Commercial Advertiser,* Sept. 27, 1839, 1.

41. Sedgwick to Tappan, Oct. 12, 1839, Tappan Papers, Corresp., 1809–72, MS Div., LC. The New York *Evening Star* probably used the law to protect slavery. See issue of Sept. 28, 1839, 2. In a later issue, the *Star* emphasized that the case was not a "struggle for freedom" and that Americans could not allow "fictitious sympathy" to approve acts of insurrection. The law had to protect civilization from the "lawless hordes of Savages." Ibid., Oct. 4, 1839, 4.

Chapter 5. "A National Matter"

1. Lewis Tappan to Rev. Leonard Bacon, Oct. 4, 1839, Bacon Family Papers, Box 5, Yale; Tappan to eds., N.Y. *Commercial Advertiser,* Oct. 1, 1839, 1.

2. *Memoirs of JQA,* 10:132–35; Ellis Gray Loring to JQA, Sept. 23, 1839, John Adams Family Papers, Corresp., MHS; Tappan to Loring, Nov. 30, 1839, Lewis Tappan Papers, Corresp., 1809–72, MS Div., LC; Bertram Wyatt-Brown, *Lewis Tappan and the Evangelical War against Slavery* (Cleveland: Case Western Reserve U. Press, 1969), 189.

3. Adams to Loring, Oct. 3, 1839, Adams Family Papers, JQA Letterbook, MHS.

4. Ibid. For the *Palmer* case, see 3 Wheaton 610 (1818). For the *Antelope,* see 10 Wheaton 66 (1825).

5. Loring to Adams, Nov. 14, 1839, Adams Family Papers, Corresp., MHS.

6. Ibid.

7. Adams to Loring, Nov. 19, 1839, JQA Letterbook, ibid.

8. *Emancipator,* Oct. 10, 1839, 94; N.Y. *Evening Star,* Oct. 24, 1839, 2; New Orleans *Times Picayune,* Oct. 17, 1839, 2; N.Y. *Morning Herald,* Oct. 1, 1839, 2; Oct. 3, 1839, 2; Oct. 4, 1839, 2; N.Y. *Advertiser & Express,* Nov. 20, 1839, 2. On racial prejudice in the antebellum North, see Leon F. Litwack, *North of Slavery: The Negro in the Free States, 1790–1860* (Chicago: U. of Chicago Press, 1961).

9. Tappan to Bacon, Oct. 4, 1839, Bacon Family Papers, Box 5; Tappan to Joseph Sturge, Oct. 19, 1839, *Side-light,* 60.

10. George E. Day to eds. of N.Y. *Journal of Commerce,* Oct. 8, 15, 1839, in *African Captives,* iii–v.

11. Tappan to Bacon, Oct. 4, 1839, Bacon Family Papers, Box 5; Tappan to Sturge, Oct. 19, 1839, Tappan Papers, Corresp., 1809–72, MS Div., LC; Tappan to Roger S. Baldwin, Oct. 12, 1839, Baldwin Papers, Box 35, Yale.

12. Tappan Papers, Journals and Notebooks, 1814–69, 93–96, MS Div., LC; N.Y. *Times & Commercial Intelligencer,* Oct. 19, 1839, 2; N.Y. *Commercial Advertiser,* Oct. 18, 1839, 2; N.Y. *Morning Herald,* Oct. 18, 1839, 2; Tappan to Sturge, Oct. 19, 1839, *Side-light,* 60.

13. Tappan to Sturge, Oct. 19, 1839, *Side-light,* 55; Joseph Sturge, *A Visit to the United States in 1841* (London: Hamilton, Adams, 1842), 5; Theodore Weld to Gerrit Smith, Oct. 23, 1839, Gilbert H. Barnes and Dwight L. Dumond, eds., *Letters of Theodore Dwight Weld, Angelina Grimké Weld, and Sarah Grimké, 1822–1844,* 2 vols., (N.Y.: D. Appleton-Century, 1834), 2:811.

14. Bayard Tuckerman, ed., *The Diary of Philip Hone, 1828–1851,* 2 vols. (N.Y.: Dodd, Mead, 1889), 1:385; N.Y. *Times & Commercial Intelligencer,* Oct. 19, 1839, 2; N.Y. *Evening Star,* Oct. 19, 1839, 2; Oct. 22, 1839, 2; Wash. *Globe,* Oct. 30, 1839, 3; N.Y. *Democratic Republican New Era,* Oct. 24, 1839, 2; N.Y. *Advertiser & Express,* Oct. 19, 1839, 4; New Orleans *Times Picayune,* Oct. 29, 1839, 2; Richmond *Enquirer,* Oct. 25, 1839, 4. A sojourner slave was a personal servant taken by his master in travel. Arguments developed over whether the slave automatically became free upon entering a free state. The Supreme Court held in *Groves* v. *Slaughter* in 1841 that the Constitution protected a citizen's right as sojourner to carry his property anywhere—even if that property included a slave. Many Northern courts, however, denied such right. On the *Groves* case see 15 Peters 449 (1841).

15. Spanish paper quoted in *Emancipator,* Oct. 24, 1839, 102; Pedro Alcántara de Argaiz to Sec. of State John Forsyth, Oct. 18, 1839, Leg. 5584, Exp. 1, no. 8, AHN; Argaiz to Forsyth, Oct. 22, 1839, U.S. DS, Notes from the Spanish Legation in the U.S. to the DS, 1790–1906, NA.

16. Eastern newspapers' views summarized in Oberlin *Evangelist* (Ohio), Oct. 23, 1839, 180; Forsyth to Argaiz, Oct. 24, 1839, U.S. DS, Notes to Foreign Legations in the U.S. from the DS, 1834–1906, NA. Note also in Leg. 5584, Exp. 1, AHN. Lewis Tappan was confident that the president would not return the blacks to the Spanish. To his brother Benjamin, a United States senator from Ohio, he wrote, "Mr. V. B. will hardly attempt it. Too many of his personal friends are interested on the other side." Lewis Tappan to Benjamin Tappan, Oct. 8, 1839, Benjamin Tappan Papers, MS Div., LC.

17. Forsyth to Argaiz, Oct. 24, 1839, U.S. DS, Notes to Foreign Legations in U.S., NA. Note also in Leg. 5584, Exp. 1, AHN.

18. Forsyth to Benjamin F. Butler, Oct. 24, 1839, *H. Exec. Doc.* 185, p. 64. A copy of this note is in Leg. 5584, Exp. 1, AHN.

19. N.Y. *Commercial Advertiser,* Oct. 23, 1839, 2; Tappan Papers, Journals and Notebooks, 1814–69, 95, MS Div., LC; "The Spaniards—Ruiz and Montes," ca. Oct. 26, 1839, unpublished letter to ed. of *Emancipator,* not signed, but clearly written by Tappan. In AMA Papers, Box 197, "Sierra Leone" folder, ARC. The records consulted in this study did not include Judge Inglis's first name.

20. N.Y. *Commercial Advertiser,* Oct. 26, 1839. The N.Y. *Evening Post* agreed with the judge's observations on slavery. If he had decided in favor of the Spaniard, Cinqué's counsel could have argued that this took away the plaintiff's action since a slave could have no remedies by civil action against his master. *Post* cited in Richmond *Enquirer,* Nov. 1, 1839, 2.

21. N.Y. *Commercial Advertiser,* Oct. 26, 1839, 1; Richmond *Enquirer,* Nov. 1, 1839, 2; N.Y. *Evening Post* cited ibid. The *Emancipator* criticized Inglis for deciding, in chambers, "one of the gravest points of law as easily as he could light his cigar.—He says that a slave cannot bring an action against his master in the courts of New York, because he is property." No man, the *Emancipator* insisted, could be the property of another in the free state of New York. See issue of Nov. 7, 1839, 110.

22. Richmond *Enquirer,* Nov. 1, 1839, 2.

23. N.Y. *American,* Oct. 28, 1839, 2; N.Y. *Evening Post* cited in Richmond *Enquirer,* Nov. 1, 1839, 2; Tappan Papers, Journals and Notebooks, 1814–69, 95–96, MS Div., LC.

24. Argaiz to Forsyth, Nov. 5, 1839, U.S. DS, Notes from the Spanish Legation in the U.S., NA.

25. Richmond *Enquirer,* Nov. 5, 1839, 2, 3; *Emancipator,* Nov. 7, 1839, 110.

26. Butler to Forsyth, Oct. 28, 1839, *H. Exec. Doc.* 185, p. 65; Aaron Vail, acting sec. of state, to Butler, Nov. 9, 1839, U.S. DS, Domestic Letters, NA; Butler to Vail, Nov. 18, 1839, *H. Exec. Doc.* 185, pp. 66–67.

27. N.Y. *Evening Journal,* Feb. 5, 1840, cited in Richmond *Enquirer,* Feb. 27, 1840, 1; Butler to Richmond *Enquirer,* Feb. 10, 1840, ibid.; N.Y. *Evening Star,* Feb. 1, 1840, 2; N.Y. *Advertiser & Express,* Feb. 8, 1840, 3; N.Y. *Semi-Weekly Express,* Feb. 12, 1840, 2; N.Y. *American,* Feb. 7, 1840, 2; Tappan to John Scoble, Dec. 10, 1839, *Side-light,* 61.

28. Richmond *Enquirer,* Nov. 5, 1839, 2; N.Y. *Evening Star,* Feb. 12, 1840, 2; *Emancipator,* Nov. 7, 1839, 110; N.Y. *American,* Feb. 7, 1840, 2; Tappan to Scoble, Dec. 10, 1839, *Side-light,* 61.

29. Argaiz to Forsyth, Nov. 29, Dec. 25, 1839, U.S. DS, Notes from the Spanish Legation in the U.S., NA. Argaiz's charges of intrigue are in the note dated Dec. 25. For the Forsyth quotation, see Argaiz to First Sec. of DS, Oct. 24, 1839, Leg. 5584, Exp. 1, no. 9, AHN. In this same note, Argaiz explained that he had asked a fellow Spaniard to accompany him as a witness to hear the secretary of state's position on the arrests. Argaiz later called Van Buren a "Northern man with Southern principles" who could not free the *Amistad* blacks because of the "numerous Southern votes that he was counting on." Argaiz to First Sec. of DS, March 20, 1841, Leg. 5584, Exp. 1, no. 88, AHN. Forsyth wrote Argaiz an elaborate defense of the administration's policy of nonintervention in the judicial process in New York. See Forsyth to Argaiz, Dec. 12, 1839, U.S. DS, Notes to Foreign Legations in U.S., NA.

30. N.Y. *Evening Star,* Feb. 1, 1840, 2; New Orleans *Times Picayune,* Feb. 21, 1840, 2; Vindex letter in N.Y. *Advertiser & Express,* Feb. 8, 1840, 3; Fiat Justitia letter in N.Y. *Semi-Weekly Express,* Feb. 12, 1840, 2.

Chapter 6. "Neither Slave ..."

1. Wendell P. and F. J. Garrison, *William Lloyd Garrison, 1805–1879: The Story of His Life Told by His Children,* 4 vols. (N.Y.: Houghton, Mifflin, 1885–89), 1:320, 322.

2. Henry Wilson, *History of the Rise and Fall of the Slave Power in America,* 3 vols. (Boston: J. R. Osgood, 1872–77), 1:458.

3. Merton L. Dillon, *The Abolitionists: The Growth of a Dissenting Minority* (De Kalb: Northern Ill. U. Press, 1974), 92–93.

4. For accounts of the Crandall affair, see Bernard C. Steiner, *History of Slavery in Connecticut,* in Johns Hopkins University Studies in Historical and Political Science (Baltimore: Johns Hopkins U. Press, 1893), 45–52; Jarvis M. Morse, *A Neglected Period of Connecticut's History, 1818–1850* (New Haven, Conn.: Yale U. Press, 1933), 193–96; Alice F. Tyler, *Freedom's Ferment: Phases of American Social History from the Colonial Period to the Outbreak of the Civil War* (Minneapolis: U. of Minnesota Press, 1944), 506–8; Russel B. Nye, *William Lloyd Garrison and the Humanitarian Reformers* (Boston: Little, Brown, 1955), 62–64; Louis Filler, *The Crusade against Slavery, 1830–1860* (N.Y.: Harper & Row, 1960), 64–65; Dwight L. Dumond, *Antislavery: The Crusade for Freedom in America* (Ann Arbor: U. of Mich. Press, 1961), 211–17; Leon F. Litwack, *North of Slavery: The Negro in the Free States, 1790–1860* (Chicago: U. of Chicago Press, 1961), 126–31; Leonard L. Richards, *"Gentlemen of Property and Standing": Anti-Abolition Mobs in Jacksonian America* (N.Y.: Oxford U. Press, 1970), 38–40; Edmund Fuller, *Prudence Crandall: An Incident of Racism in Nineteenth-Century Connecticut* (Middletown, Conn.: Wesleyan U. Press, 1971); Gerald Sorin, *Abolitionism: A New Perspective* (N.Y.: Praeger, 1972), 66; Philip S. Foner and Josephine F. Pacheco, *Three Who Dared: Prudence Crandall, Margaret Douglass, Myrtilla Miner—Champions of Antebellum Black Education* (Westport, Conn.: Greenwood, 1984), 5–46.

5. Tappan to John Scoble, Jan. 20, 1840, Lewis Tappan Papers, Correspondence, 1809–72, MS Div., LC.

6. Garrison, *William Lloyd Garrison*, 1:322–23; Steiner, *History of Slavery in Connecticut*, 48–50.

7. Judson quoted in Dumond, *Antislavery*, 214.

8. Ibid., 215.

9. Ibid., 216.

10. Ibid., 212.

11. Harold M. Hyman and William M. Wiecek, *Equal Justice under Law: Constitutional Development, 1835–1875* (N.Y.: Harper & Row, 1982), 94–95; William M. Wiecek, *The Sources of Antislavery Constitutionalism in America, 1760–1848* (Ithaca, N.Y.: Cornell U. Press, 1977), 162–67. In the Dred Scott case of 1857, Chief Justice Roger B. Taney of the Supreme Court tried to resolve the question by ruling that the word *citizen* in the Constitution did not include blacks. Associate Justice Benjamin R. Curtis vigorously dissented, arguing that at the time the Founding Fathers adopted the Constitution free blacks had been citizens of individual states under the Confederation. Surely, he declared, the Constitution did not take away citizenship from any of the people by whom it was established. Furthermore, every native-born free person who was a citizen of the state in which he resided was also a citizen of the United States. Individual states, Curtis argued, had the power to decide which people should become citizens. As citizens of the several states, they therefore enjoyed the rights of national citizenship guaranteed by the Constitution. For the Scott case see 19 Howard 393 (1857). Although Curtis's argument at first appeared more charitable than Taney's, a close examination of the matter suggests that Curtis meant only that free blacks born in states allowing their citizenship were also to have national citizenship; no state could grant citizenship to a resident born in another state. Thus, a free black with citizenship did not lose his rights by moving to a state denying black citizenship, but neither did a free black born in a state barring black citizenship gain those rights by moving into a state recognizing them. On this matter see Don E. Fehrenbacher, *The Dred Scott Case: Its Significance in American Law and Politics* (N.Y.: Oxford U. Press, 1978), 407–8. See also James H. Kettner, *The Development of American Citizenship, 1608–1870* (Chapel Hill: U. of North Carolina Press, 1978), 329–31.

12. Morse, *Neglected Period of Connecticut's History*, 192.

13. Richards, *"Gentlemen of Property and Standing,"* 40.

14. Morse, *Neglected Period of Connecticut's History*, 192–93. Although slavery was legal in Connecticut until 1848, no more than forty slaves were in the state by the 1830s. Ibid.

15. Ibid., 193, 196–97.

16. N.Y. *Commercial Advertiser*, Nov. 20, 1839, 2; Garrison to Lewis Tappan, Arthur Tappan, Joshua Leavitt, or James G. Birney, Nov. 1, 1839, AMA Papers, Box 197, "Sierra Leone" folder, ARC.

17. N.Y. *Commercial Advertiser*, Nov. 20, 1839, 2; N.Y. *Advertiser & Express*, Nov. 23, 1839, 4.

18. Ibid. The records consulted for this study fail to mention Isham's first name.

19. Ibid.

20. Ibid.

21. N.Y. *Commercial Advertiser*, Nov. 20, 1839, 2; ibid., Nov. 21, 1839, 2; testimony of Captain Peletiah Fordham, Nov. 19, 1839, 15, U.S. Dis. Ct. Records for Conn., FARC. Defense argument by Staples and Baldwin, Nov. 19, 1839, 42–

45, ibid.; Adams to Loring, Nov. 19, 1839, John Adams Family Papers, JQA Letterbook, MHS.

22. N.Y. *Commercial Advertiser,* Nov. 21, 1839, 2.

23. Ibid.

24. Ibid.

25. Defense argument by Staples and Baldwin, Nov. 19, 1839, 42–43, U.S. Dist. Ct. Records for Conn., FARC.

26. Ibid., 43–45.

27. N.Y. *American,* Nov. 21, 1839, 2; N.Y. *Commercial Advertiser,* Nov. 21, 1839, 2; Joshua Leavitt's account of district court proceedings, in *Emancipator,* Nov. 28, 1839, 122.

28. Thomas M. Madden, ed., *The Memoirs (Chiefly Autobiographical) from 1798 to 1886 of Richard Robert Madden* (London: Ward & Downey, 1891), 82; Smith letter referred to ibid., 81–82.

29. Louis Ruchames, ed., *The Letters of William Lloyd Garrison,* vol. 2 (Cambridge, Mass.: Harvard U. Press, 1971), 535 n. 1; Thomas M. Madden, ed., *Memoirs . . . of Richard Robert Madden,* 74–77; Deposition by Richard R. Madden, Nov. 20, 1839, 133, U.S. Dist. Ct. Records for Conn., FARC.

30. Thomas M. Madden, ed., *Memoirs . . . of Richard Robert Madden,* 77–80; David Turnbull, *Travels in the West: Cuba, with Notices of Porto Rico and the Slave Trade* (London: Longman, Orme, Brown, Green, and Longmans, 1840), 42, 164.

31. Thomas M. Madden, ed., *Memoirs . . . of Richard Robert Madden,* 96.

32. Garrison to Lewis Tappan, Arthur Tappan, Joshua Leavitt, or James G. Birney, Nov. 1, 1839, AMA Papers, Box 197, "Sierra Leone" folder, ARC.

33. Trist to Forsyth, Sept. 9, 1839, U.S. DS, Dispatches from U.S. Consuls in Havana, 1783–1906, NA; Trist to Joseph Tuckerman (the friend), Dec. 2, 1839, Nicholas Trist Papers, MS Div., LC; Richard R. Madden, ed., *Letter to W. E. Channing, D.D., on the Subject of the Abuse of the Flag of the United States in the Island of Cuba, and the Advantage Taken of Its Protection in Promoting the Slave Trade* (Boston: William D. Ticknor, 1839), 3; Christopher Fyfe, *A History of Sierra Leone* (London: Oxford U. Press, 1962), 217–18. On accusations against Trist, which a congressional and State Department inquiry in 1840 did not substantiate, see Warren S. Howard, *American Slavers and the Federal Law, 1837–1862* (Berkeley: U. of Calif. Press, 1963), esp. chap. 2; Arthur F. Corwin, *Spain and the Abolition of Slavery in Cuba, 1817–1886* (Austin: U. of Texas Press, 1967), 63. On Madden's charges against Trist, see his letter to Channing cited above, and David R. Murray, *Odious Commerce: Britain, Spain and the Abolition of the Cuban Slave Trade* (Cambridge, Eng.: Cambridge U. Press, 1980), 105–6.

34. N.Y. *Commercial Advertiser,* Nov. 5, 1839, 2; Walker Lewis, *Without Fear or Favor: A Biography of Chief Justice Roger Brooke Taney* (Boston: Houghton Mifflin, 1965), 343–44.

35. Leavitt's account of district court proceedings, in *Emancipator,* Nov. 28, 1839, 122.

36. Madden deposition, Nov. 20, 1839, 133, 135, U.S. Dist. Ct. Records for Conn., FARC; Madden testimony in N.Y. *Commercial Advertiser,* Nov, 25, 1839, 2; *Side-light,* 60 n. 14; 15 Peters 534 (1841).

37. Madden deposition, Nov. 20, 1839, 134, U.S. Dist. Ct. Records for Conn., FARC; 15 Peters 534 (1841); N.Y. *Commercial Advertiser,* Nov. 25, 1839, 2.

38. Madden deposition, Nov. 20, 1839, 136, U.S. Dist. Ct. Records for Conn., FARC; 15 Peters 535 (1841).

39. Madden deposition, Nov. 20, 1839, 133, U.S. Dist. Ct. Records for Conn., FARC; 15 Peters 536-37 (1841); N.Y. *Commercial Advertiser,* Nov. 25, 1839, 2.

40. Madden deposition, Nov. 20, 1839, 137-39, U.S. Dist. Ct. Records for Conn., FARC; 15 Peters 536-37 (1841); N.Y. *Commercial Advertiser,* Nov. 25, 1839, 2.

41. Ibid.

42. Tappan to Joseph Sturge, Nov. 23, 1839, Lewis Tappan Papers, Corresp., 1809-72, MS Div., LC. At one point during Madden's visit to the United States, he talked with President Van Buren, who criticized the abolitionists and agreed with Andrew Jackson's earlier assessment that they were dangerous to the Union. See Lewis Tappan to Benjamin Tappan, Nov. 14, 1839, ibid.

Chapter 7. " . . . Nor Free"

1. See R. Earl McClendon, "The *Amistad* Claims: Inconsistencies of Policy," *Political Science Quarterly* 48 (Sept. 1933): 391; Argaiz to Forsyth, Nov. 26, 1839, U.S. DS, Notes from the Spanish Legation in the U.S. to the DS, 1790-1906, NA. The reference is to Holabird's statement before the circuit court on September 21, 1839. For this statement see above, chap. 4.

2. Forsyth to Argaiz, Dec. 12, 1839, U.S. DS, Notes to Foreign Legations in the U.S. from the DS, 1834-1906, NA.

3. Argaiz to Forsyth, Dec. 30, 1839, ibid.; Memorandum from DS to Sec. of Navy James K. Paulding, Jan. 2, 1840, *H. Exec. Doc.* 185, pp. 67-68; Paulding to Forsyth, Jan. 3, 1840, ibid., 68; Forsyth to Argaiz, Jan. 6, 1840, ibid., 38.

4. Forsyth to Holabird, Jan. 6, 12, 1840, *H. Exec. Doc.* 185, pp. 55, 56.

5. Of numerous studies on the Van Buren presidency, only a few call attention to its questionable actions during the *Amistad* affair. According to Samuel Flagg Bemis, the president was bent upon maintaining his Southern constituency and used every power at his command to support the Spanish government's stand regarding the blacks. Bemis, *John Quincy Adams and the Union* (N.Y.: Knopf, 1956), 393, 393-94 n. 22. An earlier writer accuses Van Buren of "indecent haste" in trying to dispense with the problem. See William H. Smith, *A Political History of Slavery,* 2 vols. (N.Y.: Putnam's, 1903), 1:57. Another historian speaks of the administration's "shameful attempt to deceive the people of the United States, including the courts." John R. Spears, *The American Slave-Trade: An Account of Its Origin, Growth and Suppression* (London: Bickers, 1901), 188. A recent biographer of Van Buren calls his policies a "total and reprehensible disregard for the Africans' rights." See John Niven, *Martin Van Buren: The Romantic Age of American Politics* (N.Y.: Oxford U. Press, 1983), 467.

6. Memo from DS to Paulding, Jan. 2, 1840, *H. Exec. Doc.* 185, pp. 67-68; Forsyth to Holabird, Jan. 6, 1840, ibid., 55.

7. Lt. John S. Paine to Paulding, Jan, 5, 1840, U.S. Naval Records, Letters Received from Officers, NA.

8. Paulding to Paine, Jan. 6, 1840, U.S. Dept. of the Navy, Sec. of Navy Letters to Officers, Ships of War, NA; Paulding to Gedney, Jan. 8, 1840, ibid.; Paulding to Commander James Renshaw, Jan. 8, 1840, ibid.; Paulding to Paine, Jan. 8, 1840, ibid.; Paulding to Charles Robinson, officer on *Grampus,* Jan. 7, 1840, ibid.; Forsyth to Paulding, Jan. 7, 1840, *H. Exec. Doc.* 185, p. 68.

9. Paine to Paulding, Jan. 10, 1840, U.S. Navy, Letters Received by Sec. of Navy from Officers below the Rank of Commander, 1802–1884, NA; Paulding to Willcox, Jan. 10, 1840, encl. ibid.; Willcox to Paine, Jan. 10, 1840, encl. ibid.

10. Paine to Paulding, Jan. 10, 1840, ibid. See president's order and DS letter in Forsyth to Paulding, Jan. 7, 1840, U.S. DS, Domestic Letters, NA. It is noteworthy of Paine's feelings against the slave trade that in March of that same year, he, without authorization from Washington, signed an agreement for cooperation with the British commander William Tucker of the *Wolverine* for mutual suppression of the African slave trade. The White House repudiated the Paine-Tucker agreement of March 11, 1840. See Tucker to Paine, March 10, 1840, U.S. DS, Notes from British Legation in U.S. to the DS, 1791–1906, NA; Paine to Tucker, March 10, 1840, ibid.; Tucker to Rear Admiral George Eliot, March 12, 1840, ibid.; Fox to Forsyth, Aug. 15, 1840, ibid.

11. Paine to Paulding, Jan. 14, 1840, U.S. Navy, Letters Received by Sec. of Navy from Officers below Rank of Commander, NA; Tappan to JQA, May 8, 1840, John Adams Family Papers, MHS.

12. Paulding to Paine, Jan. 13, 1840, U.S. Dept. of Navy, Sec. of Navy Letters to Officers, Ships of War, NA.

13. *Emancipator,* Nov. 28, 1839, 122.

14. Baldwin to eds. of Wash. *National Intelligencer,* Dec. [?] 1839, Baldwin Family Papers, Box 35, Yale.

15. Ibid.

16. Ibid.

17. Tappan to Scoble, Dec. 10, 1839, *Side-light,* 61–62; Tappan to Loring, Nov. 30, 1839, Lewis Tappan Papers, Corresp., 1809–72, MS Div., LC.

18. Tappan to Sturge, Dec. 14, 1839, *Side-light,* 63–64.

19. Tappan to Scoble, Jan. 20, 1840, Tappan Papers, Corresp., 1809–72, MS Div., LC; Tappan to Richard R. Madden, n.d., but probably Jan. 20, 1840, ibid.; Simeon E. Baldwin, "The Captives of the *Amistad,*" *Papers of the New Haven Colony Historical Society* 4 (1888): 347; *Side-light,* 69 n. 32; N.Y. *Commercial Advertiser,* Jan. 10, 1840, 2; N.Y. *Advertiser & Express,* Jan. 11, 1840, 4.

20. N.Y. *Commercial Advertiser,* Jan. 10, 1840, 2; N.Y. *Advertiser & Express,* Jan. 11. 1840, 4; Claims by José Antonio Tellenicas and House of Aspe & Laca of Cuba, 3, U.S. Dist. Ct. Records for Conn., FARC. Holabird announcement ibid., 4.

21. Defense argument, 47–51, U.S. Dist. Ct. Records for Conn., FARC; Haley testimony, 17, ibid.; Janes testimony, 17, ibid.; N.Y. *Commercial Advertiser,* Jan. 10, 1840, 2. As was shown earlier, Janes's official position was uncertain, but he probably was a customs officer. See above, chap. 2, n. 30. Presumably Haley held a similar position.

22. N.Y. *Advertiser & Express,* Jan. 11, 1840, 4.

23. Ibid.

24. Ibid.; N.Y. *Commercial Advertiser,* Jan. 10, 1840, 2; Haley testimony, 17, U.S. Dist. Ct. Records for Conn., FARC; Janes testimony, 17, ibid. The black who spoke some English was Burnah.

25. N.Y. *Advertiser & Express,* Jan. 7, 1840, 4; N.Y. *Commercial Advertiser,* Jan. 10, 1840, 2; Covey testimony, 18, U.S. Dist. Ct. Records for Conn., FARC; Pratt testimony, ibid., 1–2. Tappan wrote the captain of the British *Buzzard* that someone would take care of Covey while he waited to testify. Tappan to Captain

Charles Fitzgerald, Nov. 1, 1839, Tappan Papers, Corresp., 1809–72, MS Div., LC.

26. N.Y. *Advertiser & Express,* Jan. 11, 1840, 2, 4; N.Y. *Commercial Advertiser,* Jan. 10, 1840, 2; Gibbs's testimony, 24, U.S. Dist. Ct. Records for Conn., FARC; Tappan to Madden, n.d., but probably Jan. 20, 1840, Tappan Papers, Corresp., 1809–72, MS Div., LC. This Gibbs was the elder.

27. Ibid. For Gibbs's article in the New Haven *Palladium,* see its reprint in Boston *Liberator,* Nov. 15, 1839, 184.

28. N.Y. *Advertiser & Express,* Jan. 11, 1840, 2; N.Y. *Commercial Advertiser,* Jan. 10, 1840, 2.

29. Ibid.; Cinqué testimony, 19–20, U.S. Dist. Ct. Records for Conn., FARC.

30. Ibid.

31. Ibid. See above, chap. 2, for Cinqué's earlier account given to Tappan and others in the New Haven jail.

32. N.Y. *Commercial Advertiser,* Jan. 10, 1840, 2; N.Y. *Advertiser & Express,* Jan. 11, 1840, 2.

33. N.Y. *Advertiser & Express,* Jan. 11, 1840, 2.

34. *Daily Herald* (N.Y.), Jan. 10, 1840, clipping encl. in Baldwin Family Papers, Box 186, Yale.

35. Ibid.

36. N.Y. *Advertiser & Express,* Jan. 15, 1840, 1.

37. Ibid.; N.Y. *Commercial Advertiser,* Jan. 11, 1840, 2.

38. N.Y. *Advertiser & Express,* Jan. 15, 1840, 1; John W. Barber, *A History of the Amistad Captives: Being a Circumstantial Account of the Capture of the Spanish Schooner Amistad* . . . (New Haven, Conn.: E.L. & J.W. Barber, 1840), 8.

39. Statement by Vega, 145, U.S. Dist. Ct. Records for Conn., FARC; N.Y. *Advertiser & Express,* Jan. 15, 1840, 1.

40. N.Y. *Advertiser & Express,* Jan. 15, 1840, 2. In circuit court in 1839, Isham declared, "We intend to claim salvage for the Slaves but we do not propose to ask to have them sold with the vessel & Cargo." Isham to Charles A. Ingersoll (not to be confused with Charles J. Ingersoll, representative from Pennsylvania), clerk, U.S. Dist. Ct. Records for Conn., FARC. Either Isham mixed his stories or he did not regard slaves as "human flesh."

41. N.Y. *Advertiser & Express,* Jan. 15, 1840, 2.

42. N.Y. *Commercial Advertiser,* Jan. 15, 1840, 2; Judson's decision, 56ff., U.S. Dist. Ct. Records for Conn., FARC. See also Boston *Liberator,* Jan. 24, 1840, 13–14. For Webster's argument in the *Bevans* case, see 3 Wheaton 336 (1818).

43. Judson's decision, 56, 58, U.S. Dist. Ct. Records for Conn., FARC; N.Y. *Commercial Advertiser,* Jan. 15, 1840, 2.

44. Judson's decision, 58, U.S. Dist. Ct. Records for Conn., FARC; N.Y. *Commercial Advertiser,* Jan. 15, 1840, 2.

45. Judson's decision, 66–68, U.S. Dist. Ct. Records for Conn., FARC; N.Y. *Commercial Advertiser,* Jan. 15, 1840, 2.

46. Judson's decision, 66–67, 69–70, U.S. Dist. Ct. Records for Conn., FARC; N.Y. *Commercial Advertiser,* Jan. 15, 1840, 2. Judson never acknowledged the validity of the Spanish government's charge of murder, because, in his view, the blacks had mutinied in self-defense after being kidnapped. But even if he had recognized the charge as valid, he could still have refused to approve the blacks'

return to Cuba as criminals, because there was no treaty provision between the nations for extradition.

47. Judson's decision, 69–70, U.S. Dist. Ct. Records for Conn., FARC; N.Y. *Commercial Advertiser,* Jan. 15, 1840, 2.

48. Ibid.

49. N.Y. *Commercial Advertiser,* Jan. 15, 1840, 2; Tappan to Madden, n.d., but probably Jan. 20, 1840, Tappan Papers, Corresp., 1809–72, MS Div., LC.

50. N.Y. *Commercial Advertiser,* Jan. 15, 1840, 2.

51. Baldwin, "Captives of the *Amistad,*" 349; Charles A. Dinsmore, "Interesting Sketches of the *Amistad* Captives," *Yale University Library Gazette* 9 (Jan. 1935): 51–55.

52. Judson's decision, 70, U.S. Dist. Ct. Records for Conn., FARC; N.Y. *Commercial Advertiser,* Jan. 15, 1840, 1. Maurice G. Baxter shows that the *Eugénie* case left unresolved the question of whether America's courts could enforce another country's legislation. Ultimately the U.S. Supreme Court decided in the negative. See his *One and Inseparable: Daniel Webster and the Union* (Cambridge, Mass.: Harvard U. Press, 1984), 162. For the *Eugénie* case see 26 Federal Cases 832 (1822). For the *Antelope* see 10 Wheaton 66 (1825). See also R. Kent Newmyer, *Supreme Court Justice Joseph Story: Statesman of the Old Republic* (Chapel Hill: U. of North Carolina Press, 1985), 347–50.

53. Lewis Tappan wrote his brother Benjamin that the blacks were either slaves or freemen; "and being freemen they ought to be free." Their return to Africa was "another matter." To a friend, Lewis Tappan wrote, "They ought to have been liberated here." And to Madden, Tappan declared that the abolitionists believed that Judson should have "instantly liberated them." Lewis Tappan to Benjamin Tappan, Jan. 15, 1840, Lewis Tappan Papers, Corresp., 1809–72, MS Div., LC; Lewis Tappan to G. Bailey, Jan. 15, 1840, ibid.; Lewis Tappan to Madden, Feb. 3, 1840, ibid.

54. Boston *Liberator,* Jan. 17, 1840, 11; N.Y. *Commercial Advertiser,* Jan. 15, 1840, 2; N.Y. *Evening Post,* Jan. 15, 1840, 2; Ludlow quoted in N.Y. *Commercial Advertiser,* Jan. 15, 1840, 2; Sedgwick to Baldwin, Jan. 16, 1840, Baldwin Family Papers, Box 36, Yale.

55. Sedgwick to Baldwin, Jan. 16, 1840, Baldwin Family Papers, Box 36, Yale; Tappan quote in Lewis Tappan Papers, Journals and Notebooks, 1814–69, Jan. 19, 1840, 115, MS Div., LC; Lewis Tappan to Benjamin Tappan, Jan. 15, 1840, ibid., Corresp., 1809–72; Lewis Tappan to Scoble, Jan. 20, 1840, ibid.; Lewis Tappan to William W. Ellsworth, Jan. 21, 1840, ibid.; Lewis Tappan to Benjamin Griswold, Jan. 30, 1840, ibid.

56. Forsyth to Holabird, Jan. 17, 1840, *H. Exec. Doc.* 185, p. 57; U.S. district attorney appeal, 70–71, U.S. Dist. Ct. Records for Conn., FARC; Spanish owners' appeal, 71, ibid.

Chapter 8. The Politics of Democracy

1. Lewis Tappan to Benjamin Tappan, April 27, 1840, Lewis Tappan Papers, Corresp., 1809–72, MS Div., LC; Staples to Baldwin, Jan. 21, 1840, Baldwin Family Papers, Box 36, Yale; Sec. of Navy James K. Paulding to Lt. John S. Paine of *Grampus,* Jan. 25, 1840, U.S. Dept. of Navy, Letters to Officers, Sec. of Navy to Ships of War, NA.

2. Hartford and New Haven papers cited in N.Y. *Commercial Advertiser,* Feb. 12, 1840, 2. See also Boston *Liberator,* Feb. 28, 1840, 36. One of the president's supporters, the attorney Ralph Ingersoll of Connecticut, did not believe the charge and asked Van Buren for a written denial that he could show voters in the state. There is no record of a reply from the White House. See Ingersoll to Van Buren, Feb. 15, 1840, Martin Van Buren papers, MS Div., LC.

3. N.Y. *Commercial Advertiser,* Feb. 12, 1840, 2.

4. N.Y. *Express,* June 9, 1840, 2.

5. British and Foreign Anti-Slavery Society, *Proceedings of the General Anti-Slavery Convention, Called by the Committee of the British and Foreign Anti-Slavery Society, and Held in London, from Friday, June 12th, to Tuesday, June 23rd, 1840* (London: British and Foreign Anti-Slavery Society, 1841), 508–11. In ARC.

6. On British relations, see U.S. DS, Diplomatic Instructions of the DS, 1801–1906: Great Britain, NA; U.S. DS, Dispatches from U.S. Ministers to Great Britain, 1791–1906, ibid.

7. Forsyth to Vail, July 15, 1840, William R. Manning, ed., *The Diplomatic Correspondence of the United States: Inter-American Affairs, 1831–1860,* 12 vols. (Wash., D.C.: Carnegie Endowment for International Peace, 1932–39), 11:23–24. On America's interest in Cuba see Lester D. Langley, *The Cuban Policy of the United States: A Brief History* (N.Y.: John Wiley, 1968), esp. 21–24.

8. *Times* of London, Oct. 7, 1839, 4; Resolution by abolitionists in Glasgow, calling on British government to intercede in behalf of *Amistad* blacks, Oct. 15, 1839, cited in N.Y. *Commercial Advertiser,* Nov. 25, 1839, 2; Letters on *Amistad* case from John Murray, secretary of the Glasgow Emancipation Society, read into minutes of meeting of Nov. 26, 1839, of British and Foreign Anti-Slavery Society, item 394, 470–71, in Papers of Brit. and For. Anti-Slavery Soc., London, Rhodes House Library, Oxford, Eng. The British *Emancipator* of London referred to an address by John Scoble and others that led a delegation of the British and Foreign Anti-Slavery Society to see Lord Palmerston, who stated that the *Amistad* case had been referred to the queen's advocate for advice on the approach the British government should use in the case. Cited in Richmond *Enquirer,* Jan. 9, 1840, 4. See also minutes of meeting of Nov. 26, 1839, item 97, 120, Papers of Brit. and For. Anti-Slavery Soc.; "Case of the *Amistad,*" Memorials and Petitions, Nov. 1839 to Aug. 1843, 1–3, ibid. Madden to Fox, Nov. 25, 1839, in AMA Papers, Box 197, "Sierra Leone" folder, ARC; Madden to Joseph Sturge, Dec. 22, 1839, in minutes of Brit. and For. Anti-Slavery Soc., item 111, 132–33, Papers of Brit. and For. Anti-Slavery Soc. See also Betty Fladeland, *Men and Brothers: Anglo-American Antislavery Cooperation* (Urbana: U. of Ill. Press, 1972), 326–27.

9. Fox to Palmerston, Nov. 29, 1839, Great Britain, *British and Foreign State Papers,* 116 vols. (London: James Ridgway, 1812–1925), 28:927–28; Palmerston to Fox, Dec. 21, 1839, ibid., 926–27; Palmerston to Minister J. J. Jernigham, Dec. 21, 1839, ibid., 574–75; Palmerston to secretary of Brit. and For. Anti-Slavery Soc., Dec. 23, 1839, read into minutes of meeting of Dec. 27, 1839, item 111, 131–32, Papers of Brit. and For. Anti-Slavery Soc. The papers of Lord Palmerston, temporarily housed in the Royal Historical Manuscripts Commission in London, contain nothing important on the *Amistad.*

10. Jernigham to H. E. D. Evaristo Perez de Castro in Madrid, Jan. 5, 1840, Great Britain, Foreign Office, FO 185/184/1840, Embassy & Consular Archives: Spain: Corresp., Public Record Office, Kew Gardens, Eng.; D. R. Clarke, acting

superintendent of liberated Africans in Havana, to Lord John Russell, May 12, 1840, encl. in Palmerston to Arthur Aston in Madrid, Aug. 6, 1840, in ibid., FO 185/182/1840; Palmerston to Aston, Aug. 6, 1840, ibid.; Jernigham to Spanish minister of foreign affairs, Don Joaquín María de Ferrer, Nov. 11, 1840, ibid.; Aston to Palmerston, Nov. 14, 1840, ibid., FO 185/183/1840; reference to parliamentary papers in N.Y. *National Anti-Slavery Standard,* Dec. 17, 1840, 110.

11. Argaiz to Forsyth, Jan. 24, 1840, Leg. 5584, Exp. 1, no. 29, AHN; memorandum encl. in Argaiz to Forsyth, March 20, 1840, U.S. DS, Notes from the Spanish Legation in the U.S. to the DS, 1790–1906, NA; Argaiz to Forsyth, April 24, 1840, ibid.

12. Forsyth to Argaiz, May 9, 1840, U.S. DS, Notes to Foreign Legations in the U.S. from the DS, 1834–1906, NA.

13. Tappan to Baldwin, Jan. 27, 1840, Baldwin Family Papers, Box 36, Yale.

14. Gilpin to Sec. of Navy, April 11, 1840, *Official Opinions of the Attorneys General of the U.S.,* 3:510. The Richmond *Enquirer* declared that, according to defenders of the blacks, if slaves rose in rebellion, the whites would become captives to "black masters" and everyone would owe the murderers *"compassion"* and *"sympathy."* See edition of Jan. 2, 1840, 4.

15. Motion for dismissal of appeal by U.S. district attorney, by Staples and Baldwin, April 7, 1840, U.S. Circuit Ct. Records for Conn., FARC.

16. Report by Tappan on Thompson's decision, printed in N.Y. *Commercial Advertiser,* May 2, 1840, 2; Tappan to Scoble, May 2, 1840, *Side-light,* 70; Boston *Liberator,* May 8, 1840, 73. See 15 Peters 519, 532 (1841). After the circuit court upheld the appeal to the Supreme Court, Staples tried another approach. He argued that there could be no appeal from the circuit court in cases involving property valued at less than $2,000. The basis for his claim lay in Section 22 of the Judiciary Act of 1789: "And upon a like process, may final judgments and decrees in civil actions, and suits in equity in a circuit court, brought there by original process, or removed there from courts of the several States, or removed there by appeal from a district court where the matter in dispute exceeds the sum or value of two thousand dollars, exclusive of costs, be re-examined and reversed or affirmed in the Supreme Court, the citation being in such case signed by a judge of such circuit court, or justice of the Supreme Court, and the adverse party having at least thirty days' notice." *U.S. Statutes at Large,* 1:84. Thompson, however, explained that that principle had no bearing on admiralty cases. He was correct. The Judiciary Act of 1789 applied the monetary stipulation only to civil suits and equity cases, and Article III of the Constitution states that the country's judicial power extends to "all Cases of admiralty and maritime Jurisdiction." See N.Y. *Commercial Advertiser,* May 2, 1840, 2.

17. N.Y. *Commercial Advertiser,* May 2, 1840, 2.

18. Ibid.

19. Baldwin to William L. Storrs, Connecticut representative in Congress, May 4, 1840, John Adams Family Papers, MHS. The letter is addressed to John Quincy Adams, rather than to Storrs, which probably is an error. In any case, the letter is also in the Baldwin Family Papers, Box 36, Yale. Forsyth to Baldwin, March 3, 25, 1840, U.S. DS, Domestic Letters, NA.

20. Baldwin to Storrs, May 4, 1840, Adams Family Papers, MHS.

21. Tappan to Baldwin, April 24, 27, 1840, Baldwin Family Papers, Box 36, Yale; Lewis Tappan to Benjamin Tappan, April 24, 1840, Lewis Tappan Papers,

Corresp., 1809–72, MS Div., LC. This letter is also in the Van Buren Papers, MS Div., LC. See Forsyth to Staples and Sedgwick, March 14, 1840, U.S. DS, Domestic Letters, NA; Forsyth to Baldwin, March 25, 1840, ibid.

22. Baldwin to Storrs, May 4, 1840, Adams Family Papers, MHS; *Memoirs of JQA,* 10:287, 296.

23. N.Y. *Express,* June 12, 1840, 2.

24. *Memoirs of JQA,* 10:370. By this time Adams had joined the blacks' defense team with Baldwin and Sedgwick. Staples had been removed. Explanation follows in text.

25. Ibid.; N.Y. *National Anti-Slavery Standard,* Dec. 17, 1840, 111.

26. N.Y. *National Anti-Slavery Standard,* Dec. 17, 1840, 111.

27. Ibid.; *Memoirs of JQA,* 10:373; U.S. Cong., *House of Representatives,* House Report 51, "Alteration of Doc. H. R. No. 185—*Amistad* Case," Jan. 4, 1841, 26th Cong., 2d sess., 1.

28. *Memoirs of JQA,* 10:377, 379; *House of Reps.,* HR 51, "Alteration of Doc. H.R. No. 185," 1, 3, 4, 6–7; Boston *Liberator,* Dec. 18, 1840, 202; ibid., Jan. 15, 1841, 11.

29. *Memoirs of JQA,* 10:382, 385–86, 389.

30. Ibid., 391.

31. Tappan to Baldwin, May 5, 1840, Baldwin Family Papers, Box 36, Yale; Baldwin to Forsyth, Sept. 9, 1840, ibid.; Tappan to Scoble, May 5, 1840, *Sidelight,* 70; Townsend to Tappan, Sept. 14, 1840, AMA Papers, Box 197, "Sierra Leone" folder, ARC.

32. N.Y. *National Anti-Slavery Standard,* Oct. 22, 1840, 78.

33. Tappan to Rev. Bacon, April 15, 1840, Bacon Family Papers, Box 5, Yale; Conn. *Observer* quoted in *African Repository* 16 (1840):301; Peale's Museum reference in N.Y. *Evening Star,* June 16, 1840, 2; Amory Hall reference in Boston *Liberator,* July 10, 1840, 111.

34. Unsigned letter pertaining to painting, April 25, 1840, AMA Papers, Box 197, "Sierra Leone" folder, ARC. The letter was probably written by Lewis Tappan. On the same day, he wrote a friend in New Haven expressing the same complaints. See Tappan to Benjamin Griswold, April 25, 1840, Tappan Papers, Corresp., 1809–72, MS Div., LC. The artist was A. Hewins.

35. Boston *Liberator,* May 15, 1840, 79.

36. Tappan to Baldwin, Sept. 9, 1840, Baldwin Family Papers, Box 36, Yale.

37. See Forsyth to Holabird, April 30, 1840, U.S. DS, Domestic Letters, NA.

38. Birney to Tappan, Oct. 2, 1840, AMA Papers, Box 197, "Sierra Leone" folder, ARC; Townsend to Tappan, Oct. 3, 1840, ibid.; Boston *Liberator,* Oct. 23, 1840, 170.

39. Tappan to Baldwin, Oct. 16, Nov. 3, 11, 21, 1840, Baldwin Family Papers, Box 36, Yale.

40. *Emancipator* story in Boston *Liberator,* Oct, 23, 1840, 111.

41. Tappan to Baldwin, April 24, 1840, Baldwin Family Papers, Box 36, Yale. To Ellis Gray Loring, Tappan wrote that Staples had "learning, weight of character," but did "not feel greatly, nor possess the boldness becoming this occasion." Tappan to Loring, Oct. 19, 1839, Tappan Papers, Corresp., 1809–72, MS Div., LC. Assessment of Sedgwick ibid. Tappan to Webster, May 10, 1840, Harold D. Moser, ed., *The Papers of Daniel Webster: Correspondence,* vol. 5, *1840–1843* (Hanover, N.H.: Dartmouth College and U. Press of New England, 1982),

36–37. Moser could find no reply from Webster to Tappan and concluded that he declined the offer. Ibid., 37 n. 2. The Amistad Research Center recently acquired the letter containing Webster's refusal and confirming Moser's supposition. See Webster to Tappan, May 13, 1840, ARC. Tappan to Baldwin, Oct. 16, 1840, Baldwin Family Papers, Box 36, Yale; Baldwin to Tappan, Oct. 19, 1840, ibid.; Tappan to Baldwin, Oct. 28, 1840, ibid.

42. For Webster's views on slavery, see Maurice G. Baxter, *One and Inseparable: Daniel Webster and the Union* (Cambridge, Mass.: Harvard U. Press, 1984), 90, 414–15, 418. On Choate see Jean V. Matthews, *Rufus Choate: The Law and Civic Virtue* (Philadelphia: Temple U. Press, 1980), 195–96, 241.

43. Tappan to Baldwin, Oct. 28, 1840, Baldwin Family Papers, Box 36, Yale. Simeon Jocelyn from the *Amistad* Committee considered Adams a man of "honesty and opinion." Jocelyn to Tappan, Oct. 21, 1840, AMA Papers, Box 197, "Sierra Leone" folder, ARC. A Virginian accused Adams of being so "diseased" on the subject of slavery that his name had become "odious" in the South. Because of this, the writer told Adams, "your name will descend to the latest posterity with this blot on it: Mr. Adams loves the negroes too much, *unconstitutionally.*" Letter from a Virginian to JQA, Dec. 31, 1839, Adams Family Papers, MHS.

44. *Memoirs of JQA,* 10:358; Tappan to Baldwin, Oct. 28, 1840, Baldwin Family Papers, Box 36, Yale.

45. Tappan to Baldwin, Oct. 28, 1840, Baldwin Family Papers, Box 36, Yale; Adams to Baldwin, Nov. 11, 1840, ibid.; Baldwin to Adams, Nov. 2, 1840, ibid.

46. *Memoirs of JQA,* 10:359–60; Tappan to Baldwin, Nov. 21, 1840, Baldwin Family Papers, Box 36, Yale; Townsend to Tappan, Oct. 3, 1840, AMA Papers, Box 197, "Sierra Leone" folder, ARC.

47. *Memoirs of JQA,* 10:361–62, 372.

Chapter 9. "Oh How Shall I Do Justice . . .?"

1. *Memoirs of JQA,* 10:383.

2. John Niven, *Martin Van Buren: The Romantic Age of American Politics* (N.Y.: Oxford U. Press, 1983), 471; Donald B. Cole, *Martin Van Buren and the American Political System* (Princeton, N.J.: Princeton U. Press, 1984), 373.

3. Major L. Wilson, *The Presidency of Martin Van Buren* (Lawrence: U. Press of Kansas, 1984), 207; Robert G. Gunderson, *The Log-Cabin Campaign* (Lexington: U. Press of Kentucky, 1957), 255, 256 n. 14.

4. Niven, *Van Buren,* 470–72; Cole, *Van Buren and the American Political System,* 373; James C. Curtis, *The Fox at Bay: Martin Van Buren and the Presidency, 1837–1841* (Lexington: U. Press of Kentucky, 1970), 190.

5. Tappan to Baldwin, Dec. 24, 1840, Baldwin Family Papers, Box 36, Yale; N.Y. *Commercial Advertiser,* Jan. 13, 1841, 2; Walton Perry, "The Mysterious Case of the Long, Low, Black Schooner," 360, in ARC. Wilson to Adams, Dec. 25, 29, 1840, John Adams Family Papers, MHS. Wilson also wrote Baldwin about Hyde, although Baldwin had been aware of Hyde's story over a year earlier. See Wilson to Baldwin, Dec. 29, 1840, Baldwin Family Papers, Box 36, Yale; Tappan to Baldwin, Nov. 11, 1839, ibid., Box 35.

6. See Adams to Loring, Oct. 3, Nov. 19, 1839, Adams Family Papers, JQA Letterbook, MHS.

7. Baldwin brief ibid., Corresp.; *Memoirs of JQA,* 10:383, 387, 397, 402, 409–10. To his son Charles Francis, John Quincy Adams explained that in 1783 he had seen in the British Museum in London the signature and seal of Saer de Quincy on the original parchment of the Magna Carta. That he was a descendant of Saer de Quincy had never had real impact until he contemplated defending the *Amistad* captives. Gedney's seizure of the blacks was a "gross violation" of the principles underlying the Magna Carta because he had acted without a warrant. Adams's great responsibilities to liberty had caused him "agony of soul" from the day he agreed to serve as counsel. See JQA to Charles Francis Adams, April 14, 1841, Adams Family Papers, MHS.

8. Kale and Kinna to Adams, Jan. 4, 1841, Adams Family Papers, MHS; Cinqué to Baldwin, Feb. 9, 1841, Baldwin Family Papers, Box 37, Yale.

9. Adams's notes on *Amistad* case, Feb. 7, 1841, Adams Family Papers, MHS.

10. Ibid.

11. Ibid.

12. Ibid.

13. See Angel Calderón de la Barca to Forsyth, Sept. 6, 1839, U.S. DS, Notes from the Spanish Legation in the U.S. to the DS, 1790–1906, NA; Argaiz to Forsyth, Nov. 26, 1839, ibid. The Spanish text in the latter note was: "resultando de aqui que la vindicta publica no se halla aun satisfecha; porque es preciso no olvidar que la Legacion de Espana no pide la estradicion de esclavos, sino la de asesinos."

14. Argaiz to Forsyth, Jan. 19, 1841, ibid.

15. Ibid.

16. The Spanish minister's changing emphases become apparent upon reading the following notes to the Department of State: Calderón to Forsyth, Sept. 6, 1839, ibid.; Argaiz to Forsyth, Nov. 26, 1839, Jan. 19, 1841, ibid. In September 1839 Calderón warned that if the "crime in question" went unpunished, the result would be more "revolt and evasion." Spanish paper quoted in N.Y. *Advertiser & Express,* Sept. 11, 1839, 1.

17. Vail to Forsyth, Jan. 15, 1841, U.S. DS, Dispatches from U.S. Ministers to Spain, 1792–1906, NA.

18. Ibid.

19. Townsend to Tappan, Jan. 18, 1841, AMA papers, Box 197, "Sierra Leone" folder, ARC; *Memoirs of JQA,* 10:399–401; Fox to Adams, Jan. 17, 1841, Adams Family Papers, MHS.

20. Fox to Forsyth, Jan. 20, 1841, U.S. Congress, *Sen. Docs.,* No. 179, "Message from the President of U.S.," Feb. 12, 1841, 26th Cong., 2d sess., 27–28.

21. Forsyth to Fox, Feb. 1, 1841, U.S. DS, Notes to Foreign Legations in the U.S. from the DS, 1834–1906, Great Britain, NA.

22. For emphasis on the McLeod affair in Anglo-American relations, see Great Britain, Foreign Office, FO 5: U.S., vols. 359–64 (1841), PRO, Kew Gardens, Eng.

23. Townsend to Tappan, Jan. 18, 1841, AMA Papers, Box 197, "Sierra Leone" folder, ARC; Tappan to Roger M. Sherman (the friend), Jan. 20, 1841, ibid.; Tappan to Townsend, Jan. 20, 1841, ibid.; Tappan to Norton, Jan. 20, 1841, ibid.; Thomas Fessenden to Tappan, Jan. 25, 1841, ibid.

24. Townsend to Tappan, Jan. 18, 1841, ibid.

25. Townsend to Tappan, Jan. 22, Feb. 12, 1841, ibid.

26. *Memoirs of JQA*, 10:396–97; Key to Tappan, Jan. 6, 1841, Lewis Tappan Papers, Corresp., 1809–72, MS Div., LC; Tappan to Baldwin, Jan. 20, 1841, Baldwin Family Papers, Box 37, Yale.

27. "Veto" in N.Y. *National Anti-Slavery Standard*, Jan. 21, 1841, 129. See *Side-light*, 185, 185 n. 140.

28. "Veto" in N.Y. *National Anti-Slavery Standard*, Jan. 21, 1841, 129.

29. Leavitt to Tappan, Jan. 16, 1841, AMA Papers, Box 197, "Sierra Leone" folder, ARC; Townsend to Tappan, Jan. 18, 1841, ibid.

30. Jay to Tappan, Jan. 23, 1841, ibid.

31. Tappan to Adams, Jan. 8, Feb. 13, 1841, Adams Family Papers, MHS.

32. Lewis Tappan to Benjamin Tappan, March 9, 13, 1840, Papers of Benjamin Tappan, MS Div., LC.

33. Tappan to Baldwin, Jan. 20, 1841, Baldwin Family Papers, Box 37, Yale; Leavitt to Tappan, Jan. 16, 1841, AMA Papers, Box 197, "Sierra Leone" folder, ARC.

Chapter 10. "The Eternal Principles of Justice"

1. Charles Warren, *The Supreme Court in United States History*, 3 vols. (Boston: Little, Brown, 1922), 2:316. See also Carl B. Swisher, *History of the Supreme Court of the United States*, vol. 5; *The Taney Period, 1836–64* (N.Y.: Macmillan, 1974).

2. Associate Justice Joseph Story believed that only the maintenance of the constitutional compromise on slavery could preserve the Union. Worked out in Philadelphia in 1787, it provided that Congress could not interfere with the importation of slaves before 1808 and that three-fifths of the slaves in the United States would count in determining taxation apportionment and representation in the House. Six years later, in 1793, Congress passed a fugitive-slave law to help the states enforce a similar clause in the Constitution. Story used the principles underlying these specific provisions to argue that the only way to deal with the slavery question was through compromise. See R. Kent Newmyer, *Supreme Court Justice Joseph Story: Statesman of the Old Republic* (Chapel Hill: U. of North Carolina Press, 1985), 357, 365–66.

3. Swisher, *History of the Supreme Court*, 5:63, 66–67; Warren, *Supreme Court in United States History*, 2:313–15.

4. *Memoirs of JQA*, 10:431; Swisher, *History of the Supreme Court*, 5:57, 67; Newmyer, *Supreme Court Justice Joseph Story*, 354. The full name of the case was *Somerset* v. *Stewart*. Story's work on conflict theory was *Commentaries on the Conflict of Laws* (Boston: Hilliard, Gray, 1834). In it, he declared that, under the *Somerset* decision, when a slave from Africa or any other slaveholding country entered England, he became "*ipso facto* a freeman." In the United States, he wrote, "there is no doubt, that the same principle pervades the common law of the non-slaveholding states in America." Ibid., 92–93. For a penetrating analysis of the *Somerset* case, see William M. Wiecek, *The Sources of Antislavery Constitutionalism in America, 1769–1848* (Ithaca, N.Y.: Cornell U. Press, 1977), chap. 1. See also Paul Finkelman, *An Imperfect Union: Slavery, Federalism, and Comity* (Chapel Hill: U. of North Carolina Press, 1981), 16–17, 38–40, and numerous other references to the case.

5. Swisher, *History of the Supreme Court,* 5:11–13. See also Charles G. Haines and Foster H. Sherwood, *The Role of the Supreme Court in American Government and Politics, 1835–1864* (Berkeley: U. of Calif. Press, 1957), 96–110.

6. *Memoirs of JQA,* 10:429, 437; U.S. Supreme Court, "Minutes of the Supreme Court of the United States," 4373, 4376, NA; U.S. Sup. Ct., "Dockets of the Supreme Court of the United States," case 2310, *The United States* v. *The Libellants & Claimants of the Schooner Amistad & c. and the Africans mentioned & described in the General Libels & claims,"* ibid.; 15 Peters 541–47 (1841).

7. 15 Peters 547–49 (1841).

8. *Memoirs of JQA,* 10:429; U.S. Sup. Ct., "Minutes," 4379; 15 Peters 549, 551, 560 (1841).

9. 15 Peters 550 (1841). Baldwin's notes on the case showed that he based his motion on the following factors: the appellees owed no allegiance to Spanish law or dependencies; they were not assassins; they were not guilty of crimes or violations of laws; no power existed in any government department of the United States—by Constitution, law, or treaty—to surrender them for trial as fugitives or criminals upon the demand of the Spanish minister; the blacks had never been property belonging to Ruiz and Montes, but had been and were free; the United States had not instituted a suit here or in the lower courts charging the blacks with a crime or any other act justifying imprisonment; and, in a point not upheld by law (see above, chap. 8, n. 16), he declared that if they were slaves, none was valued at $2,000, the minimum necessary for property questions to come before the Supreme Court. See Baldwin's notes for January term of Supreme Court, in Baldwin Family Papers, Box 37, Yale. For the *Miln* case, see 11 Peters 102 (1837).

11. Harold M. Hyman and William M. Wiecek, *Equal Justice under Law: Constitutional Development, 1835–1875* (N.Y.: Harper & Row, 1982), 103; 15 Peters 550–51, 556, 560–61 (1841). Madison's notes on the Constitutional Convention were published in 1840.

11. 15 Peters 550–51, 553, 554 (1841).

12. Ibid., 558–59.

13. Ibid., 551–52, 554.

14. Ibid., 565–66.

15. N.Y. *American,* Feb. 27, 1841, 2; *Memoirs of JQA,* 10:430.

16. U.S. Sup. Ct., "Minutes," 4381; *Memoirs of JQA,* 10:427, 431.

17. John Quincy Adams, *Argument of John Quincy Adams, before the Supreme Court of the United States, in the Case of the United States, Appellants, vs. Cinque, and Other Africans, Captured in the Schooner Amistad* (N.Y.: S. W. Benedict, 1841), 3–4, 6, 8–9, reprinted in The Basic Afro-American Reprint Library (N.Y.: Arno Press, 1969). See manuscript of Adams's speech before Supreme Court on *Amistad* case, in Lewis Tappan Papers, Corresp., 1809–72, MS Div., LC. Adams's argument did not appear in Peters's *Reports,* because he failed to get his manuscript to the court reporter on time. For this reason, it is impossible to be sure how much of Adams's *Argument* was actually delivered before the Court, and how much he later added to his own published version of the proceedings. He probably managed to present most of the points he intended. In any case, he had made most of his charges before the House of Representatives and, in one form or another, in the newspapers. See Adams to Peters, May 3, 19, 1841, John Adams Family Papers, JQA Letterbook, MHS.

18. JQA, *Argument,* 11.

19. Ibid., 49–50.

20. Ibid., 79; Joseph Sturge, *A Visit to the United States in 1841* (London: Hamilton, Adams, 1842), app. E, xxxviii–xl.

21. MS of Adams's speech, Tappan Papers, Corresp., 1809–72, MS Div., LC.

22. Ibid.; Sturge, *Visit,* app. E, xxxix.

23. JQA, *Argument,* 65–66.

24. Ibid., 15, 29, 30.

25. Ibid., 13–14, 20–21, 42. Adams was referring to the Adams-Onís Treaty.

26. JQA, *Argument,* 23, 42.

27. Ibid., 16, 38, 42–43, 71.

28. Ibid., 46–47.

29. *Memoirs of JQA,* 10:396–97, 431, 435.

30. Joseph Pickering (the observer) to Adams, March 12, 1841, Adams Family Papers, MHS; N.Y. *Commercial Advertiser,* March 4, 1841, 2; N.Y. *American,* Feb. 27, 1841, 2; N.Y. *Evening Post,* March 2, 1841, 2; Garrison to Elizabeth Pease, March 1, 1841, Walter M. Merrill, ed., *The Letters of William Lloyd Garrison,* vol. 3 (Cambridge, Mass.: Harvard U. Press, 1973), 18; Norton to Tappan, Feb. 27, 1841, AMA Papers, Box 197, "Sierra Leone" folder, ARC. Barbour reference in extract of letter by unidentified writer, published in Richmond *Enquirer,* March 9, 1841, 3; William W. Story, ed., *Life and Letters of Joseph Story,* 2 vols. (Boston: Little & Brown, 1851), 2:348.

31. *Memoirs of JQA,* 10:431–32; U.S. Sup. Ct., "Minutes," 4382; N.Y. *American,* March 4, 1841, 2.

32. *Memoirs of JQA,* 10:437; 15 Peters 572, 591 (1841).

33. 15 Peters 570–71 (1841); U.S. Sup. Ct.,"Minutes," 4395.

34. 15 Peters 575–76 (1841).

35. Ibid., 576–79.

36. Ibid., 578.

37. Ibid., 580–81.

38. Ibid., 581–82.

39. Sedgwick to Tappan, Oct. 12, 1839, Tappan Papers, Corresp., 1809–72, MS Div., LC.

40. 15 Peters 583 (1841).

41. Ibid., 583–84.

42. Ibid., 584–86.

43. Ibid., 586–87.

44. Maurice G. Baxter, *Daniel Webster and the Supreme Court* (Amherst: U. of Mass. Press, 1966), 20; 15 Peters 593 (1841); Robert M. Cover, *Justice Accused: Antislavery and the Judicial Process* (New Haven, Conn.: Yale U. Press, 1975), 102; Newmyer, *Supreme Court Justice Joseph Story,* 355–58.

45. Sedgwick to Tappan, Oct. 12, 1839, Tappan Papers, Corresp., 1809–72, MS Div., LC.

46. 15 Peters 596–97 (1841). For the congressional act of March 3, 1819, see *U.S. Statutes at Large,* 3:532–34. There is nothing of importance on the *Amistad* in the Joseph Story Papers housed in either the Library of Congress or the Massachusetts Historical Society.

47. U.S. Sup. Ct., "Minutes," 4415–16; Swisher, *History of the Supreme Court,* 5:194; 15 Peters 519–20, 592, 597 (1841). See also Newmyer, *Supreme Court Justice Joseph Story,* 368–69. Taney's opinions in other cases indicate that he con-

sidered blacks to be subject to the states in which they were at the time, and probably not open to federal intervention. He undoubtedly did not concur with Story's statements relating to "eternal principles of justice." See Carl B. Swisher, *Roger B. Taney* (N.Y.: Macmillan, 1936), 418.

48. 15 Peters, 520, 593 (1841).

49. Ibid., 593–94; Joseph Story, *Commentaries on the Constitution,* 3 vols. (Boston: Hilliard, Gray, 1833), 1:276. See also Cover, *Justice Accused,* 105, 112.

50. 15 Peters 595–96 (1841); Cover, *Justice Accused,* 112.

51. 15 Peters 520, 594–95 (1841).

52. Ibid., 597.

53. For correspondence relating to Adams's failure to have the manuscript ready for publication, see n. 17 above. Peters even delayed publication of the volume including the *Amistad* case to give Adams more time to submit his manuscript. When Adams still failed to furnish it, Peters explained, "As many of the points presented by Mr. Adams, in the discussion of the cause, were not considered by the Court essential to its decision: and were not taken notice of in the opinion of the Court, delivered by Mr. Justice STORY, the necessary omission of the argument is submitted with less regret." See 15 Peters 566 (1841).

54. Ibid., 597. Leavitt told Tappan that he was "not very sorry" that the blacks were "in the hands of Daniel Webster instead of John Forsyth." Leavitt to Tappan, Feb. 15, 1841, AMA Papers, Box 197, "Sierra Leone" folder, ARC. Though Webster had not accepted the invitation to defend the *Amistad* captives before the Supreme Court, the abolitionists had reason to believe that he would not uphold his predecessor's position on the case. In late 1819, during the debate over Missouri's admission to the Union, Webster had set out his position on slavery— that Congress should prohibit its extension on constitutional grounds. See Maurice G. Baxter, *One and Inseparable: Daniel Webster and the Union* (Cambridge, Mass.: Harvard U. Press, 1984), 89, 90.

55. Cover, *Justice Accused,* 109, 114–16.

56. Leavitt quoted in William Jay, *A View of the Action of the Federal Government, in Behalf of Slavery* (Utica, N.Y.: G. F. Hopkins, 1844; originally published in 1839), app.

57. Adams to Tappan, March 9, 1841, Adams Family Papers, MHS; Adams to Baldwin, March 9, 1841, Baldwin Family Papers, Box 37, Yale.

Chapter 11. In Perspective

1. *Emancipator,* Oct. 10, 1839, 94; Mobile *Commercial Register & Patriot,* March 24, 1841, 2; Charleston *Courier,* March 15, 1841, 2; New Orleans *Times Picayune,* March 23, 1841, 2; N.Y. *Commercial Advertiser,* March 11, 1841, 2; March 20, 1841, 2; Baldwin to Adams, March 12, 1841, Baldwin Family Papers, Box 37, Yale; Baldwin to *Amistad* Committee, March 12, 1841, ibid.; Samuel Peckham (observer) to Tappan, Feb. 3, 1841, AMA Papers, Box 197, "Sierra Leone" folder, ARC. Leavitt to Adams, March 18, 1841, John Adams Family Papers, MHS; Smith to Weld, March 14, 1841, Gilbert H. Barnes and Dwight L. Dumond, eds., *Letters of Theodore Dwight Weld, Angelina Grimké Weld, and Sarah Grimké, 1822–1844,* 2 vols. (N.Y.: D. Appleton-Century, 1934), 2:863. Despite this favorable reaction to the decision, Adams criticized the Supreme Court in a long letter to the *Amistad* Committee, which the New York *Commer-*

cial Advertiser published. Adams believed that the Court sidestepped many of the issues, including the charge of executive interference. See Adams to *Amistad* Committee, March 17, 1841, Adams Family Papers, JQA Letterbook, MHS; N.Y. *Commercial Advertiser,* March 23, 1841, 2.

2. N.Y. *Commercial Advertiser,* March 20, 1841, 2.

3. Ibid.

4. Ibid.; Townsend to Tappan, March 11, 1841, AMA Papers, Box 197, "Sierra Leone" folder, ARC; Banna to Tappan, March 12, 1841, ibid.; Kinna to Tappan, March 13, 20, 28, 1841, ibid.

5. Harold M. Hyman and William M. Wiecek, *Equal Justice under Law: Constitutional Development, 1835–1875* (N.Y.: Harper & Row, 1982), 104; Tappan to Baldwin, April 9, 1841, Baldwin Family Papers, Box 37, Yale; Leavitt to Adams, Aug. 29, 1841, AMA Papers, Box 197, "Sierra Leone" folder, ARC. At one public exhibition attended by Joseph Sturge, Tappan's friend and a leader of the British and Foreign Anti-Slavery Society, a large crowd jammed the assembly, paying the high price of half a dollar, which went into a fund to transport the blacks back to Africa. Fifteen of them were present, including Kale and the three girls, and Cinqué spoke Mende in a "very animated and graceful" manner. Kale spoke English, and each of the others read from the New Testament. These public displays, Sturge wrote, made it "impossible for any one to go away with the impression, that in native intellect these people were inferior to the whites." Joseph Sturge, *A Visit to the United States in 1841* (London: Hamilton, Adams, 1842), 50–51. For accounts of this exhibition, see N.Y. *Commercial Advertiser,* May 13, 1841, 2, and *African Repository* 17 (1841): 164–65. See also Lewis Tappan Papers, Journals and Notebooks, 1814–69, 35, MS Div., LC.

6. Tappan to Baldwin, March 26, April 1, 1841, Baldwin Family Papers, Box 37, Yale; *Amistad* Committee to Baldwin, April 15, 1841, ibid.; *The Amistad Case,* 210 (personal copy of Tappan's), in ARC. Whereas Staples and Sedgwick were reimbursed for expenses, Adams declined any compensation. *Amistad* Committee to JQA, April 15, 1841, Adams Family Papers, MHS.

7. *Amistad* Committee to Adams, March 24, 1841, Adams Family Papers, MHS; Leavitt to Alexander, March 25, 1841, AMA Papers, Box 197, "Sierra Leone" folder, ARC; Leavitt to Committee of British and Foreign Anti-Slavery Society, April 28, 1841, ibid.; *Memoirs of JQA,* 10:455. Adams undoubtedly based his stand on the Logan Act of 1798, which prohibits private citizens from negotiating with foreign governments.

8. *Amistad* Committee to Baldwin, March 11, 24, 1841, Baldwin Family Papers, Box 37, Yale; Baldwin to Leavitt, March 12, 1841, ibid.; Tappan to Baldwin, April 1, 1841, ibid.; Baldwin to Tappan, et al., April 2, 1841, ibid.; Adams to *Amistad* Committee, April 3, 1841, Adams Family Papers, JQA Letterbook, MHS (letter also in ARC); Extract of letter from Adams, April 3, 1841, encl. in Tappan to Baldwin, April 13, 1841, Baldwin Family Papers, Box 37, Yale; Staples to Tappan, April 9, 1841, Tappan Papers, Corresp., 1809–72, MS Div., LC; Sedgwick to Tappan, March 18, 1841, ibid.

9. *Amistad* Committee to Baldwin, March 11, 24, 1841, ibid.; Baldwin to Leavitt, March 12, 1841, ibid.

10. Horatio T. Strother, *The Underground Railroad in Connecticut* (Middletown, Conn.: Wesleyan U. Press, 1962), 77; Extract of letter from Adams, April 3, 1841, encl. in Tappan to Baldwin, April 13, 1841, Baldwin Family Papers, Box

37, Yale; Tappan to Baldwin, April 1, 1841, ibid.; E. B. Sherman to Simeon E. Baldwin, Feb. 16, 1888, ibid., Box 87; John Dougall to Leavitt, April 26, 1841, AMA Papers, Box 197, "Sierra Leone" folder, ARC; *Long Island Farmer* (N.Y.), May 11, 1841, 2; N.Y. *Commercial Advertiser,* May 13, 1841, 2.

11. Kinna to Baldwin, March 15, 1841, Baldwin Family Papers, Box 37, Yale; New Haven *Herald,* March 16, 1841, cited in N.Y. *Commercial Advertiser,* March 19, 1841, 1.

12. N.Y. *Commercial Advertiser,* March 19, 1841, 1. Ralph Ingersoll had appeared as attorney against the *Amistad* blacks during the hearings before Judge Smith Thompson in Hartford in September 1839. Charles A. Ingersoll was a clerk during the early stages of the *Amistad* court proceedings in Connecticut. He is not to be confused with Charles *J.* Ingersoll, the Democratic representative from Pennsylvania.

13. Ibid., March 20, 1841, 2. At Baldwin's request, Tappan retained the legal assistance of General [?] Kimberly. Ibid.

14. Ibid.; Tappan to Simeon Jocelyn, March 18, 1841, AMA Papers, Box 197, "Sierra Leone" folder, ARC.

15. N.Y. *Commercial Advertiser,* March 20, 1841, 2.

16. Ibid.; Tappan to Jocelyn, March 18, 1841, AMA Papers, Box 197, "Sierra Leone" folder, ARC.

17. Tappan to *Amistad* Committee, March 19, 1841, printed in N.Y. *Journal of Commerce* and reprinted in Boston *Liberator,* March 26, 1841, 50.

18. *American Missionary* (published by AMA of N.Y.), Jan. 1858, 2, in ARC; Tappan to Jocelyn, March 18, 1841, AMA Papers, Box 197, "Sierra Leone" folder, ibid.; A. F. Williams to Tappan, June 3, 4, Aug. 18, Sept. 7, 1841, ibid.; L. M. Booth (the contact) to Tappan, June 4, 1841, ibid.; John F. Norton (abolitionist in Connecticut) to Tappan, Aug. 9, 1841, ibid.; New Haven *Herald* (n.d.) cited in Richmond *Enquirer,* March 30, 1841, 2; *Niles' National Register* (Balt.), Aug. 21, 1841, 400; *Amistad* Committee pamphlet (n.d.), A1258, 4, in ARC.

19. Kale letter in *Emancipator,* March 25, 1841, quoted in Strother, *Underground Railroad in Connecticut,* 74–76.

20. Scoble to Aberdeen, Dec. 10, 1841, "The *Amistad* Captives," 77, Papers of the British and Foreign Anti-Slavery Society, London, Rhodes House Library, Oxford, Eng.; Strother, *Underground Railroad in Connecticut,* 78–79.

21. Baldwin to Adams, March 12, 1841, Baldwin Family Papers, Box 37, Yale; Baldwin to Leavitt, March 12, 1841, ibid.; Augustus F. Beard, *The Story of the "Amistad,"* pamphlet published by AMA (n.d.), A1437, ARC: Tappan to Benjamin Griswold, Jan. 30, 1840, Tappan Papers, Corresp., 1809–72, MS Div., LC; Tappan to Dr. Richard R. Madden, Feb. 3, 1840, ibid.

22. Adams to Baldwin, March 17, 1841, Adams Family Papers, JQA Letterbook, MHS; Adams to Baldwin, March 17, 1841, Baldwin Family Papers, Box 37, Yale.

23. *Memoirs of JQA,* 10:446–47.

24. Ibid., 11:23–24; Leavitt to Tappan, June 30, 1841, AMA Papers, Box 197, "Sierra Leone" folder, ARC; Leavitt to Adams, Aug. 29, 1841, ibid.; Jocelyn and Tappan to Pres. Tyler, ca. late Aug. 1841, in Adams Family Papers, MHS; Tappan to Adams, April 21, 1841, ibid.; Tappan to Sturge, Sept. 25, 1841, *Side-light,* 83–84; Fletcher Webster, acting sec. of state, to Tappan, Oct. 6, 1841, U.S. DS,

Domestic Letters, NA; Tyler to Tappan, Oct. 20, 1841, Tappan Papers, Corresp., 1809–72, MS Div., LC; *African Repository* 17 (1841): 35.

25. Leavitt to Alexander, March 25, 1841, AMA Papers, Box 197, "Sierra Leone" folder, ARC; Leavitt to Buxton, March 29, 1841, ibid.; Scoble to Tappan, Oct. 19, 1841, ibid. Neither the papers of Lord Aberdeen nor those of Sir Robert Peel, both housed in the British Library (formerly called the British Museum) in London, contain anything important relating to the *Amistad*. There is nothing on the *Amistad* in the Lord John Russell Papers stored in the PRO in Kew Gardens, Eng.

26. Covey to Tappan, April 29, 1841, AMA Papers, Box 197, "Sierra Leone" folder, ARC; Tappan to Leavitt, Nov. 15, 1841 (public letter), Sturge, *Visit*, app. E, xli–xliii, xlvi–xlvii, li; *Long Island Farmer* (N.Y.), Dec. 17, 1841, 2; William W. Anderson in N.Y. to Commanders of Brit. vessels on African coast, Nov. 19, 1841, in James B. Covey Corresp., "Sierra Leone" folder, ARC; Fox to Tappan, Nov. 20, 1841, ibid.; Fox to Lt. Col. Sir John Jeremie, Brit. gov. of Sierra Leone, Nov. 20, 1841, encl. ibid.; Tappan to Jed [?] Frye, Nov. 23, 1841, ibid.; N.Y. *National Anti-Slavery Standard,* Dec. 9, 1841, 105–6; *African Repository* 17 (1841): 345; Scoble to Aberdeen, Dec. 10, 20, 1841, 77–80, Papers of Brit. and For. Anti-Slavery Soc.; Stratford Canning to Scoble, Dec. 25, 1841, ibid., 80; Brit. lt. gov. of Sierra Leone, W. Fergusson, to Tappan, et al. (n.d.), encl. in Tappan to J. H. Tredgold, Dec. 18, 1841, ibid., 81–82; *Oberlin Evangelist,* Dec. 22, 1841, 206; *Niles' National Register* (Balt.), April 23, 1842, 128; Strother, *Underground Railroad in Connecticut,* 80; Robert S. Fletcher, *A History of Oberlin College from Its Foundation through the Civil War,* 2 vols. (Oberlin, Ohio: Oberlin College, 1943), 1:258; T. J. Alldridge, *A Transformed Colony: Sierra Leone* (London: Seeley, 1910), 260.

27. Most of the blacks returned to Mende, although some stayed in Sierra Leone to work with the missionaries. Ten of the males, including Covey, joined the three females in choosing not to return to Mende. In 1846 the *Amistad* Committee merged with other missionary societies to form the American Missionary Association, and in 1849 one of the three female captives of the *Amistad,* Margru (renamed Sarah Kinson), began work as a missionary after studying at Oberlin College at AMA expense. Some writers believe that Cinqué returned to his people and worked as interpreter for the AMA mission at Kaw-Mende until his death about 1879. See *Amistad* Committee pamphlet (n.d.), A1258, ARC; *Long Island Farmer* (N.Y.), April 19, 1842, 2; *Niles' National Register* (Balt.), July 16, 1842, 311; *African Repository* 18 (1842): 158; 19 (1843): 154–56; *Oberlin Evangelist,* Oct. 12, 1842, 167; Nov. 5, 1845, 182; Tappan to Scoble, April 25, 1843, *Side-light,* 133; *American Missionary,* Jan. 1847, 20; Nov. 1847, 2; Feb. 1851, 26; Nov. 1850, 4; June 1854, 59; Jan. 1858, 1; Charles A. Dinsmore, "Interesting Sketches of the *Amistad* Captives," *Yale University Library Gazette* 9 (Jan. 1935): 55; Michael E. Strieby, "Oberlin and the American Missionary Association" (Address delivered at Oberlin, Oct. 23, 1891), in ARC; Benjamin Quarles, *Black Abolitionists* (N.Y.: Oxford U. Press, 1969), 76, 78–79; Simeon E. Baldwin, "The Captives of the *Amistad,*" *Papers of the New Haven Colony Historical Society* 4 (1888): 364; Strother, *Underground Railroad in Connecticut,* 81; Fletcher, *History of Oberlin College,* 1:259–60; Alldridge, *Transformed Colony,* 261. On the AMA, see Clifton H. Johnson, "The American Missionary Association, 1846–1861: A Study of Christian Abolitionism," Ph.D. diss., University of North Carolina,

1958. The Spanish could not have known, but Fox had assured Palmerston that the Supreme Court's "just and virtuous decision" eliminated the need for "all further interference" in Spanish-American affairs. Fox to Palmerston, March 9, 1841, Grea. Britain, Foreign Office, FO 185/184/1841, Slave Trade: Corresp., PRO, Kew Gardens, Eng.

28. Argaiz to First Sec. of DS, March 9, 1841, Leg. 5584, Exp. 1, no. 86; March 20, 1841, ibid., no. 88, AHN; Argaiz to Webster, March 17, April 5, 11, May 27, 29, Sept. 24, 1841, U.S. DS, Notes from the Spanish Legation, NA.

29. Fletcher Webster, acting sec. of state, to Argaiz, May 3, 1841, U.S. Congress, *House Documents,* 191, 17 Cong., 3d sess., 5:3; Webster to Argaiz, Sept. 1, 1841, June 21, 1842, U.S. DS, Notes to Foreign Legations in the U.S. from the DS, Spain, 1834–1906, NA.

30. Argaiz to Webster, Sept. 24, 1841, June 27, 1842, Notes from the Spanish Legation, NA; Aaron Vail, U.S. chargé in Madrid, to Webster, Nov. 30, 1841, William R. Manning, ed., *The Diplomatic Correspondence of the United States: Inter-American Affairs, 1831–1860,* 12 vols. (Wash., D.C.: Carnegie Endowment for International Peace, 1932–39), 11:326–28; Vail to Webster, Dec. 28, 1841, U.S. DS, Dispatches from U.S. Ministers to Spain, 1792–1906, NA. Spanish authorities in Cuba demanded that London withdraw its consul, David Turnbull, whom they regarded as the "avowed and unblushing tool of the British Society of Abolitionists." Even a high-ranking British official in Madrid thought Turnbull had "allowed his zeal to get the better of his discretion." See Hubert H. S. Aimes, *A History of Slavery in Cuba, 1511–1868* (N.Y.: Putnam's, 1907), 135–39, 141–43; Arthur Aston to Lord Palmerston, Feb. 23, 1841, GC/AS/171/3, Lord Palmerston Papers, Broadlands MSS, Royal Historical MSS Commission, London, Eng. By permission of the Trustees of the Broadlands Archives. See also Forsyth to Vail, July 15, 1840, U.S. DS, Instructions, Spain, NA; Vail to Webster, Dec. 28, 1841, U.S. DS, Dispatches from U.S. Ministers to Spain, NA. The Spanish were also concerned that the United States itself might be looking for a reason to intervene in Cuba. See Aimes, *History of Slavery in Cuba,* 138.

31. Vail to Webster, Feb. 12, 1842, U.S. DS, Dispatches from U.S. Ministers to Spain, NA; Irving to Webster, Dec. 5, 1842, Kenneth E. Shewmaker, ed., *Papers of Daniel Webster: Diplomatic Papers, vol. 1, 1841–1843* (Hanover, N.H.: Dartmouth College and U. Press of New England, 1983), 226–28; Argaiz to Webster, Sept. 24, 1841, U.S. DS, Notes from the Spanish Legation, NA.

32. Tyler to House of Representatives, Feb. 27, 1843, in James D. Richardson, ed., *A Compilation of the Messages and Papers of the Presidents,* 11 vols. (N.Y.: Bureau of National Literature, 1896–1910), 4:232; *House Docs.,* 191, 1–2; Legaré to Webster, March 2, 1842, Shewmaker, ed., *Papers of Webster,* 1:204; Argaiz to Webster, June 27, 1842, U.S. DS, Notes from the Spanish Legation, NA. On the *Creole,* see Howard Jones, "The Peculiar Institution and National Honor: The Case of the *Creole* Slave Revolt," *Civil War History* 21 (March 1975): 28–50. Questions had arisen about the legality of Gedney's request for salvage, but Secretary of the Navy James K. Paulding investigated the matter and found the claim "perfectly satisfactory." See Paulding to Gedney, Feb. 3, 7, 1840, U.S. Dept. of Navy, Sec. of Navy, Letters to Officers, Ships of War, NA.

33. Upshur to Irving, Jan. 9, 1844, Manning, ed., *Dipl. Corresp. of U.S.,* 11:31–32; Irving to Upshur, March 2, 1844, ibid., 336.

34. Report from Committee on Foreign Affairs, April 10, 1844, U.S. Cong., *House Reports,* 426, 28th Cong., 1st sess., 2:1–3. The committee members were Ingersoll, chairman; Robert B. Rhett of South Carolina (Dem.); Lemuel Stetson of New York (Dem.); William H. Hammett of Mississippi (Dem.); John White of Kentucky (Whig); John B. Dawson of Louisiana (Dem.); Samuel C. Sample of Indiana (Whig); William P. Thomasson of Kentucky (Whig); and Henry Williams of Massachusetts (Dem.). This Ingersoll, of course, was not the one earlier involved in the *Amistad* Case.

35. Ingersoll Committee Report, *House Reports,* 426, 28th Cong., 1st sess., 2:3.

36. Ibid., 9.

37. Ibid., 9–12.

38. Ibid., 12–14.

39. Ibid., 1: U.S. Cong., *Congressional Globe, App., 1843–44,* 28th Cong., 1st sess., 13:500.

40. The Papers of Charles J. Ingersoll, MS Div., LC, contain no references to the *Amistad.*

41. *Cong. Globe, App., 1843–44,* 28th Cong., 1st sess., 13:500–504. Congress passed the "gag resolution" in 1836 to halt debates on petitions to end the domestic slave trade in the nation's capital. John Quincy Adams led the fight against the rule as a violation of freedom of speech and finally won its repeal in 1844.

42. Ibid., 504, 534, 538; *Memoirs of JQA,* 12:12–13. The House vote was eighty-six to sixty-two.

43. Adams's public letter to inhabitants of his home congressional district in Mass., printed in Wash. *National Intelligencer,* April 3, 1845, 2; *Memoirs of JQA,* 12:186.

44. Calderón to Calhoun, Dec. 4, 1844, U.S. DS, Notes from the Spanish Legation, NA; Calderón to Buchanan, Jan. 29, 1846, ibid.

45. Buchanan to Ingersoll, March 19, 1846, *House Reports,* 753, 29th Cong., 1st sess., 4:1; Calderón to Buchanan, June 18, 1846, U.S. Cong., *Senate Docs.,* 29, 31st Cong., 2d sess., 3:8.

46. *House Reports,* 753, 29th Cong., 1st sess., 4:4–17; Calderón to Buchanan, Sept. 20, Dec. 29, 1846, U.S. DS, Notes from the Spanish Legation, NA; *Cong. Globe, App. 1846–47,* 29th Cong., 2d sess., 16:437–38, 506; *House Journal,* 29th Cong., 2d sess., 483. The margin was 113 to 40. Of the 113 nays, 97 were Northerners, leaving only 16 from the South (including one representative from Missouri who was born in Virginia). Among the 40 yeas were only 4 from the North; the remaining 36 included one representative from Missouri who had retired on an Arkansas plantation. Political differences were less distinct: among the 113 nays were 55 Whigs, 51 Democrats, 2 Republicans, 3 "Americans," and 2 with no announced party affiliation; among the 40 yeas were 3 Whigs, 36 Democrats, and 1 with no affiliation. Ibid., 483–84.

47. Polk's Third Annual Message to Congress, Dec. 7, 1847, in Richardson, ed., *Messages and Papers of the Presidents,* 4:551; Buchanan to James J. McKay, chairman, House Ways and Means Committee, March 2, 1847, *Sen. Docs.,* 29, 31st Cong., 2d sess., 3:11; Calderón to Buchanan, March 11, 1847, U.S. DS, Notes from the Spanish Legation, NA; Buchanan to Calderón, March 19, 1847, U.S. DS, Notes to Foreign Legations in U.S., Spain, NA; T. C. Reynolds, sec. of U.S. Legation in Madrid, to Buchanan, July 8, 1847, U.S. DS, Dispatches, Spain, NA; Buchanan to Romulus Saunders, U.S. minister to Spain, Sept. 29, 1847, U.S. DS,

Instructions, Spain, ibid.; John B. Moore, ed., *The Works of James Buchanan: Comprising His Speeches, State Papers, and Private Correspondence,* 12 vols. (N.Y.: Antiquarian Press, 1960; originally published in 1908–11), 7:423–24.

48. Judson to Baldwin, Dec. 18, 1847, Baldwin Family Papers, Box 44, Yale.

49. *Cong. Globe, 1847–48,* 30th Cong., 1st sess., 17:101.

50. *Cong. Globe, App. 1847–48,* 30th Cong., 1st sess., 17:1126, 1128–29.

51. Chase to Van Buren, Aug. 21, 1848, Martin Van Buren Papers, MS Div., LC; Butler to Van Buren, Oct. 3, 1848, ibid.; James R. Beys (the other supporter) to Van Buren, Oct. 19, 1848, ibid.; Van Buren to Beys, Oct. 24, 1848, ibid.; Salmon P. Chase Papers, ibid.

52. *Cong. Globe, App., 1847–48,* 30th Cong., 1st sess., 17:1129.

53. Calderón to Buchanan, Aug. 22, 1848, U.S. DS, Notes from the Spanish Legation, NA; Calderón to Sec. of State John M. Clayton, Nov. 20, 1849, ibid.; Calderón to Webster, Aug. 14, 1850, ibid.; Calderón to Webster, Jan. 8, 1851, ibid. As in previous years, the United States warned that cession of Cuba to any foreign power would be the "instant signal for war." See Clayton to Daniel M. Barringer, U.S. minister to Spain, Aug. 2, 1849, Manning, ed., *Dipl. Corresp. of U.S.,* 11:70. See also R. Earl McClendon, "The *Amistad* Claims: Inconsistencies of Policy," *Political Science Quarterly* 48 (Sept. 1933): 386–412.

54. *Cong. Globe, 1850–51,* 31st Cong., 2d sess., 30:385, 401–3. The vote was forty-three to six. Clay's notoriety was not always deserved. The Compromise of 1850, usually considered his handiwork, but more rightfully attributable to Senator Stephen A. Douglas of Illinois, stipulated the following: California's admission to the Union as a free state; abolition of the slave trade in Washington, D.C.; establishment of a federally enforced fugitive-slave law; institution of the principle of "popular sovereignty" in determining the existence of slavery in the territories of Utah and New Mexico; and an amicable settlement of a boundary controversy between Texas and New Mexico.

55. *Sen. Reports,* 301, 31st Cong., 2d sess., 1:2–7; *Sen. Reports,* 158, 32d Cong., 1st sess., 1:1–78; *Cong. Globe, 1851–52,* 32d Cong., 1st sess., 21, pt. 1:702, pt. 2:902–3; John B. Moore, *A Digest of International Law,* 8 vols. (Wash., D.C.: GPO, 1906), 5:854; Moore, ed., *Works of Buchanan,* 10:141, 252–53, 349–50; *Cong. Globe, 1857–58,* 35th Cong., 1st sess., 27, pt. 1:517; ibid., 2d sess., 28, pt. 1:1–2; *Sen. Reports,* 36, 35th Cong., 1st sess., 1:1–7; *Sen. Journal,* 35th Cong., 2d sess., 7; Sec. of State Lewis Cass to Augustus Dodge, U.S. minister to Spain, Jan. 6, 1858, Manning, ed., *Dipl. Corresp. of U.S.,* 11:226. Both Democratic presidents during the late 1850s, Franklin Pierce and James Buchanan, appealed to Congress to honor the *Amistad* claims. They were derisively called "doughfaces" because they were Northerners with Southern policies. See Pierce's First Annual Message to Congress, Dec. 5, 1853, in Richardson, ed., *Messages and Papers of the Presidents,* 5:209; Buchanan's First Annual Message to Congress, Dec. 8, 1857, ibid., 446; Buchanan's Second Annual Message to Congress, Dec. 6, 1858, ibid., 511; Buchanan's Third Annual Message to Congress, Dec. 19, 1859, ibid., 561.

56. *Cong. Globe, App., 1854–55,* 33d Cong., 1st sess., 23:55; *Cong. Globe, 1857–58,* 35th Cong., 1st sess., 27, pt. 1:442–45. For the Dred Scott Case, see Don E. Fehrenbacher, *The Dred Scott Case: Its Significance in American Law and Politics* (N.Y.: Oxford U. Press, 1978).

57. *Cong. Globe, 1858–59,* 35th Cong., 2d sess., 28, pt. 1:1–2, 904–5.

58. Calderón to Webster, April 19, 1852, U.S. DS, Notes from the Spanish Legation, NA; Spanish Minister Manuel Bertran de Lis to Sec. of State Edward Everett, Nov. 11, 1852, *Sen. Exec. Docs.,* 19, 32d Cong., 2d sess., 3; Bertran to Calderón, Nov. 11, 1852, *House Docs.,* 20, 32d Cong., 2d sess., 3:3; Calderón to Everett, Jan. 6, 1853, U.S. DS, Notes from the Spanish Legation, NA; Moore, *Digest of International Law,* 5:853–54; Sec. of State William L. Marcy to Pierre Soulé, U.S. minister to Spain, July 23, 1853, Manning, ed., *Dipl. Corresp. of U.S.,* 11:160–61; Calderón to Soulé, April 18, 1854, ibid., 759–60; Soulé to Calderón, April 20, 1854, ibid., 761–64. For Southern territorial objectives during the 1850s, see Robert E. May, *The Southern Dream of a Caribbean Empire, 1854–1861* (Baton Rouge: Louisiana State U. Press, 1973).

59. Dodge to Cass, Aug. 15, 1857, Manning, ed., *Dipl. Corresp. of U.S.,* 11:926–29; Dodge to Cass, Aug. 25, 1858, ibid., 951. The Cuban-claims issue stemmed from a hurricane on the island in 1844, after which the government in Havana permitted duty-free importation of goods for six months, only to revoke the decree suddenly. Among those importers hurt by this action were Americans, who had lodged a claim for indemnification with the Spanish government.

60. R. Earl McClendon, "The Two-Thirds Rule in Senate Action upon Treaties, 1789–1901," *American Journal of International Law* 16 (Jan. 1932): 45–46; Moore, *Digest of International Law,* 5:854; Moore, ed., *Works of Buchanan,* 11:28, 29; 12:237; Richardson, ed., *Messages and Papers of the Presidents,* 5:642; William Preston, U.S. minister to Spain, to Cass, March 6, June 28, 1860, Manning, ed., *Dipl. Corresp. of U.S.,* 11:977, 977 n. 2; Preston to Cass, Oct. 25, 1860, ibid., 993–94.

61. Sir William Blackstone, *Commentaries on the Laws of England,* 12th ed., 4 vols. (London: Strahan and Woodfall, 1793), 1:62.

Index